Black Barons of Birmingham

Black Barons of Birmingham

The South's Greatest Negro League Team and Its Players

LARRY POWELL

Foreword by CLAYTON SHERROD

McFarland & Company, Inc., Publishers
Jefferson, North Carolina, and London

Acknowledgments

Dozens of people assisted in the compilation of this work, but the author wishes to identify several who were particularly helpful. Without their assistance, this book would not have been completed. These include: the past and present members of the Alabama Negro League Association, who willingly gave of their time to be interviewed. Many also provided important photos; David Brewer, of the Friends of Rickwood, who provided access to the organization's files and photos; Dr. Jean Bodon and David Knight, both of whom assisted in the video-recording of many of the interviews; Anita Williams, who transcribed many of the interviews; Bert Brouwer, Dean of Arts and Humanities at the University of Alabama–Birmingham, who supported this research; and my wife, Clarine Powell, who understands why I take baseball so seriously.

LIBRARY OF CONGRESS CATALOGUING-IN-PUBLICATION DATA

Powell, Larry, 1948–
Black Barons of Birmingham : the south's
greatest Negro League team and its players /
Larry Powell ; foreword by Clayton Sherrod.
    p.   cm.
Includes bibliographical references and index.

ISBN 978-0-7864-3806-8
softcover : 50# alkaline paper ∞

1. Birmingham Black Barons (Baseball team)—History.
2. Negro leagues—History. 3. Baseball—Alabama—
Birmingham—History. I. Title.
GV875.B57P68   2009   796.357'6409761781—dc22   2009022660

British Library cataloguing data are available

©2009 Alabama Negro League Players Association. All rights reserved

*No part of this book may be reproduced or transmitted in any form
or by any means, electronic or mechanical, including photocopying
or recording, or by any information storage and retrieval system,
without permission in writing from the publisher.*

On the cover: Members of the Birmingham Black Barons pose in
front of the team bus in 1950; background ©2009 Shutterstock

Manufactured in the United States of America

*McFarland & Company, Inc., Publishers
Box 611, Jefferson, North Carolina 28640
www.mcfarlandpub.com*

Table of Contents

Acknowledgments iv
Foreword by Clayton Sherrod 1
Preface 3

PART I. THE BLACK BARONS BEFORE INTEGRATION

Introduction 7
1. The Black Barons in the 1920s 10
2. The Black Barons in the 1930s 33
3. The Black Barons in the 1940s 42

PART II. THE BLACK BARONS AFTER INTEGRATION

Introduction 53
4. Post–Robinson Era Black Barons 62
5. Players and Tryout Camps 112
6. Black Barons in the White Minor Leagues 125
7. Black Barons in the Major Leagues 165

Afterword 199
Chapter Notes 201
Bibliography 211
Index 215

Foreword
by Clayton Sherrod

As a young boy growing up in ACIPCO (American Cast Iron Pipe Company) during the 1940s, my Sundays consisted of early morning church services, the best home-cooked dinners imaginable, and, of course, the very best sport ever — baseball. As a child, I did not have many heroes, not even imaginary ones. Most young children in my community grew up pretty fast because family responsibilities were shared by all, even the very young. However, my father loved baseball and felt that we should be given time to learn about and enjoy the sport he played and loved as a youth. It was on the dirt playing field, and later at Rickwood Field, that I found a gold mine of heroes.

During the early years of the leagues, segregation had prevented black and white teams from playing together or against each other. My dad would say, "It's a shame that they won't let them play in white leagues and on teams everywhere." I remember vividly thinking to myself, "I feel sorry for the white people that they won't get to play with the greatest players in the world." I felt it was unfair that they would have to miss out on what I felt was the best thing in life, Negro League Baseball.

Looking into the faces and eyes of the players, I saw pride, courage, strength and determination. Their bodies seemed to be machines that combined skill, talent, speed and agility beyond the imagination. Their bodies are no longer the well-tuned machines that would allow them to run effortlessly from base to base, steal home, or hit a home run over the walls of Rickwood Field. Watching them play was transfixing; for the span of the game, there seemed to be no racial issues — segregation, discrimination — and no national issues — unemployment and war. All that mattered in those precious moments was the game, the team and the players I had grown to idolize.

My friends and I would run as fast as we could to get to the field. We had a special place where we liked to sit so that we could see every movement of the game. We would scream and yell our support to our heroes in hopes that they would notice us in the crowd and nod in our direction as they approached the plate to bat. We knew the stats on each player without having to check our record books. If the Birmingham Black Barons had been a course in school, we would have been scholars.

As an adult, I reflect back on those years and experiences of watching the local baseball players in my community and players that are now known as the legendary Birmingham Black Barons, and I feel wealthy beyond comprehension. When members of the industrial league joined the Negro League, my heroes became greater in my sight and also gave me a chance to see Rickwood Field. I became a bat boy for the Birmingham Black Barons!

Rickwood was not merely a baseball field, it was an arena for only the best and greatest in baseball. The first time I walked into Rickwood Field, it was unbelievable! I had the opportunity to see the legends, my heroes during the prime of their lives and athletic careers. I owe a great deal of gratitude to each of them for following their passion for the sport of baseball. To me and others like me, they represented hope, pride, skill and physical perfection. They were masters of the game of baseball, and they were living giants in our young eyes and hearts. Because of their lives and experience in baseball, many young black men remained hopeful that other barriers would indeed come down as well.

Looking into the eyes and faces of my heroes today, I see wisdom, heritage, and the wear and tear of sacrifice and courage. Their hair may have grown silver and they bodies no longer the epitome of strength, but — in the eyes of this much older man from ACIPCO — they remain my childhood heroes. I will admire and celebrate them for the remainder of my lifetime. I will continue to support efforts to have their story told for generations to come.

Clayton Sherrod, CEC, AAC, is chairman of the Alabama Negro League Foundation.

Preface

As a young man, the first televised baseball game I ever saw was a 1955 World Series contest between the New York Yankees and the Brooklyn Dodgers. I saw Duke Snider hit a home run as the Dodgers won the first world championship in the team's history. I was an instant Dodger fan, quickly learning the Dodgers' key players — Gil Hodges, Jackie Robinson, Pee Wee Reese, Roy Campanella, Don Newcombe, Johnny Podres. As a seven-year-old, the entire event seemed perfectly normal, and yet it was different than anything I had ever seen before. The game featured black and white players, playing together. On the same team. And winning. Nothing like that happened at the small segregated elementary school I attended. Still, it seemed quite natural.

Six years later, when the civil rights movement was starting to erupt, it was a little difficult for me to understand what the problem was. Blacks and whites played together on the Dodgers and (by then) most other teams in the major leagues. Why shouldn't they be playing together on high school teams and attending those same schools together? My reaction apparently represented those of many others of my generation. That's why so many people today credit baseball with paving the way for integrated society.

They did it by serving two distinct functions. First, the Negro Leagues became a way of coping with the inequities of a segregated society during years of oppression. As Fullerton noted:

> The Birmingham Black Barons offer a classic study in the ironies of segregation. The team stood as an example of a successful black enterprise and brought real and psychological rewards to the players and a sense of pride to the black community of Birmingham. Success also meant living within a social and economic system that was separate, but far from equal.[1]

I started this book because I saw an important story going untold. Further, it was a story that had affected my own life, even if the players had never met me before. My only trepidation was a question about my own ability as a Southern white boy to accurately relate their stories. And would the players feel comfortable recounting their experiences for me? I handled the first problem by making sure that the final product was theirs, not mine; each player has reviewed his own chapter, and the Alabama Negro

League Players Association retains rights to this work. As for the players' willingness to open up — more on that later.

The book is divided into two large sections. Part One looks at the Birmingham Black Barons in the years before the integration of the major leagues. Chapter 1 covers the 1920s, including the founding of the team in 1920 and its first venture into the Negro Leagues in 1923. Chapter 2 reviews the 1930s and some of the more notable players from that decade. Chapter 3 looks at the years 1940 to 1946, these years immediately before Jackie Robinson joined the Brooklyn Dodgers in 1947.

Part Two reviews the history of the Black Barons following the integration of Major League Baseball. Rather than taking the chronological approach used in Part One, this section divides its content in terms of how that racial change affected different players. Chapter 4 looks at most of the post–Robinson era Black Barons, those who maintained the legacy of the team but never got a chance to move into so-called organized baseball. Chapter 5 covers the careers of players invited to major league tryout camps but never received contracts in white baseball. In some cases, the evidence suggests that the outcome of the tryout was never in doubt. But a significant number made it into the white minor leagues, and their stories are recounted in Chapter 6. Finally, those rare few who reached the major leagues are the topic of Chapter 7.

The process for collecting the stories was simple. The players gathered once a month at the Smithfield Library in Birmingham, convening for Alabama Negro League Player Association meetings. At one of those meetings I shared my plans for the book project and set up interviews with each of them. Many of those interviews were conducted there at the library, either following the meeting or on other days during the weeks that followed.

University of Alabama–Birmingham video technician David Knight was extremely helpful in this early stage, converting a small library meeting room into a makeshift video studio. There we interviewed many of the organization's core group of players — the Rev. Bill Greason, Jake Sanders, Tony Lloyd, Earnest Harris, Willie Harris, Jessie Mitchell, and Cleophus Brown. For those who had trouble traveling to the library, we went to them. David accompanied me on trips to visit Willie Curry and Henry Elmore.

Many of the players, though, lived in other cities and did not attend the monthly meetings. For most of those, I waited until the players held their annual banquet. David set up a makeshift studio at the Alabama Sports Hall of Fame for one session, where we did a number of interviews — including those with Frank Evans, Elmer Knox, and Elijah Gilliam. The latter interview became especially important, since Mr. Gilliam died shortly thereafter. University of Alabama–Birmingham film professor Jean Bodon offered his services for two other sessions prior to the banquet.

That still didn't cover everybody. To catch up with others, I carried a small audio recorder with me to all of the group's meetings. If a player I hadn't interviewed turned up, I requested an interview after the meeting. A few other interviews were done by telephone, including Sam Williams. Mr. Williams, a California resident, interrupted his yard work to talk with me. He was an engaging man who made me smile just to talk with him. Unfortunately, he died a few weeks after the interview.

In fact, several of those who participated in this project have passed on since its inception. That was one reason that this project needed to be done. Too many of the players who can speak of this era are not with us anymore, and we're losing too many too fast. Their stories need to be part of the record.

That brings us to the second problem that concerned me, i.e., would I be accepted by these players? Would they feel comfortable recounting their stories to me? That turned out not to be a problem.

Baseball, it seems, transcends racial differences. And that's the way it should be.

Part I. The Black Barons Before Integration

Introduction

Contrary to popular opinion, Jackie Robinson was not the first black American to play baseball in the major leagues. In fact, he doesn't even rank among the first three. The first black player in the major leagues was probably William White, who played one game with the Providence Grays in 1879.[1] Moses Fleetwood "Fleet" Walker is generally credited with being the first African American with a major league contract, playing 42 games for Toledo in the American Association in 1883.[2] Soon after Fleet joined Toledo, his brother, Welday, became a teammate. But neither was able to play his career in the major leagues. Welday Walker only had six games. Fleet Walker had the longest career of the three, hitting .263 in his 42 games. Further, he will go down in the history of the sport as the *last* African American to play in the majors until Robinson joined the Dodgers in 1947.

If Fleet Walker is credited as the last black major leaguer before Robinson, Cap Anson is the man popularly credited with helping Walker gain that unwanted distinction. In August of 1883, when Anson's Chicago White Stockings were scheduled to face Walker's Toledo Blue Stockings, at first Anson refused to let his team take the field, demanding Walker be removed from the park. Though Anson's behavior backfired — the Blue Stockings manager Charlie Morton promptly inserted Walker's name in the lineup and, after Morton threatened to withhold Chicago's share of the gate receipts, the game was played — the story made the papers.[3] Before long, black players were finding themselves out of work, teams having apparently decided that integration posed too great a threat to the smooth operation of their business.

Until Robinson's historic role with the Brooklyn Dodgers, black players were limited to playing in the Negro Leagues or in all-black corporate leagues. They played their careers in semi-obscurity, heroes within the black community but largely unknown to the predominantly white United States. Yet their games featured some of the best athletes to ever play the sport. Today's modern major leagues look to the likes of Hank Aaron and Willie Mays as among the best in the history of professional baseball. But those names overlook similarly talented players who roamed the playing fields between the turn of the century and the end of World War II. Major league fans rooted for Babe Ruth, Lou Gehrig, and Ty Cobb. They rarely heard of such black legends as Satchel Paige and Josh Gibson.

Even worse were the hundreds (maybe thousands) of talented athletes whose names have faded into obscurity. They toiled in forgotten leagues, on barnstorming tours, and in the Caribbean to scratch out a living playing baseball.[4] Many of them were, as Donn Rogosin described them, "invisible men."[5] Similarly, *Sports Illustrated* called them "baseball's forgotten pioneers,"[6] while Cal Fussman called them "baseball's forgotten heroes."[7] They were barely given the recognition they deserved at the time. By the 1990s, most were not only forgotten, but often living in poverty.[8] As Randy Horick noted, Negro League players "and the fans who saw them in action, memory is the impermanent and sometimes imperfect keeper of the game."[9]

Their names have since faded, but their achievements have not. Playing in the Negro Leagues was fun, and a way to make a living that beat toiling in coal mines or cotton fields. But their willingness to play the game under adverse conditions served a social function for the black community and an important cultural role for the nation. The quality of baseball was high. On those rare occasions when Negro League players faced an all-star team of major leaguers, the Negro Leaguers won more than 60 percent of the time.[10]

Some recognition has started to come. Art Rust, a sportswriter who covered the Negro Leagues, recalled their contributions to the game in his classic work, *Get That Nigger Off the Field*.[11] Robert Peterson captured the essence of their story in his marvelous book, *Only the Ball Was White*.[12] Christopher Hauser compiled a chronological history of the Negro Leagues.[13] Leslie Heaphy compiled a broader history of black baseball,[14] and several oral histories have included Negro League players in their compilations.[15] Recognition started to increase in the 1990s, with a number of books, banquets, and awards in their honor.[16] Most importantly, a museum honoring the Negro League was opened in Kansas City in 1990.[17] It is housed in the very building where Rube Foster first organized the Negro National League in 1920.[18] Guiterrez wrote that the museum "is testimony to the will and spirit of athletes whose perceived sin was the color of their skin."[19]

Such attention has led to specific teams within the Negro Leagues receiving recognition. Other books have looked at such teams as the Chicago American Giants[20] and the Homestead Grays.[21] Darrell Howard examined black baseball in Virginia.[22] The Birmingham Black Barons have also received some recognition, particularly through Christopher Fullerton's fine book, *Every Other Sunday*, issued in 1999.[23] Four years before its release, the Birmingham Public Library honored 50 former members of the Negro League and sponsored a traveling exhibit—"Discover Greatness: An Illustrated History of the Negro Leagues Baseball."[24]

The individual players of the Birmingham Black Barons, though, have not received their due. They were arguably the most successful team in the history of the leagues. The Black Barons didn't win as many Negro League championships as the Kansas City Monarchs, they didn't have the sluggers of the Homestead Grays, and they didn't play that humorous brand of baseball that distinguished the Indianapolis Clowns. But they were usually among the teams that challenged for the championships, they were financially among the most successful (always drawing strong crowds), and—most importantly—they outlasted all of their contemporaries.

They played their home games in Rickwood Field. Fans who visit the historic stadium today can experience the feeling of watching baseball during the 1940s. They can't, however, appreciate the park in which the Black Barons played. The original design was laid out by baseball legend Connie Mack, who angled "the field to keep the sun from blinding the outfielders."

Home runs were rare in old Rickwood, where the left field fence as 405 feet from home plate and centerfield was a monstrous 470 foot shot. Only right field, with its 334-foot line, was comparable to today's park. Left field is now 80-feet shorter at just 325, while centerfield is a more reasonable 393 feet, but the Rickwood Field of the Black Barons was one that intimidated home run hitters while making pitchers happy. It was also the venue that allowed the Black Barons and other Negro League players to exhibit their talents in front of major league scouts.

Chapter 1

The Black Barons in the 1920s

The Birmingham Black Barons were organized in 1920 as part of the Negro Southern League. That same year, Rube Foster organized the Negro National League — the first true major league for black baseball.[1] The Birmingham Black Barons were one of the first eight teams invited to join the new league. The Black Barons were already viewed as a talented "professional team created in the aftermath of World War I from the city's industrial league."[2]

Frank Perdue paid $200 for the rights to own the Birmingham Stars in the Negro Southern League in 1920. The Stars nickname was quickly discarded, though, as the team became known as the Black Barons — a reference to the white team in the city.

Perdue sold the team to hotel owner Joe Rush in 1923, and Rush took the team to Foster's Negro National League. The Black Barons joined the new league as an associate member in 1923, finishing with a 23–15 record. In 1925, they became full members of the Negro National League.

The Black Barons managers during the 1920s included Joe Hewitt and Reuben Jones. Most of the players came from poor areas around Birmingham, playing baseball in the street as kids and getting jobs at local companies so they could play in Birmingham's industrial league. Those in outlying rural areas were often hired by the coal mines, where they could also play baseball. Baseball became a way to escape the hard labor and professional limitations that segregation imposed on African American society in the South at the time.

The industrial teams provided a feeder system for the Negro Leagues, particularly for the Black Barons. As Einstein noted, "There were the Negro 'minor leagues.' And there were the major leagues, and the Birmingham Black Barons were major league."[3] Elmer Knox, a member of the Atlanta Crackers who got his start in the steel industry, noted that the industrial teams had a professional atmosphere. "Don't let nobody fool you now," Knox said. "The steel industry has developed more baseball players that any other industry in this country.... They say it's amateur baseball, but how in the world are you going to play amateur baseball when you hire a man to play?"

The powerhouse of industrial teams in the city was ACIPCO, an acronym for the American Cast Iron & Pipe Company. The company was founded in Georgia in 1905,

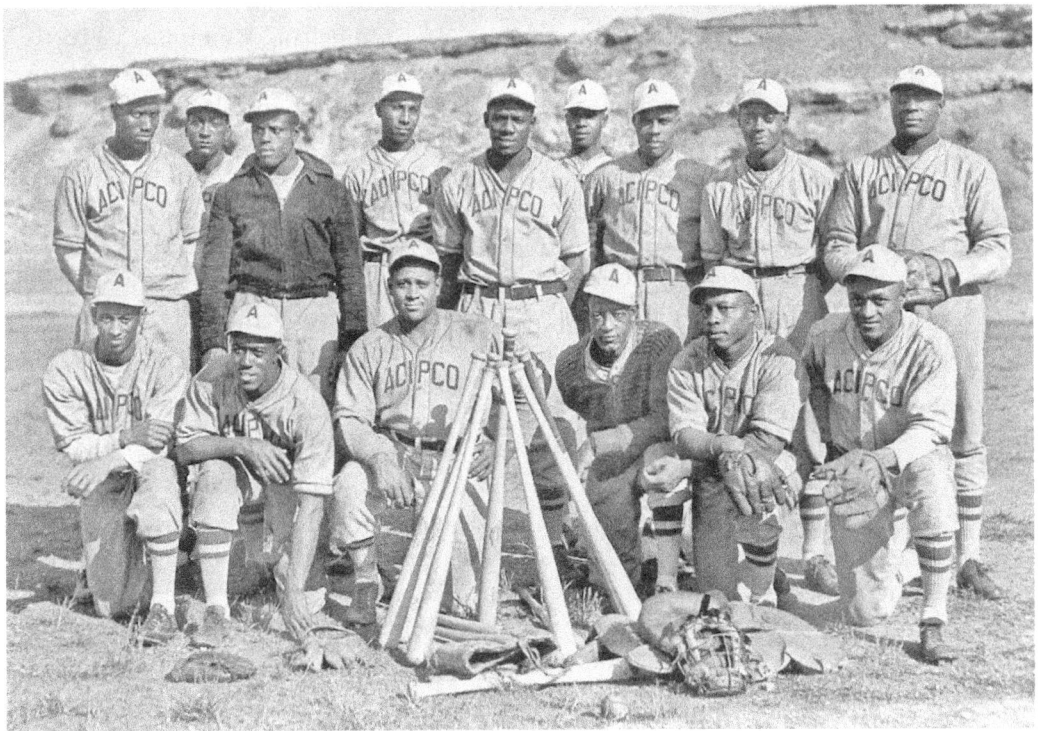

The 1924 (top) and 1936 ACIPCO teams of the Birmingham Industrial League. Sponsored by the Alabama Cast Iron Pipe Company, ACIPCO was for years a powerhouse in local amateur baseball, and a handful of Black Barons got their start with the team.

but the Birmingham area was the site of its pipe plant—a major employment center that had its own town ("ACIPCO"). Like many companies of the day, ACIPCO often hired some workers because of their baseball talent. ACIPCO and the other companies that sponsored the industrial league found that baseball teams helped to develop employee loyalty.

Critics complained that the practice was merely an "exercise in corporate paternalism"[4] in which the companies used the teams to teach "the values they wanted in their workers—self control, respect for authority, the importance of a good performance—but also increased a sense of identity among the workers with the factory."[5] More forceful critics have labeled it as a modern form of slavery.[6]

Regardless, baseball was in integral part of the industrial community, leading many of the companies to develop teams that "rivaled their professional counterparts in Birmingham both in talent and salaries,"[7] while the players became heroes to the other workers in the company.[8]

The exact role of the industrial league and ACIPCO in the establishment of the Black Barons has been debated. Cary believed that most of the original team came from ACIPCO.[9] Whitt argued that most of the players came from two teams, ACIPCO and their chief rival, Stockham Valve.[10] Regardless, the all-black industrial league became the equivalent of the local minor leagues, the feeder system for the Birmingham Black Barons. There were similar structures elsewhere, including coal company teams in Pennsylvania[11] and textile teams in the Carolinas.[12] In Birmingham, young black players played in the streets and on playgrounds until they had a chance to get a job with an industrial team. That, in turn, gave them a chance to play with the Black Barons. And, when the Negro Leagues finally died, many returned to the fields of the industrial leagues.

A combination of reasons—the formation of a competing league in the South, long and expensive travel schedules to play teams from the North, and the economic downturns associated with the Great Depression—contributed to financial problems during the 1920s and 1930s. The Black Barons bounced between the Negro National League and the Southern Negro League during this period.

Some Other Players from the 1920s

The Birmingham Black Barons had their share of heroes during that time, but many of those players were overlooked. They included superb athletes and some players who approached celebrity status within the African American community. Many of their records have been lost to history, but some became so well known that they continue to demand respect from baseball aficionados. What follows is a sample of the players on the rosters during the 1920s.

THEODORE "BUBBLES" ANDERSON

Bubbles Anderson had a four-year career in the Negro Leagues, playing from 1922 until 1925. Anderson was a second baseman for the Kansas City Monarchs, Washington Potomacs, Birmingham Black Barons, and the Indianapolis ABCs. His interesting nickname made him memorable, but a medical problem ended his career in 1925.

Larry "Iron Man" Brown

Iron Man Brown spent only one year with the Birmingham Black Barons, in 1919, before the team became a member of the Negro Leagues. That season was his first in professional baseball. He went on to have a 31-year career as a catcher and a manager with ten different teams, becoming a star on the Memphis Red Sox and Chicago American Giants during the 1920s and '30s. He received his "Iron Man" nickname during the 1930 campaign with the New York Lincoln Giants when he set a Negro League record by catching 234 games during the season.[13]

Brown was born September 5, 1905, in Pratt City, Alabama. After breaking in with the Barons in 1919, he would go on to become a six-time all-star and would play on three championship teams. He was the starting catcher for the victorious Chicago American Giants in the 1927 World Series. He was the team's catcher again in 1933 when it went to the World Series, and was on the 1934 team that fell one win short of qualifying for another championship.

Brown was a top defensive player who became famous for making plays while wearing his catcher's mask. Most catchers remove the mask and toss it to one side, particularly when looking for pop foul balls. Brown chased down the balls with his on.

Brown was also known for a strong and accurate arm and consistently threw out baserunners. Riley reported an oral tradition that says Brown once threw out speedster Ty Cobb on five consecutive steal attempts while playing against the Hall of Famer in Cuba. One version of the story says Cobb was so impressed that he considered getting the light-skinned Brown into the major leagues by claiming he was a Cuban.[14]

Brown finished his baseball career as a manager for the Philadelphia Stars from 1936 until 1938. He died April 7, 1972, in Memphis.

Black Bottom Buford

Buford had an eight-year career in the Negro Leagues (1927–34), playing for five different teams. Buford was primarily a third baseman, but occasionally played other positions; on rare occasions, he used his strong arm to pitch.

Buford is best remembered as a member of the Nashville Elite Giants. He broke in with the team in 1927 and stayed with them through 1932. During that span, he spent part of the 1931 season with the Birmingham Black Barons. A short stay, but his colorful nickname made him hard to forget.

Melvin "Slick" Coleman

Slick Coleman was a shortstop for the Birmingham Black Barons from 1937 until 1939. Coleman made his Negro League debut with the Barons in 1937, hitting sixth in the batting order. His three years with the Barons were mostly as a shortstop, although he occasionally picked up some games as a catcher. In 1940, he joined the Ethiopian Clowns. He remained with the Clowns for two years, playing under the clown name of "Macon."[15]

ANTHONY "ANT" COOPER

Ant Cooper was a 5'4" infielder whose small size and given name led to his nickname. He was a light hitter and slow runner, but his defensive skills kept him in the Negro Leagues for eight seasons.

Cooper broke into professional baseball in 1928 with the Birmingham Black Barons. He hit .253 in 1929 but dropped to .218 in 1930. He left the Barons after the 1930 season, joining the Louisville White Sox and the Cleveland Stars. After that, he played briefly with a number of other teams — the Homestead Grays (1932), Baltimore Black Sox (1933), Pittsburgh Crawfords (1933), Cleveland Red Sox (1934), and the Newark Dodgers (1935). Cooper was out of baseball for six seasons before signing a one-year contract with the New York Black Yankees in 1941.

WILLIE "SUG" CORNELIUS

Willie Cornelius is best remembered for his ten years as a pitcher for the Chicago American Giants (1936–43, 1945–46), but he spent the 1930 season with the Birmingham Black Barons.

Cornelius broke into professional baseball in 1928 with the Nashville Elite Giants. He also played for the Memphis Red Sox before joining Chicago. His best season came in 1936 when he posted a 20–4 record and was the starting pitcher for the West in the East-West All-Star Game. It was one of three All-Star Game appearances for the pitcher, all of which came with the American Giants. He was the winning pitcher in relief in the 1935 contest and was again the starting pitcher in the 1938 game.

SAM CRAWFORD

Sam Crawford was a pitcher whose start to his professional career preceded the Negro Leagues. He began playing for the New York Black Sox in 1910, and finished his career with the Indianapolis Athletics in 1937. In between, he played or managed 13 different teams. That included two seasons (1925 and 1938) with the Birmingham Black Barons.

Some of his achievements in the game were legendary. In 1912, while pitching for the Chicago Giants, he tossed a pair of five-inning no-hitters in the same day during an exhibition double-header against a local team in Braidwood, Illinois, called the Coal Citys. He struck out 27 batters on the day, getting all 15 outs in the first game on whiffs before adding 12 more in the second contest.

The highlight of his Negro League career came in 1926 with the Chicago American Giants. The Giants won the pennant and won the Negro League World Series. Crawford pitched in one of the series games, in relief.

SAUL DAVIS

Saul Davis was a Louisiana native who became an infielder and manager in the early days of black baseball. He spent portions of four seasons with the Birmingham Black Barons, from 1923 to 1926.

Born February 22, 1901, in Bayou, Louisiana, Davis broke into professional baseball with the Houston Black Buffalos in 1918. He joined the Barons in 1923. He left the Barons for the Memphis Red Sox and then the Chicago American Giants. He finished his career in 1937 as the manager of the Zulu Grass Skirts, a touring comedy team that traveled in the Midwest.

WILLIAM "DIZZY" DISMUKES

Dizzy Dismukes had a 19-year career as a pitcher and manager in the Negro Leagues, but he really made his mark as an executive. He started playing professionally in 1910, was still in the game in 1951, and played a role in seeing Jackie Robinson break the major league color barrier. In between, he spent two years with the Birmingham Black Barons—1924 and 1938.

Dismukes was born March 15, 1890, in Birmingham. He broke into professional baseball as a submarine pitcher in 1910 with the West Baden Sprudels. He played or worked with 20-plus teams in his career, but was best known for his tenure with the Indianapolis ABCs. He was with the team from 1914 until 1924, missing two years to military service. Dismukes served with the 803rd Pioneer Infantry for World War I.

He had a brief stint as a pitcher for the Black Barons in 1924. He returned to the Barons in 1938 as the team's manager.

Dismukes served as the traveling secretary for the Kansas City Monarchs for 11 years, from 1942 until 1952. He played a major role in signing Jackie Robinson to the Monarchs, and also recommended that Robinson shift positions, from shortstop to second base. The change resulted in a more natural position for Robinson. It also made it easier for him to reach the major leagues, since he wouldn't have to compete with Pee Wee Reese of the Dodgers for the shortstop job.

Once the color barrier was broken, Dismukes served as a scout for the major leagues, working for the New York Yankees for the 1953 and 1954 seasons. He shifted to the Chicago White Sox for 1955 and 1956.

Dismukes died June 30, 1961, in Campbell, Ohio.

BILL FOSTER

One memorable player of the 1920s was Bill Foster. The pitcher spent the 1925 season with the Black Barons as part of a Hall of Fame career. He finished his career as athletics director at Alcorn State University.

Foster was a brother to Rube Foster, the founder of the Negro Leagues.[16] Willie was a pitcher best known for his career with the Chicago American Giants, but he spent one season with Birmingham, in 1925. Over those years, he compiled a record that includes the most wins in the history of the Negro Leagues.[17] Dewey and Acocella described him as "the Negro Leagues' greatest lefthanded pitcher."[18] Negro League veteran Dave Malacher once said Bill Foster "was the greatest pitcher of our time, not even barring Satchel."[19] In 1996, Foster became the third former Black Baron to be inducted into the Baseball Hall of Fame.

Born June 12, 1904, in Clavert, Texas, Foster broke into the Negro Leagues with the Memphis Red Sox in 1923, but joined Chicago later in the season. He posted a 5–2 record in his rookie year, and a 6–1 mark in 1924. In 1925, he got an break from the Giants and played for the Black Barons. He posted a 7–1 mark.

In 1926, he spent his first full season with Chicago and won 26 consecutive games while the Giants earned the second-half title. In the playoffs against the Kansas City Monarchs, Foster pitched and won both games of a double-header to win the pennant for the Giants. In the World Series, he pitched two complete games and made one relief appearance. He won two of the games, including one shutout, while posting a 1.27 ERA for the series.

His 1927 season was almost as good as the previous one. He posted an overall 32–3 record, including 21–3 in league play. In the World Series, he again won two games, starting two and pitching in two others in relief.

That 1927 season was also the heyday of the New York Yankees. Babe Ruth hit 60 home runs, while he and Lou Gehrig led a team that is sometimes considered the greatest in the history of baseball. But as one baseball historian noted, "Babe Ruth and Lou Gehrig did not have to face Bill Foster."[20]

Foster posted a 14–10 record in 1928 and an 11–7 mark in 1929. After the 1929 season, Foster was the Negro League pitcher chosen to face an American League all-star team in a two-game series. The major league players hit him rather well in the first game, but he overwhelmed them in the second match-up by tossing a shutout, striking out nine, and allowing no hits for the first eight innings. Future Hall of Famer Charlie Gehringer reportedly told Foster after the game, "If I could paint you white I could get $150,000 for you right now."

Dave Malacher, Foster's manager with the American Giants, described Foster's approach to pitching for Robert Peterson:

> Willie Foster's greatness was that he had this terrific speed and a great, fast-breaking curve ball and a drop ball, and he was really a master of the change-of-pace. He could throw you a real fast one and then use the same motion and bring it up a little slower, and then a little slower yet. And then he'd use the same motion again, and Z-zzzz![21]

In 1930, he became both pitcher and manager of the team and posted a 16–10 record. After the season, Foster left the team and signed in 1931 with the Homestead Grays. In a September game, he was the starting pitcher in a win over the Kansas City Monarchs, and then switched teams — joining the Monarchs for the remainder of the season. He finished the slate with a 9–2 record.

He returned to the Giants in 1932 and notched a 15–8 record as the team won a pennant. His 9–3 mark in 1933 was also part of a pennant-winning year. He was also the starting pitcher for the West team in the inaugural East-West All-Star Game, where he tossed a complete-game victory.

Foster led the Giants to a first-half championship in 1934, and then put together a 6–3 record in 1935. He finally left the Giants in 1936, joining the Pittsburgh Crawfords. He spent two years with the team, with 1937 being his last full season in the Negro Leagues. He finished out his baseball career in 1938, splitting time with a white semi-pro team in Elgin, Illinois, and a black team in Yakima, Washington.

Late in his career, Foster relied less on his fastball and more on pitching knowledge. As Bill Yancey recalled of Foster's later years, "That guy would give you 10 hits and shut you out. He could really pitch!"[22]

Foster left the game with the distinction of having won more Negro League games than any pitcher in history. After retiring, Foster pursued a career in academics, becoming a dean and baseball coach at Alcorn State College, his alma mater, in 1960. In 1995, Foster was inducted into the Alcorn State Hall of Fame.

By the 1990s, baseball historians were calling for Foster's election to the Baseball Hall of Fame.[23] In 1996, the Hall of Fame agreed, and he was inducted into the National Baseball Hall of Fame in Cooperstown on August 4, 1996,[24] becoming the third former member of the Black Barons to receive the honor.

Foster died in Lorman, Mississippi, on September 16, 1978, at the age of 74.

BILL GATEWOOD

Bill Gatewood had a 25-year career in black baseball. He spent much of that time as a pitcher for 15 different teams, but two seasons (1927–28) as the manager of the Birmingham Black Barons. During his career, he gave "Cool Papa" Bell his nickname and tutored a future Hall of Fame pitcher, Satchel Paige.

Gatewood broke into professional baseball with the Leland Giants in 1905, 15 years before the formation of the Negro League. He played briefly with the Chicago Giants, and then went with the Chicago American Giants when the team split in 1912.

Statistical data from those early years is sparse, but Gatewood was good enough to keep playing for a variety of teams, including the Philadelphia Giants, Indianapolis ABCs, St. Louis Stars, Toledo Tigers, Milwaukee Bears, and the Memphis Red Sox.

He had a 6–8 record and a .433 batting average in 1914 with the New York Lincoln Giants. He posted a 6–9 record with the Detroit Stars in 1921; his six wins included one documented no-hitter.

Gatewood joined the St. Louis Stars in the dual role of pitcher and manager in their inaugural season in the Negro League. His players included a 19-year-old, left-handed pitcher named James Thomas Bell. Impressed with the youngster's calmness in clutch situations as well as his maturity, Gatewood nicknamed him "Cool Papa." He also moved Bell off the mound and made him a left-handed hitter in order to better utilize his speed in getting to first base.

In 1926, Gatewood joined the Albany Giants in the Negro Southern League, again as player-manager. His tenure there included another documented no-hitter, this time against his future team, the Birmingham Black Barons.

He joined the Black Barons in 1927, posting a 1–2 mark on the mound. His major contribution to the game, though, may have come from tutoring Leroy "Satchel" Paige on the finer points of pitching. Gatewood is credited with teaching Paige how to throw his famous hesitation pitch.[25]

JAMES "JIM" GURLEY

Jim Gurley had an eleven-year career in the Negro Leagues, mostly in the 1920s, as an outfielder and pitcher. That included two seasons—1927 and 1929—with the Birmingham Black Barons. He split time with the Memphis Red Sox and Barons in 1927, hitting .243 as an outfielder. He was a backup on the Barons in 1929, hitting only .176. He made his professional debut in 1922 with the St. Louis Stars. He spent some time with the Indianapolis ABCs, Chicago American Giants, and the Nashville Elite Giants before joining the Barons. His last season in professional baseball was in 1932 with the Montgomery Grey Sox, where he tried playing first base before retiring from the game.[26]

REUBEN JONES

Reuben Jones had a baseball career that spanned four decades in the early years of the Negro Leagues. He broke into pro ball in 1918 with the Dallas Giants. He next shows up on baseball rosters in 1923 with the Birmingham Black Barons. He stayed with the team for five of the next six years, spending the 1926 season with the Indianapolis ABCs.

Jones' major contribution to the Black Barons took place in 1927, when he played three different roles for the team — manager, center fielder, and clean-up hitter. He hit for a .295 average for the year and guided the team to the second-half title in the Negro National League. The Barons lost the playoffs, though, to the Chicago American Giants.

Jones joined the Giants for the 1928 season. In 1932, he was on the roster of the Little Rock Black Travelers, batting .341 for the year. He was the leadoff hitter for the Cleveland Red Sox in 1934.[27] After an extended absence from the game, he returned in 1949 for a one-year stint as the manager of the Houston Eagles.

GEORGE MCALLISTER

McAllister spent 11 years in professional baseball, from 1923 until 1934. He broke into the Negro Leagues with the Birmingham Black Barons in 1923. He spent a total of eight years with the team, finally moving on after the 1932 season.

His best season came in 1927 when he hit .305 as the Barons' leadoff hitter and guided them to the second-half championship of the Negro American League. He posted a .287 average in 1929 before taking a one-year stint with the Memphis Red Sox.

After leaving the Barons again following the 1932 season, McAllister played for the Homestead Grays (1933) and the Cleveland Red Sox (1934) before hanging up his bat and glove.

BUFORD "GEETCHIE" MEREDITH

Geetchie Meredith was a shortstop/second baseman for the Black Barons during the 1920s, breaking in with the team in 1923. He was the Barons' starting second baseman in 1927, posting a .240 average as the team won the second-half championship. He posted a .273 average in 1929 before joining the Nashville Elite Giants in 1930. Geetchie returned to the Barons in 1931 for what would prove to be his final year. He was killed in a mining accident following the 1931 season.

LEROY "SATCHEL" PAIGE

After a losing season, on the field and at the gate, the Black Barons returned to the Negro Southern League in 1926, but their stay was short. They rejoined the Negro League and its higher level of competition in 1927 and qualified for the post-season championship games behind the pitching of rookie Satchel Paige. However, the team lost the Negro League World Series to the Chicago American Giants in four straight.

Paige would later become the first African American inducted into the National Baseball Hall of Fame. He pitched in more than 2,500 games (including 153 in one season), tossed more than one hundred no-hitters, and was still pitching professional ball while in his fifties. From the 1920s through the late 1940s, Paige dominated Negro League baseball.

If not the best pitcher in the history of baseball, Leroy "Satchel" Paige was at least the most durable. As Peterson wrote, "During the late 1930s and through the middle Forties, Satchel Paige dominated Negro baseball as Babe Ruth had dominated the major leagues earlier."[28] Dewey and Acocella had a similar assessment, writing, "As a pitcher, Paige was without peer; as a legend, only Babe Ruth was in his league."[29]

Most fans didn't get to see him until the 1950s — well past his prime — but that was enough to get a glimpse of a great player. In 1956, at the age of 50, he was the top pitcher in the International League. In 1965, at the age of 59, he made a one-game appearance for the Kansas City Athletics, pitching three innings of shutout game against the Boston Red Sox.[30] And, as Jeff Kisseloff noted, Satchel Paige was the only professional pitcher who could match Dizzy Dean for confidence on the mound.[31]

A major part of Paige's career came with the Birmingham Black Barons. Paige signed with the Chattanooga Black Lookouts in 1926, but was sold to the Black Barons after the 1927 season. "Big Bill" Gatewood was named the manager for the team in 1927, and he wanted a third pitcher to join his rotation, behind Sam Streeter and Harry Salmon. Gatewood and owner Joe Rush traveled to Chattanooga to sign the young pitcher.[32]

Paige had signed with Chattanooga for $50 per month. The Black Barons upped his salary to $250 a month.

The new relationship started out as a rocky one. Gatewood thought Paige was talented but unskilled. He tried to teach the youngster some of the intricacies of the game. Paige balked at the effort. When the manager tried to show him how to grip a curveball, Paige simply responded, "I don't do it that way."[33]

The problem was multiplied by the young pitcher's lack of control. Within a few years, Paige would be known as one of the best control pitchers in the history of baseball; that wasn't true at the beginning of the season. Jelly Gardner, an outfielder for the Chicago American Giants, faced Paige in the pitcher's first game for the Barons. As Gardner later recalled, "One time [the ball came] at you, one time behind you, the next time at your feet.... You had to be an acrobat to hit against him."[34]

Paige also refused to take signs from the catcher, mainly because his primary pitches were variations of a fastball. "There ain't no need for signs," he told Gatewood and his catchers. "All you gotta do is show me a glove and hold it still. I'll hit it."[35]

That described his later years, not his first season with the Black Barons. As biographer Mark Ribowsky noted, Satchel hit the catcher's target "roughly as often as high tide, and his frustration only made him more perilous to people's health."[36]

In a June 27 game against the St. Louis Stars, Satchel hit the first three batters who came to the plate. The third Star to get plunked, catcher Mitch Murray, charged the mound with his bat in hand, chasing Paige back toward second base. There he threw that bat at the pitcher's head, narrowly missing. Paige picked it up and then chased Murray around the field. Both benches emptied. When the umpires finally got the riot settled, Murray and Satchel were both ejected and the Barons forfeited the game.

Years later, Paige denied that he hit the batters from lack of control. "I hit a few batters that day, but I meant to," he wrote in his autobiography. "Why, I haven't hit more than two batters in my entire life except when I wanted to."[37]

Gatewood adjusted by using Satchel as a reliever until he learned the strike zone. And, despite his reluctance to take instructions, he gradually learned more about pitching. Streeter corrected a flaw in his delivery. Salmon taught him how to hold runners on base.

He also teamed up with a catcher, George Perkins, that he called "one of the best ball players of all time — Negro or white."[38] Perkins, Satchel once said, "handled a pitcher like nobody's business."[39] More to the point, according to Ribowsky, Perkins didn't use signs and let Satchel call his own game.[40]

By August, he was beginning to get it together. On August 14, he struck out nine Kansas City Monarchs in $6\frac{2}{3}$ innings. He followed that with two shutouts — a 2–0 win and a 10–0 win — over the Memphis Red Sox. In the 2–0 contest, he also went 2-for-3 at the plate, while striking out ten.

On September 12, he tossed a complete-game, four-hit shutout in a 5–0 win over the Cuban stars. Then, on the last day of the season, he won both games of a doubleheader — one as a starter and the other in relief.

In 1929, he set a league record of 164 strikeouts in a season — a record that was never broken. On July 29, 1929, he struck out 17 batters in a 5–1 win over the Detroit Stars. That remained the league record until he broke it in 1935.

In another game, he boasted that he would strike out the first six batters on the opposing team. After whiffing the first five, the opponents waved a white flag from the dugout. The sixth batter hit a harmless pop-up. When someone pointed out that the didn't strike out all six, he said, "They'd already surrendered. When Ol' Satch needs a strikeout, he gets it."[41]

By then, he was a star and major drawing card in black baseball. New Barons owner R. T. Jackson started renting Satchel out to other teams for an occasional game. Jackson, Paige, and the local promoter split the proceeds.

One such game, though, created a problem. Paige was hired out for a game in Albany, Georgia, but got into an argument with the local sheriff, who was doubling as an umpire for the contest. The sheriff ruled Satchel was out for not touching second base on a trip around the bases. An irate Paige had to be restrained, with the sheriff threatening to put him in jail. He stayed on the mound, though, and won.

"If there had been anybody else to pitch, I think he would have thrown me in jail," Satchel later recalled. "I didn't dare go back to Albany until I heard that sheriff had been beaten in an election."[42]

Paige stayed with the Barons through the 1930 season. By then, as Ribowsky noted, "he had overrun the team's ability to pay him."[43]

Still, the Birmingham Black Barons were the team where Paige "learned both control and the power of myth."[44] As Paige would later say, "Birmingham showed me a new world of baseball."[45]

Born July 7, 1906, in Mobile, Satchel was the seventh of eleven children. As a youngster, he had a part-time job carrying luggage at the local train depot, a job that gave him his lifelong nickname.[46] Baseball became his career of choice after a minor run-in with the law.

In 1918, Satchel received a five-year sentence in a juvenile detention center following a shoplifting charge. In his 1962 autobiography, *Maybe I'll Pitch Forever*, Paige credits the facility with making him a professional ballplayer. "You might say I traded five years of freedom to learn how to pitch," he wrote. "Those five and a half years there did something for me ... they made a man out of me. If I'd been left on the streets of Mobile to wander with those kids I'd been running around with, I'd of ended up as a big bum or crook."[47]

Following his release, Satchel returned to Mobile and played in the local semi-pro leagues. Stints with Chattanooga and Birmingham followed. By 1929, he played year-round baseball — spring, summer, winter, and fall — until 1958. "I played almost every day ... for those twenty-nine years, and I didn't quit then; I just cut out winter ball," he said.[48]

He received his first exposure to major league competition in 1930 while barnstorming against the Babe Ruth All-Stars. In one game, he struck out 22 of the major league players. "During the whole tour, I never pitched against Babe Ruth," he noted afterwards. "When I was pitching, he was bench-managing, and when I was getting a day off he was playing."[49]

From 1930 to 1931, he played in Baltimore, Nashville, and Cleveland, averaging 20-plus wins a season and 15 strikeouts per game. His reputation really started growing when he joined the Pittsburgh Crawfords in 1931, where he won more than 100 games in three years.

In 1933, he pitched in 41 games, won 31, and tossed sixteen shutouts. Toward the end of 1934, he jumped to a higher-paying club in Bismarck, North Dakota. There he pulled one of the many stunts that made him famous. After yelling at his outfielders for their casual play, the three angry players refused to take the field the following inning. He pitched without them and struck out the side.

The following season, Satchel's Bismarck team won the first National Baseball Congress tournament in Wichita, Kansas. Satchel was the tournament MVP after pitching four games, including one contest in which he struck out a tournament-record 17 batters.

He faced major league competition again in 1935 when he toured against Dizzy Dean's barnstormers, beating Dizzy four out of six times. Dean became one of Satchel's biggest admirers. "My fastball looks like a change of pace alongside that little pistol bullet Old Satchel shoots up to the plate," Dizzy said. "If Satch and I were pitching on the same team, we'd cinch the pennant by July 4 and go fishing until the World Series," he said on another occasion.[50]

The game that brought Paige the most attention was a 1936 exhibition in Oakland against another team of major leaguers. Satchel lost, 2–1, but only because he had little offensive or defensive support. "After that game, the talk about getting me in the major leagues really flew," he remembered in his book.[51]

One of his opponents was Joe DiMaggio, who was scheduled to join the Yankees the following season. After getting an infield hit, DiMaggio reportedly said, "Now I know I can make it with the Yankees. I finally got a hit off Ol' Satch."[52]

Frank Evans recalled another all-star exhibition game in 1941 at Chicago's Wrigley Field between Negro League players and major league all-stars. "I watched Satchel walk the bases loaded for nine innings and no one got a hit off of him," Evans recalled. "Ted Williams fouled two off of him, and Joe DiMaggio fouled one and from then on, it was history. No one could touch it. This was 1941 in Wrigley Field."

In 1936, Satchel returned to the Pittsburgh Crawfords. One of his games during that season was in Louisville, Kentucky, before a crowd of 15,000. The batters he faced that day included a 17-year-old rookie named Robert Abernathy. Abernathy later recalled his first at-bat against the legend for writer Randy Horick:

> I got up against Satchel, and I looked at the first two pitches [both were balls], and he said, "Woo, you got a pretty good eye."
>
> The next one I hit long but foul. He threw another one and I hit it long but foul again, and Satchel said, "I see you can hit too." I worked the count to 3 and 2, and then he stared at me and said, "Do you know who I am?"
>
> Then he threw another pitch and I didn't swing until the catcher was throwing it back. It was that fast. He blew it by me.[53]

Paige jumped to the Mexican League in 1937. The move backfired for Satch when he got sick, injured his arm and nearly ruined his career. One doctor said he would probably never pitch again, but he was still famous enough to join the Kansas City Monarchs in 1938 as a drawing card. "I was still pulling some fans, but to the boys on my team I was just the old man without an arm anymore," Satchel said.[54]

Toward the end of the season, his arm strength returned. By 1939, he was back to his original form. Behind his pitching, the Monarchs won the '39 Negro American League title and won the overall championship, from 1940 to 1942.

If anything, his arm seemed more durable than ever. In 1941, he once pitched 30 consecutive days. On another occasion, he won three games in one day, winning the opener and night game as a starter and the middle contest in relief.

As former Black Baron Willie Curry noted, Paige became so popular that he was frequently hired by a variety of teams for exhibition games. "He might pitch for the Black Barons this Sunday. Next Sunday, he might be with the Memphis Red Sox," Curry said. "The next Sunday, he might be with the Kansas City Monarchs. He was a drawing card. When Satch would be there, everybody was coming and the whole park would be full."

During this time, Black Baron legend Bill Greason got a chance to bat against Paige in Nashville. "I was a pretty good hitter, I thought," Greason recalled. "Satch said he wanted to know who the little youngster was who thought he could hit.

"I know I can hit," Greason replied.

"Where do you want it, high or low?" Satchel asked.

Satchel Paige's traveling All-Stars team was a major attraction on the Negro League circuit, sometimes playing local African American teams and sometimes facing teams of Major League All-Stars. This particular group of all-stars was barnstorming with Bob Feller's All-Stars.

Greason called for three pitches down the middle of the plate. "I didn't hardly get the bat off of my shoulder, he was so fast," Greason recalled. "He threw three 'right there' and I never got the bat off my shoulder. He was up in age then and could still throw.

"He didn't have a breaking ball," Greason added. "He just had that hesitation pitch. People didn't know what it was. He would just stride out, stop, and then throw. They outlawed it when he was in the majors."

Paige also had pinpoint control. Veteran minor leaguer Ed Mickelson had a brief career with the St. Louis Browns while Paige was on the team. He recalled one incident in which Paige used a matchbox as a pitching target. The other players on the team scoffed at the idea that a pitcher could hit the corners of such a target, much less toss one over it.

"Satch took ten pitches to warm up with Les Moss, our catcher," Mickelson said. "Satch stepped on the mound as someone placed the match box on home plate. He said, 'This is going to be inside.' He missed his call by an inch. Out of ten pitches, only one pitch was more than 2½ inches from the corner. The scoffers were now believers."[55]

"He could throw that ball right where he wanted it," Greason agreed. "I've seen him warm up with a matchbox. He said, if you pitch high and tight, low and away, you could win. That's what Satch would do. He would pitch up tight then go low and outside. That was pretty hard to catch up with when a man is throwing at ninety five miles an hour."

Another Negro League legend, Ted "Double Duty" Radcliffe, said Greason's estimate of Paige's speed was too conservative. Radcliffe once said of Paige, "He could throw 105 miles an hour and hit a mosquito over the outside corner of the plate."[56]

Rumors started circulating that blacks would soon be playing in the major leagues. If the barrier was broken, most Negro League fans assumed Satchel Paige would do it. Yankee pitcher Lefty Gomez was one of those advocates. "Paige could win in any league consistently," he said. "And don't forget he was pitching three or four times a week. If he had the rest a big leaguer gets, I don't know what club could beat him."[57]

When the barrier was finally broken by Satchel's teammate, Jackie Robinson, the pitcher was disappointed. "Somehow I'd always figured it'd be me," he said afterwards. "Maybe it happened too late and everybody figured I was too old. But signing Jackie like they did still hurt me deep down. I'd been the guy who'd started all that big talk about letting us in the big time."[58]

In retrospect, Paige had little chance of breaking the barrier. "He had age working against him," Negro historian Larry Lester noted. "His best years were behind him. He was overused."[59] Indeed, as Lester added, in 1947 Paige pitched in every game of the Negro League World Series.

His disappointment did not interfere with his pitching, though. In 1946, the Monarchs won both the first and second half of the Negro League season. Satchel had a 21–0 record at the age of 40. He finally made it to the majors in 1948, signed by the Cleveland Indians on July 7—his 42nd birthday. Two days later, he made a relief appearance against the St. Louis Browns, pitching two scoreless innings; he was the first African American to pitch in the American League, the fifth to play the game, and the oldest rookie in the history of the majors.[60]

Clarence M. Markham, writing in a 1948 issue of the *Negro Traveler*, called it one of the most momentous events in the history of the Negro Leagues. "Not even the signing of Jackie Robinson, Larry Doby, or Roy Campanella meant as much to Negroes as a whole as the signing of LeRoy Paige, who had been the baseball hero of Negro America for years."

Satchel created controversy immediately. Browns manager Zack Taylor protested when Satchel tossed his hesitation pitch. The umps ruled it legal, but American League president Will Harridge soon banned the pitch. "I almost got worried," Satchel said afterwards. "I was afraid if I showed any of my other tricks he might ban them too."[61]

Still, his irrepressible humor could not be contained. Ed Mickelson recalled a game when he was playing first base and Paige was pitching for the Browns against the Chicago White Sox. Mickelson was holding a runner at first base when Satchel lifted his left leg, and with a flick of his wrist, tossed the ball into Mickelson's glove without even looking toward first base.

"I tagged the runner coming back to first base," Mickelson said. "Satchel surprised me and the runner, and the umpire. If Satch had not made a perfect throw, the ball would have hit me in the gut. The umpire being fooled too called the runner out but quickly came to his senses when he realized Satch did not step with his left foot toward first base."[62] Paige, meanwhile, was on the mound, doubled over with laughter. He knew he had balked, but also knew that he had fooled all three men at first base.

Mickelson noted that Satchel used one of his trick pitches. "After he had gone into his single, double and triple windup, he stepped with his left foot and hesitated for several seconds and threw the ball in an arching manner about 12 feet in the air," Mickelson said. "Both the batter and umpire were bewildered as the ball descended toward home plate. The batter did not swing and the umpire did not know what to call. Again, the sound of laughter came from the mound."[63]

Paige's first start was a 5–3 victory on August 3 over the Washington Senators; his second was a shutout over the Senators. Cleveland went on to win its first pennant in 28 years, and Satch finished the season with a 6–1 record and two shutouts. His 2.47 ERA was second best in the league. In the World Series against the Braves, Satchel became the first African American to pitch in the post-season classic. He appeared in one game, pitching two-thirds of an inning in relief, and held the Braves scoreless.

For the 1949 season, he posted only four wins against seven losses, but his 3.04 ERA was in the league's top ten. The 1950 season was a year of barnstorming, but he returned to the majors in 1951 as a reliever for the St. Louis Browns. He was 3–4 for the cellar-dwelling club, with 48 strikeouts in 62 innings.

Satchel was a major drawing card for the last-place Browns. His showmanship, honed over years in exhibition games, delighted the fans. On one occasion, with two outs and two runners on base, the ball was hit directly back to Satchel, who fielded it, started walking toward third base, and then flipped the ball backhand to first without looking.

The Browns gained even further exposure from joking about his age. The team bought him a special contour chair for the bullpen. "I'd just sit there and doze a little until (manager) Marty Marion signaled for me to come in. Then I'd just loaf out to the pitching mound," Satch remembered.[64]

In the 1952 press guide for the team, Satchel's birthday was listed as, "September 11, 1892-Z, 1896-Z, 1900-Z, 1904-Z." At the end of the pitcher's information, they had another line: "Z — Take your pick."

Interestingly, none of those dates is correct; Satchel's official birthday is dated July 7, 1906. And that may be wrong too. According to Ted "Double Duty" Radcliffe, who grew up with Paige in Mobile, Satchel arbitrarily assigned himself the birth date July 7, 1906, when he entered professional baseball. Radcliffe argued that Paige was actually born in 1900. "He was always two years older than me when we was kids" Radcliffe said. "He was always two years older than me when we was in school together."[65]

But it was no joke for the rest of the league. Yankee manager Casey Stengel said, "If the Yanks don't get ahead in the first six innings, the Browns bring in that damned old man and then we're sunk."[66]

Indeed, in 1952 Paige was the best reliever in baseball with a 12–10 record, 10 saves, and a 3.07 ERA — all at the (real) age of 46. But in 1953, his record was a dismal 3–9;

when the Browns were sold and moved to Baltimore the next season, Satchel was released.

He spent the next few seasons barnstorming prior to joining the Miami Marlins of the International League in 1956. He pitched a shutout in his first game and finished the season with an 11–4 record and an ERA of 1.86. At the age of 50, he was the top pitcher in the league.

In 1957, he was 10–8 with a 2.42 ERA for Miami, walking only 11 batters in 40 games. In 1961, he signed with Portland in the Pacific Coast League; he was 55 years old and pitched only 25 innings, but he tallied 19 strikeouts with a 2.88 ERA.

In 1965, Paige made another appearance in the major leagues with Kansas City, pitching three scoreless innings against the Boston Red Sox. At the age of 59, he was the oldest player to ever pitch in a major league game.

How could one man pitch so well for so long? Part of it was pure talent. His control was so sharp he would win bets by using a handkerchief as home plate and throwing eight strikes out of ten pitches across it. "It got so I could nip frosting off a cake with my fastball," he said. "If you know where that ball is going, you can do a lot no one else can, and you can stay around long after the real good stuff you throw is gone."[67]

Part of it was the seriousness to which he approached his profession. "I never joked when I was pitching," he once said, "Between pitches, okay."[68]

Part of it came from his year-round pitching routine. "A man rusts sitting in one spot, and if you don't rust you can keep going long after the other guy stops," he said.[69]

And part of it came from a determination to let others know how good he was. "When you weren't in the major leagues, you had to keep proving it," he said.[70]

Paige kept proving it. "Even without the tall tales that grew up around it, the righthander's career often reads like fiction," Dewey and Acocella wrote. "Ultimately, Paige's ability, longevity, and showmanship gave the Negro Leagues much of whatever visibility they had in the white world."[71]

Over the years, his name and abilities have become legendary. That doesn't make them any less real. As Negro League umpire Bob Motley wrote:

> Even now, some 60 years after first laying eyes on him in person, I can tell you from my personal experience, everything you have heard or read about the magnitude of his talent is not an exaggeration. Words cannot do justice to his prowess. But I'll try anyway: Satchel Paige was simply a phenom![72]

In 1971, the phenomenal Leroy "Satchel" Paige was inducted into the Hall of Fame, becoming the first Negro League player so honored. Finally, it seems, the rest of the world was convinced.

Roy "Red" Parnell

Red Parnell was an outfielder on the 1927 Black Barons team that won the second-half championship for the Negro National League. He was a major contributor to that title, registering a .426 batting average for the season.

Parnell broke into the Negro Leagues by joining the Black Barons in that pivotal 1927 season. He played well enough to be in the starting lineup for the league playoffs, getting two hits in the four games. He stayed in Birmingham for only one more year, but he put up some impressive numbers during that 1928 season. He hit for a .326 average and finished the year ranked third in the league with 18 doubles.

Parnell played with a number of teams thereafter before beginning an eight-year stint with the Philadelphia Stars in 1936.

Parnell was selected to two all-star games, playing with the East squad in 1934 as a member of the Nashville Elite Giants, and with the West in 1939 while posting a .304 average as a member of the Stars.

Parnell joined the Pittsburgh Crawfords in 1946. He finished out his career by splitting the 1950 season with the New York Cuban Stars and the Houston Eagles.

BILL PERKINS

Bill Perkins had a 21-year career as a catcher/manager in professional baseball, a career that started with the Birmingham Black Barons in 1928. He played for some of the best teams in the league, including the Pittsburgh Crawfords, Homestead Grays, and New York Black Yankees. He also played in two all-star games for the league.

Perkins, a Georgia native, broke in with the Barons in 1928 as a catcher, posting a .236 batting average. He topped out with a .308 average with the Barons in 1930, his last year with the team.[73]

In 1930, he followed Satchel Paige to the Cleveland Cubs and then to the Pittsburgh Crawfords.[74] He posted a .335 average in 1932, and upped that to .360 in 1933 with the Crawfords. Perkins made his first all-star appearance in 1934.

Playing behind Josh Gibson in Pittsburgh, Perkins eventually moved on to the Philadelphia Stars in 1938. He joined the Baltimore Elite Giants in 1940, and finished out his career by splitting time between the Stars, Giants, and the New York Black Yankees.

ROBERT "BLACK DIAMOND" PIPKIN

Black Diamond Pipkin was a charismatic pitcher who broke into the Negro Leagues with the Birmingham Black Barons in 1928. He stayed with the team in 1929, posted a 3–5 record, and moved on to the Cleveland Cubs in 1931. Pipkin returned to the Barons in 1942, registering a 5–2 record in his final season in the Negro Leagues.

ROBERT POINDEXTER

Robert Poindexter was a pitcher for the Black Barons during the 1920s. The right-hander broke into the Negro Leagues with the Barons in 1924. He left the team after the 1925 season, joining the Chicago American Giants. His 6–2 record in 1926 was a significant contribution to the Giants' pennant-winning season.

Poindexter returned to the Barons in 1927, posting a 10–12 record. He was with the team again in 1928, but his career took a significant downturn after that. He first returned to Chicago in 1929, but was soon shipped off to the Memphis Red Sox. In Memphis, he apparently was drinking heavily and was arrested for shooting a teammate. Poindexter attempted to commit suicide, but failed. Regardless, his career in the Negro Leagues was over.

Harry Salmon

Harry Salmon spent 16 years in professional baseball, and most of that was with the Birmingham Black Barons. Born May 30, 1895, in Warrior, Alabama, Salmon grew up playing baseball in the coal mining communities around Birmingham.[75] He joined the Barons in 1920. He played with the Pittsburgh Keystones for two years before returning to the Barons in 1923 when they joined the Negro League.

Salmon posted a 7–3 record in 1923, an 8–3 mark in 1924, and a 7–6 record in 1925. He blossomed in 1926, putting together a 14–3 record that included a no-hitter. He was just as good in 1927, notching a 14–6 record as the Barons faced the Chicago American Giants in a playoff for the league pennant. He made two appearances in the playoffs, losing both decisions, as the Giants won the series.

After brief stints with the Memphis Red Sox and Detroit Wolves, Salmon finished his career by playing three seasons for the Homestead Grays. He retired to Pittsburgh after the 1935 season. Salmon died in Pittsburgh in July 1983.

Sam Streeter

Sam Streeter spent 17 years as a pitcher in the Negro Leagues. He played for ten different teams during that span, but he is best remembered for his years with the Black Barons.

Born September 17, 1900, in New Market, Alabama, Streeter broke into pro ball with the Montgomery Grey Sox in 1920. He played with the Atlanta Black Crackers, the Chicago American Giants, the Atlantic City Bacharach Giants, and the New York Lincoln Giants before joining the Barons in 1924.

His first year with the Barons proved to be the best season in his career. He posted a 14–7 record and led the league in strikeouts. He had another good season in 1927, posting a 14–12 record while teaming with Harry Salmon and rookie Satchel Paige to pitch the Barons to the second-half title.

Streeter left the Barons during the 1928 season to join the Homestead Grays. He returned to the Barons in 1930, and spent part of that season with the Baltimore Black Sox, compiling a combined record of 14–12 for the year.

Streeter finished his career with the Pittsburgh Crawfords, retiring after the 1936 season. He died in Pittsburgh on August 8, 1985.

George "Mule" Suttles

Another star of the era was slugger Mule Suttles. Suttles, a member of the Baseball Hall of Fame, is the all-time home run leader for the Negro Leagues with 127 blasts. In 1926, playing with St. Louis, he led the league with a .498 average, while hitting 27 home runs and 21 triples. He became just the second player in Negro League history to hit 20 homers, 20 doubles and 20 triples in a single season, despite playing in only 78 league games. The mark has been matched by four major league players since then (including another former Black Baron, Willie Mays), but everyone else played in twice as many games.

In 2006, the National Baseball Hall of Fame received the results of the Special Committee on the Negro Leagues, which had been assigned to identify those players whose achievements in the pre–Robinson years warranted inclusion in the hall. As a result of that move, George "Mule" Suttles became the fourth former member of the Birmingham Black Barons to enter the Hall of Fame. Suttles had a 36-year career as a player that spanned two world wars.

Buck O'Neil had a simple description of Suttles. "What a hitter, man," O'Neil said. "Powerful. He hit the ball a country mile."[76]

Born March 31, 1900, in Blocton, Alabama, the 6'6", 250-pound Suttles broke into professional baseball at the age of 17 in 1918, two years before the establishment of the Negro National League. He played in one game with the New York Bacharach Giants in 1921, and then made his entry into the Negro National League by joining the Birmingham Black Barons in 1923.

He played left field for Birmingham, batting .283 with one home run in his rookie season. He improved to .317 the next year — with 10 home runs — and became a star in 1925. He finished the season with a .428 batting average, tops in the Negro Leagues. His 14 home runs also ranked third in the league. And, he started playing first base, the position that would become his favorite and the one most associated with his prime years. His homer total might have been higher if not for playing his home games in Rickwood Field. During one season, Suttles hit only one homer at Rickwood, where the left-field fence was 411 feet away and center field was 485 feet at the time.

In 1926, the first baseman joined the St. Louis Stars. The name of his new team was appropriate, because he soon became a star player in the Negro Leagues. He stayed with the team for seven seasons and led them to championships in 1928, 1930, and 1931. During that span, he also led the Negro National League in home runs twice and added single-season titles in doubles, triples, and batting average.

He was the league MVP in 1926, during which he won the batting average title and led the league in home runs. Riley credits him with a .432 average, 26 home runs, and a 1.000 slugging percentage.[77] Holway lists him with a .498 average and 27 home runs.[78] Holway also credits Suttles with 27 doubles and 21 triples in league games — both league-leading numbers.

Suttles was off to a good start again in 1927, hitting .476 about six weeks into the season. That ended when opposing pitcher Chet Brewer hit Suttles in the head with a bean ball. The injury caused the slugger to miss the rest of the campaign.

He returned in 1928 with a .372 batting average and 20 home runs, good for third in the league in both categories. On August 29 he hit three triples in a game. He topped that with three home runs in a September 9 game. He was a key figure in the Stars' championship season, going 9-for-27 in the post-season games against the Chicago American Giants.

In 1929, he posted a .351 average. Holway credits him with hitting 20 home runs — second in the league[79] — but some sources list only nine dingers. Regardless, he did hit 26 doubles, best in the league. The Stars lost the World Series to Homestead, but Suttles batted .350 in off-season exhibition games against major league teams.

Suttles moved above the .400 mark in 1930, leading the league with a .422 batting average. His 12 home runs were second in the league. He spent part of the season playing for the Baltimore Black Sox, hitting another 10 home runs and batting .389.

He dropped to .349 in 1931, good enough for fourth in the league. His 12 home runs were second best in the West Division, while his 10 homers with Baltimore led the East Division.

After the Stars disbanded, Mule split one season with the Detroit Wolves and the Washington Pilots. Holway credits him with a .315 average for Detroit and .322 for Washington. He also lists Suttles with hitting nine home runs, although some sources say he slammed two dingers for the season.[80]

In 1933, he signed with the Chicago American Giants as an outfielder. Manager Dave Malarcher shortened his swing and Suttles responded with a .283 average and made the all-star team. His average rose to .295 in 1934, and his 12 home runs were third in the league. He went 3-for-4 with a triple in the all-star game. Further, he helped the Giants win the league pennant.

In 1935, he was up slightly to .263 at the plate, while his 13 home runs were second in the league. It was his last season with the Giants, but he made all-star appearances during each of his three years with the team.

Suttles holds the distinction of hitting the first home run in the history of the East-West All-Star Game. His three-run blast — along with a double, two runs, and three RBIs — led the West to an 11–7 win in the inaugural 1933 contest. Two years later, in 1935, he hit another all-star home run. This one came in the 11th inning, another three-run blast to give the East another win.[81]

In 1936, Suttles joined the Newark Eagles and returned to his favorite position at first base. He became a member of arguably the most renowned infield in the history of the Negro Leagues — the Eagles' "million dollar infield." His teammates included Dick Seay at second, Willie Wells at shortstop, and future Hall of Fame member Ray Dandridge at third base.

He remained a force at the plate, hitting .365 with 15 home runs in 1936. He had similar numbers in 1937 — a .345 average and 16 home runs. His average dropped to .282 in 1938, but his 14 home runs led the league. He repeated the batting average in 1939, hitting the .282 mark again, while clubbing 12 home runs, good for second in the league. He again made it to the All-Star game, but was 0-for-4 as the cleanup hitter for the East.

In 1940, age was beginning to have its effect. His average dropped to .262, and his home run count dropped to the single digits (only eight) for the first time since his rookie season. Suttles continued with his all-star playing, making the East-West All-Star Game twice more as an Eagle. He finished his five all-star appearances with a .412 batting average and a .833 slugging percentage.[82]

Suttles left the Eagles after the 1940 season, signing with the New York Black Yankees in 1941. He hit only .222 for the season and returned to the Eagles in 1942, putting up a .385 average as a utility player.

He became the Eagles' manager in 1943, posting a 19–20 record, but returned to the field as their player-manager in 1944. He finished his career in 1944 with a .250 average (10-for-40) with three homers while compiling a 19–22 record as manager. He retired from the game after being replaced as manager by Willie Wells.

Suttles was considered one of the most powerful hitters in the history of the Negro

Leagues.[83] He used a 50-ounce bat that he wielded with power. Several of his home runs were listed as being more than 500 feet.

In a game at Tropicana Park in Havana, Cuba, Suttles hit one blast over a 60-foot-high screen in center field that was designed to keep balls from landing in the ocean. The blast was officially listed as 598 feet. Teammate Willie Wells remembered watching the blast and said, "He hit this damn ball so far it looked like we were playing in a lot; it didn't look like no ball park."

Such feats caused one sports writer, Chico Renfroe, to write that Suttles "had the most raw power of any player I've ever seen." "He wasn't a finesse player at all," Renfroe added. "He just overpowered the opposition."[84]

Records from the Negro League are notoriously sketchy, but Riley credits him with a .338 lifetime batting average.[85] Holway puts the number at .341, fifth on the all-time Negro League career list.[86]

Holway also credits Suttles with 237 career home runs in Negro League competition. That number puts him at the top of the Negro League career home list, 13 more than career runner-up Josh Gibson.[87] Add exhibition games to that, and some sources raise his overall batting average to .453 and innumerable home runs.

Those numbers weren't due to lack of competition. In 1929, Suttles played in a series of exhibition games against an all-star team of major leaguers, led by Hall of Fame member Charlie Gehringer. Suttles hit .341 and smashed ten home runs in 170 at-bats against major league competition. Five of those home runs and a .374 average came in the 26 games played in 1929.

Like many Negro League players, Suttles usually played baseball year-round. He spent several of his winters playing in the California Winter League, where he often faced major league competition.[88] He won two batting and six home run titles in that arena, while compiling an .869 slugging average.

He also played in an era when the spitball was legal. It didn't seem to hamper his home run total. Negro League player Charley Biot recalled one loaded pitch thrown to Suttles that the slugger knocked out of the park. "You could actually see the saliva fly off of it when it went over the center field fence," Biot said.[89]

Suttles was inducted into the National Baseball Hall of Fame in Cooperstown, New York, in 2006. His selection was no surprise. A decade earlier, Holway identified him as one of the Negro League players who deserved induction.[90] Prior to that, he came to the attention of the national baseball community with an magazine article in 1953.[91]

George "Mule" Suttles died of cancer on July 9, 1966, at the age of 66 in Newark, New Jersey.

JAMES "SANDY" THOMPSON

Sandy Thompson won the Negro League batting title in 1927 with a .441 average while leading the Birmingham Black Barons to the second-half title.

Thompson broke into pro ball with the Dayton Marcos in 1920. He played with the Milwaukee Bears before joining the Barons in 1924 and hitting .322. He stayed with the Barons through 1925, posting a .341 average, then moved to the Chicago American Giants in 1926.

He returned to the Barons in 1927 for his record-setting year, then returned to the Giants in 1928 and stayed with the team through 1930. He finished his career with a season each with the Chicago Columbia Giants (1931), Cole's American Giants (1932) and the Cuban Stars (1933).

Columbus "Luke" Vance

Luke Vance was a pitcher for the Birmingham Black Barons from 1927 until 1931. He put up a 3–0 record in his rookie season as the Barons won the second-half title. His best season came in 1930, when he posted an 8–11 record. Vance left Birmingham after the Negro National League folded in 1931. He pitched for three teams in 1932 and finished his career with a 6–7 mark for the Detroit Stars in 1933.[92]

Poindexter Williams

Poindexter Williams had a 13-year career in pro baseball, playing for six different teams, but he is most often identified with the Birmingham Black Barons. He spent seven seasons as a catcher and first baseman for the Black Barons, from 1923 until 1929. Williams posted a .389 average in 1925, hit for a .381 mark in 1937, and finished his years with the Barons with a .308 average in 1929. Williams joined the Nashville Elite Giants in 1930. He concluded his career as a backup catcher for the Homestead Grays in 1933.

CHAPTER 2

The Black Barons in the 1930s

From 1928 to 1930, the Barons fielded teams with losing records. Financial problems caused be the Great Depression sent the team back to the Negro Southern League in 1931. They tried an unsuccessful return to the big league in 1937, but were generally not competitive with the other teams. Returning to the Negro Southern League for 1938 and 1939, they rebuilt the team by recruiting stars of Birmingham's industrial leagues. They provided the foundation for a return to the Negro American League in 1940.[1]

Early players during this period included Samuel Howard "Sam" Bankhead. Bankhead had a 22-year career in baseball that included three years with the Black Barons (1929, 1931–32). He also played with the Nashville Elite Giants, the Louisville Black Caps, the Kansas City Monarchs, the Pittsburgh Crawfords, the Memphis Red Sox, and the Homestead Grays. The seven-time all-star was a member of the 1948 Grays team that defeated the Black Barons in the Negro League World Series. In 1952, he was named to the all-time Negro League team by the *Pittsburgh Courier*.

The 1930s saw Clarence Smith, W. Jones, A. M. Walker, and Black Barons legend Sam Crawford at the team's dugout helm.

A few of the more memorable players are identified below.

HERMAN "JABO" ANDREWS

Jabo Andrews had a 14-year career as an outfielder and manager in the Negro Leagues, toiling from 1930 until 1943 with 13 different teams. His career began in 1930 with the Birmingham Black Barons, when he hit .388 for the season.

Andrews spent the rest of the 1930s playing for a variety of teams before returning to Birmingham following the 1938 season to play in the industrial leagues. He returned to the Barons in 1940, and finished his career with the Philadelphia Stars in 1943.

TANK AUSTIN

Tank Austin had only a three-year career as a pitcher in the Negro League, playing from 1930 until 1932. He broke into the league with a brief stint with the Nashville Elite Giants. He joined the Birmingham Black Barons later in the season and stayed with them through the 1931 year. He finished his career with the Atlanta Black Crackers in 1932, but is best remembered for his short tenure with the Barons.

FRED BANKHEAD

Fred Bankhead followed his brother Sam into the Negro Leagues in 1936, making his debut as a reserve infielder with the Birmingham Black Barons and playing three seasons for the team (1936–1938). Born November 23, 1912, in Empire, Alabama, he had a 13-year career in the Negro Leagues — mostly with the Memphis Red Sox.

Bankhead first joined Memphis as a second baseman in 1938 and contributed to the Red Sox team winning the first-half championship. He moved to third base in 1939 and played the next nine seasons with Memphis. In 1942, he made his only East-West All-Star Game appearance, entering the contest as a pinch-runner.

Bankhead was a fast runner who contributed with his defensive play, but was a below-average hitter. He hit only .235 in 1942, his all-star year. He reached a high of .282 in 1944, but dropped to .242 in 1945 and then to .204 in 1946. He played the 1947 season with Memphis, and then spent his final year in the Negro League with the New York Black Yankees in 1948.

Bankhead died in an automobile accident in Mississippi on December 17, 1972.

SAM BANKHEAD

Of the five different Bankhead brothers from Empire, Alabama, who played in the Negro Leagues, Sam Bankhead had the most impressive career. The oldest of the five brothers was a legendary player during the 1930s and 1940s. Moffi and Kronstadt described him as "one of the finest shortstops in the Negro Leagues for nearly 20 years."[2] He was also a versatile player that former Barons manager Tommy Sampson remembered as "a guy I used to admire because he could play anywhere."[3]

Charlie Biot, one of Bankhead's teammates on the Grays, considered him the best second baseman he ever saw play, but was also impressed by his versatility. "He could catch, play third — anywhere," Biot said. "You need a center fielder, put him out there.... He was some ball player. It's hard to play all the positions."[4]

Bankhead got his start in professional baseball by playing five seasons (1929, 1930–32, and 1938) with the Birmingham Black Barons. His most notable accomplishments came with two other teams — the Pittsburgh Crawfords during the 1930s[5] and the Homestead Grays[6] during the 1940s. He was a key player in the Grays' winning the Negro League World Series over the Barons in 1948. On the positive side, Bankhead was a player that others looked to as someone who "dressed well, played smartly."[7] On the negative side, Bankhead eventually got in trouble while playing with the Grays, breaking team rules by drinking on the bus.[8]

Bankhead was born September 18, 1905, in Empire, Alabama, a mining town near Birmingham. He would become a seven-time all-star while playing for three different teams, Pittsburgh, Homestead, and Nashville, and playing five different positions — second base, shortstop, left field, center field, and right field. In 1952, he was selected as the first-team utility player on the all-time Negro Leagues All-Star team.[9]

He began his career in 1929 with the Barons. He started the 1930 season with the

Nashville Elite Giants before returning to Birmingham late in the year. He showed his versatility early, playing most of the infield and outfield positions. He also occasionally got behind the plate to catch a game and — starting in 1932 — had a few appearances as a pitcher for the Barons (posting a 2–6 career record).

After the 1938 regular season, the Memphis Red Sox signed Bankhead and David Whatley from the Barons to help them in the Negro League playoffs. That ended Bankhead's association with the Barons. The next year he was signed by the Homestead Grays, the beginning of a ten-year career with the team. It was interrupted only once — two years, in 1940 and 1941, when he played in the Mexican League.

In his later years, Bankhead became a mentor to young players. He watched after Josh Gibson, Jr., the son of one of his best friends, during the youngster's brief career in the Negro Leagues and in Canada. Maurice Peatros, another young player on the Grays during Bankhead's latter years, also credited the legendary player for watching after him. "Sam was like in my ear hole constantly," Peatros once said, "'cause he knew my dad and the idea was 'Look out for my son.'"[10]

Bankhead was the manager of the Homestead Grays when they disbanded in 1950. He finished his baseball career in Canada in 1951, serving as the manager for the Farnham club in the Provincial League. That position made him the first African American to manage a white baseball team.

Bankhead eventually retired to the Pittsburgh area. He died there on July 24, 1976.

JERRY BENJAMIN

Jerry Benjamin had a 17-year career as an outfielder and manager in the Negro Leagues that spanned from 1932 to 1948. Those years included one season — 1934 — with the Birmingham Black Barons. Benjamin is best remembered for his 14 years in center field for the Homestead Grays,[11] where he became a three-time all-star and helped the Grays to nine league championships. He became so popular that Wilson signed him to endorse the company's baseballs in 1945 and 1946.[12]

Benjamin was born November 9, 1909, in Montgomery, Alabama. He entered the Negro Leagues with the Memphis Red Sox in 1932, joined the Detroit Stars in 1933, and then became a Black Baron in 1934.

After joining the Homestead Grays in 1935, he was a key figure in the team's winning of nine Negro League pennants. Although a consistent .300 hitter, his best season came in 1944 when he hit for a .392 average. The Black Barons also won their pennant that year, but Benjamin was one of the team leaders as the Homestead Grays defeated the Barons in the Negro League World Series.

During part of his tenure with the Grays, the speedy Benjamin was a teammate of Cool Papa Bell. In 1945, he tied Bell for second place in stolen bases for the league. Benjamin finished his career as a manager for the Norfolk-Newport News Royals in the Negro American Association.

JACK BRUTON

Jack Bruton played four seasons with the Black Barons in the late 1930s (1936–38) and again in 1940. Primarily a pitcher, the Cordova, Alabama, native was good enough at the plate and versatile enough in the field to play a defensive position when he wasn't on the mound. In addition to the Barons, he played with the Philadelphia Stars (1938), the Cleveland Bears (1939), the New York Black Yankees (1940) and the New Orleans–St. Louis Stars (1940–41).

JIM CANADA

First baseman Jim Canada played three seasons for the Birmingham Black Barons (1936–37, 1946), part of an 11-year career as a player. After finishing his playing career, he stayed in the league into the 1950s as a manager.

Canada broke into professional baseball in 1933 with the Jacksonville Redcaps. He moved to the Black Barons and the Negro Southern League in 1936. He took over the third spot in the batting order and was anchored there when the Barons joined the Negro American League in 1937.

Canada moved to the Atlanta Black Crackers in 1938. He returned to his first team — Jacksonville — in 1942 and then finished his playing career with the Memphis Red Sox, from 1943 until 1945. By then his age was hindering his talent. He hit only .206 in 1944, and .209 in 1945.

Canada returned to the Birmingham Black Barons in 1946 and was associated with the team off and on until 1962. He also briefly managed the Chattanooga Choo Choos, where Willie Mays briefly played. Canada resigned from Chattanooga soon after Mays joined the team. He recommended that Piper Davis sign the youngster to the Black Barons.[13]

OLIVER FERGUSON

One Black Baron from the 1930s is still an active member of the Alabama Negro League Players Association. Oliver Ferguson had a brief career in the Negro Leagues, playing only one season as a utility player with the Birmingham Black Barons. He spent several years with other teams, mostly in Birmingham's industrial league. His memories of his playing days provide insight into black baseball in the 1930s.

Born November 26, 1920, in Woodward, Alabama, Ferguson grew up as the son of a baseball coach, which became his avenue into pro ball. "My father had a baseball team, and I was the batboy," he said. "I started with that, and he then made me play with the big men."[14]

He entered the game at a rough financial time in the history of the nation, growing up as a teenager during the Great Depression. "There was a panic from 1932 to 1935. There weren't no jobs," he said. "We didn't get no money. They'd give you meal money; that's all we got."

Things improved after Franklin D. Roosevelt won the 1936 presidential election. Roosevelt took office in 1937 and jobs started returning to the nation as well as the Birmingham area. "When Roosevelt took over in 1937, that's when we started getting jobs," he said.

Ferguson was first hired to a semi-pro job, working for a local company while playing baseball for them. "They hired all these young men for the factory," he said. "We didn't make but $16 a week. But after that, I had enough money."

Oliver Ferguson (right), pictured here with Charley Pride, played one season as a utility player with the Birmingham Black Barons in 1938. He spent several years with other teams, mostly in Birmingham's industrial league.

He joined the Barons in 1938. "I was a utility man. I played all positions, but my regular position was shortstop," he said.

As a Baron, he traveled throughout much of the South. A typical road trip included a visit to Montgomery and then to Mobile. That might be followed by a swing into New Orleans or a tour of Florida. The team would then move back toward Georgia, Tennessee, and the Carolinas before returning home to Birmingham.

Ferguson left Birmingham in 1939 and played shortstop for a team in Bluefield, West Virginia, for two years. His best game came while he was there, against a team in Virginia. He finished that game with two home runs, two doubles, and two singles. "I had near 'bout a perfect day that day," he recalled.

Ferguson returned to Birmingham in 1942 and played in the industrial league until 1950. "I got out of baseball when I was 40 years old," he said.

He remains active in sports, spending much of his time playing golf. Looking back, he has some advice for the players of the future.

"If they get with the right team and the right manager, they can do the same thing we did," he said. "But they've got to be straight and do what the manager says. If they won't do that, they won't make it."

And, he added, an education is essential for the players of today — particularly to prepare them for a life after baseball. "They need to go to school and get an education," he said. "That will take them a long way.

"In baseball, you've got to have an education so you've got somewhere to go," he added. "You can't stay in baseball all your life. You've got to come out sooner or later. If you finish high school, you've got a chance at getting some kind of job."

Victor "Vic" Harris

Outfielder Vic Harris made his reputation with the Homestead Grays with a career that spanned from the 1920s to the 1940s. After his playing days were over, he spent one season as the manager of the Birmingham Black Barons. Harris was at the helm of the club in 1950.

Born June 10, 1905, in Pensacola, Florida, Harris broke into professional baseball with the Cleveland Tate Stars in 1923, hitting for a .304 average. He played in Ohio for two years, either in Cleveland or Toledo, before hitching on with the Chicago American Giants late in the 1924 season and finishing the year with a .277 average.

In 1925, he joined the Homestead Grays, the team that would be his baseball home for 23 years. Although lacking power, he was a line-drive hitter who could handle a bat. He batted .324 for the Grays in 1930 as the team won the Eastern Division. He became the leadoff hitter in 1932, responding with a .348 average and improving to .351 in 1933. Harris signed a one-year contract with the Pittsburgh Crawfords for 1934, hitting .360 for the season, and then returned to the Grays for the 1935 campaign as player-manager, when he hit .370. When the Grays added Josh Gibson to the lineup in 1937, it was the beginning of nine straight pennants for the team.

Harris' best season as a player was in 1938 when he hit .380 with 10 home runs and 17 stolen bases. His role as the team's manager was briefly interrupted in 1943 when he took a job at a defense plan during World War II. He still continued to play for the team part-time for the '43 and '44 seasons, and returned as the Homestead manager in 1945. He again led them to the NNL championship, with the Grays defeating the Birmingham Black Barons in the Negro League World Series.

Harris built up a .299 career batting average and appeared in six East-West All-Star Games. Harris was in the starting lineup of the first All-Star Game in 1933; he was a pinch-runner in his final all-star appearance in 1947.[15] He played in a total of six East-West All-Star Games and was a key figure in the Grays' winning nine consecutive Negro National League pennants, from 1937 to 1945.[16] He also led the Grays to the 1948 World Series over the Birmingham Black Barons.

He served as the manager for the Black Barons in 1950, his final season in the Negro Leagues. Harris died February 23, 1978, in San Fernando, California.

Lester "Buck" Lockett

Lester Lockett broke into the Negro Leagues with the Birmingham Black Barons in 1938. He went on to be a three-time all-star — twice with the Black Barons (1943, 1945) and once with the Baltimore Elite Giants (1948).

Born March 26, 1912, in Princeton, Indiana, Lockett made a quick impression as an outfielder and third baseman in the league. He hit for a .328 average in his first full season in 1941. He notched a .315 mark in '42, and then hit .408 in 1943. He dropped to .249 in 1944, but came back up to .300 in 1945.

Lockett hit above the .300 mark for both of his seasons with the Baltimore Elite Giants, and finished his Negro League career in 1950 with a .301 average for the Chicago American Giants. Lockett spent the latter part of his career playing in Canada's Mandak League.

Terris "Speed" McDuffie

Speed McDuffie was a pitcher for the Birmingham Black Barons in 1930 and 1931—the beginning of a 16-year career in professional baseball. Born July 22, 1910, in Mobile, McDuffie went on to play for a dozen teams, including the Baltimore Black Sox, Newark Dodgers, New York Black Yankees, Philadelphia Stars, and Homestead Grays. In between, he also played in Cuba and in the Mexican League.

McDuffie had a reputation as an excellent pitcher. He was the starting and winning pitcher in the 1941 East-West All-Star Game. He was the starting pitcher again in the 1944 game. He faced Satchel Paige three times, winning twice. At one point after World War II, McDuffie was the highest-paid player in the eastern part of the Negro Leagues with a salary of $6,000 a year.[17]

In the 1935 season, McDuffie pitched a no-hitter against the House of David team. That probably was not his most memorable game, though. That most likely occurred in Cuba when his manager, Dolph Luque, named McDuffie as the game's starter, and McDuffie refused to take the mound. Luque pulled a gun from his hip, pointed it at McDuffie, and repeated his decision. McDuffie started and pitched a two-hitter.

In 1945, Branch Rickey took a look at McDuffie as a possible player to break the major league color barrier. McDuffie was 34 years old at the time, and well past his prime. Still, Rickey watched as McDuffie and Showboat Thomas showed their stuff. Rickey decided to pass on McDuffie, saying, "He has good control but doesn't follow through on any delivery. It may take time to break that habit."[18]

His stuff was good enough, however, to get him into the minor leagues. He finished his career in the Texas League in 1954, posting a 3–4 record and a 3.04 ERA. A leg injury ended his playing days.

Johnny Ray

Johnny Ray was the Black Barons starting center fielder in 1937. He played for the Barons for three seasons, staying with the team in 1938 and spending a second stint with them in 1945. Born in Nashville in 1907, Ray broke into professional baseball with the Montgomery Gray Sox in 1931. He moved to a minor league team, the Claybrook Tigers, in 1934 and stayed with them through '36. He made his debut with the Barons in 1937, batting in the second position in the batting order.

Ray split his time in 1939 and '40 with the Chicago American Giants and Cleveland Bears before settling in with the Jacksonville Red Caps for two seasons. That stint was followed by three seasons with the Cincinnati-Indianapolis Clowns, and part of the '45 season with the Kansas City Monarchs. He finished his career by returning to the Black Barons in 1946.

John Shackleford

John Shackleford had an five-year career in the Negro Leagues that covered three different decades. The infielder debuted in the league in 1924 with the Cleveland Browns and then played with the Harrisburg Giants (1925) and Chicago American Giants (1926). He joined the Birmingham Black Barons for one season, in 1930, hitting .286. He finished his career in the 1946 campaign as the manager for the Cleveland Clippers.

Clarence Smith

Clarence Smith was the player-manager of the Birmingham Black Barons in 1929 and 1930. He played frequently as a fill-in outfielder in 1929, posting a .390 batting average. Smith broke into pro ball in 1921 with the Columbus Buckeyes. He played with the Detroit Stars and Atlantic City Bacharach Giants before joining Birmingham. After leaving the Black Barons, he played with the Columbia American Giants and the Cleveland Cubs.

A. M. Walker

Walker was the manager for the Birmingham Black Barons in 1931, their inaugural season in the Negro American League.[19]

Jim West

Jim West played three seasons at first base for the Birmingham Black Barons, in 1930, 1932, and 1947. He is best remembered for his years with the Baltimore Elite Giants (1938–39) and the Philadelphia Stars (1939–45). He appeared in two East-West All-Star Games, making the 1936 classic with the Washington Elite Giants and repeating the honor in 1942 with the Stars. West finished his career by splitting time with the Black Barons and the Black Yankees in 1947. West worked as a bartender in Philadelphia after leaving baseball. In 1970, he was shot and killed in an armed robbery at his bar.

David "Hammerman" Whatley

David Whatley broke into the Negro Leagues as an outfielder with the Birmingham Black Barons in 1936. He picked up the nickname "Hammerman" in 1937 when he batted cleanup and served as the power hitter in the Black Barons lineup.

After the 1938 season, "Double Duty" Radcliffe signed Whatley to a post-season contract to play in the Negro American League championship season. The following season, he was signed by the Homestead Grays and became a star for the team. He was part of the Grays' four consecutive championships, from 1939 through 1942.

One of his most memorable games came in 1942 when the Grays faced the Kansas City Monarchs in a league contest. Whatley got three hits off Monarchs pitcher Satchel Paige, including a two-out RBI single in the twelfth inning that gave the Grays a 3–2 win.[20]

Released from the Grays in 1944 after they signed Cool Papa Bell to play the outfield, Whatley signed with the New York Black Yankees. He played with New York for two seasons before closing his career with the Pittsburgh Crawfords in 1946.

Parnell Woods

Parnell Woods is best known for his years with the Cleveland Buckeyes in the 1940s. He was a four-time all-star, making the team in consecutive years with different teams, from 1939 until 1942. However, he debuted in the Negro Leagues with the Birmingham Black Barons in 1933. He played with the Barons for six seasons before moving on to other teams in the league. His esteem in the league is demonstrated by Pat Patterson's description of Woods as "a fantastic third baseman" and "a great hitter and fielder."

Woods was born February 26, 1912, in Birmingham. The third baseman played with the Barons from 1933 though 1938 while refining his batting. He hit a respectable .269 in 1937 and .256 in 1938.

Midway during the 1938 season, he joined the Jacksonville Red Caps. The team moved to Cleveland for the 1939 season, changed its name to the Cleveland Bears, and Woods made the move with them. He batted .343 in 1939 and made his first appearance in the East-West All-Star Game. He started with the Bears in 1940, but returned to the Black Barons early in the season. He finished the 1940 season with a .318 average and again made the all-star team — this time as a Baron.

He returned to Jacksonville with the revamped Red Caps in 1941. He made the East-West All-Star game for his third consecutive year and with his third different team.

He started the '42 season with the Red Caps but signed with the Cleveland Buckeyes as player-manager. He was 30 years old and the youngest manager in the history of the Negro Leagues. He finished the 1942 season with a .343 batting average and made the All-Star Game for the fourth consecutive year — with his fourth different team.[21]

Woods was called into military service for World War II in the spring of 1942, but was turned down by the military. He returned to the Buckeyes as player-manager, hitting .288 in 1943 and .329 in 1944.

Woods was replaced as manager of the Buckeyes for the 1945 season, but he stayed on as the team's third baseman. He remained team captain and batted in the cleanup position. He finished the year with a .335 batting average and led the Buckeyes to the Negro American League pennant and a World Series sweep of the Homestead Grays.

When Jackie Robinson broke the major league color barrier in 1947, Woods became a hot commodity for major league scouts. He received a brief chance in the minors in 1949, playing with the Oakland Oaks in the Pacific Coast League. By then he was 39 years old and well past his prime playing years. Still, he batted .275 in 40 games for the Oaks, but spent most of the season with the relocated Louisville Buckeyes in the Negro League.

Woods joined the Memphis Red Sox in 1950, but his average dropped to .174. He spent another year, in 1951, with the Chicago American Giants before retiring from the game.

Woods' post-baseball career included a 27-year career as the business manager for the Harlem Globetrotters basketball team. He died July 22, 1977, in Cleveland, Ohio.

CHAPTER 3

The Black Barons in the 1940s

The Barons received a new owner when Tom Hayes purchased the team in 1940. Hayes had financial help from Abe Saperstein, who was best known for owning the Harlem Globetrotters. Hayes also owned the Rush Hotel on North Eighteen Street in Birmingham. It was one of the "few hotels in the state of Alabama that catered to a black clientele."[1]

Hayes' hotel provided housing to visiting teams. Saperstein, meanwhile, brought in a high-profile player in Ted "Double Duty" Radcliffe and started booking the team in profitable venues. Before Saperstein, the Black Barons were largely content to barnstorm across the nation in small towns. Saperstein began booking the team in such places as New York's Yankee Stadium. "Every time the Yankees would leave, Birmingham would be in Yankee Stadium with twenty-five to thirty thousand people," Radcliffe later recalled.[2]

The Globetrotters also became an extra source of income for the players. Some, including Radcliffe and Piper Davis, worked with or played on the team. Black Barons' catcher Paul Hardy worked in the off-season as the Globetrotters' bus driver. Reese Tatum, one of the Black Barons most popular players, set a precedent that hoops hero Michael Jordan would later emulate by playing professional baseball and basketball. Tatum, a center fielder for the Black Barons, joined the Harlem Globetrotters and became famous as "Goose" Tatum, the Clown Prince of Basketball.[3]

The decade of the '40s represents the apex of the franchise's history. Wingfield Welch led the team from 1940 until 1945. Tommy Sampson took over in 1946. A star for the team during this period was the legendary Lyman Bostock (1940–42, 1946), who was named to the 1941 East-West All-Star Game.[4] World War II interrupted his baseball career, but after fighting in Europe, he returned to the Barons before finishing his Negro League career with the Chicago American Giants (1947, 1948). When the decline of the Negro Leagues began following Robinson's breaking of the major league color barrier, Bostock missed out on a major league career, but like many black baseball players of that decade, found employment in Canada's Mandak League with the Winnipeg Buffaloes (1951–1953).[5] Although he never reached the major leagues, Bostock would sometimes barnstorm with the Jackie Robinson All-Stars.

The 1943 team, led by Negro League legend Lorenzo "Piper" Davis, won the Negro

The 1940 Black Barons were led by manager Wingfield Welch. This was also the first team under the ownership of black hotel magnate Tom Hayes and Harlem Globetrotters owner Abe Saperstein. The legendary Lyman Bostock was a star on the 1940 team, later named to the 1941 East-West All-Star Game. Dan Bankhead was a rookie, going on to play in the major leagues with the Brooklyn Dodgers.

American League pennant but lost the Negro World Series to the Homestead Grays in seven games. The Black Barons repeated as American League champs in 1944, but again lost the World Series to the Grays — this time in only five games.

EARL ASHBY

Ashby had a four-year career as a catcher in the Negro League, playing from 1945 until 1948. His one season with the Black Barons was in 1947. Ashby was born in Havana, Cuba, in 1921. He came to the United States in 1945, joining the Cleveland Buckeyes. In 1947, he joined the Homestead Grays, hired to replace the legendary Josh Gibson after the slugger's death. Ashby simply wasn't up to the job, and was sent to the Birmingham Black Barons for the rest of the season. He signed with the Newark Eagles in 1948, his last season in the Negro League, and then played in Canada until completing his baseball career after the 1950 season.

LYMAN BOSTOCK, SR.

Bostock was a star first baseman for the Birmingham Black Barons during the 1940s, becoming one who was closely identified with the team.[6] Born March 11, 1918,

Back, left to right: Felix McLaurin, John Britton, Leroy Morney, Artie Wilson, Jimmy Newberry, Butch Huber. Middle, left to right: Lester Lockett, Lafayette Washington, Alfred Saylor, Tommy Sampson, Lloyd "Pepper" Bassett, Piper Davis. Front, left to right: Johnny Scott, Ed Steele, Ted "Double Duty" Radcliffe, Winfield Welch, Bubber Gipson, Leandry Young.

in Birmingham, he broke into professional baseball with the Brooklyn Royal Giants in 1938. He stayed there for two seasons before joining the Black Barons in 1940. He played two seasons, making the 1941 East-West All-Star Game where he had an RBI single.

His career was interrupted by World War II, where Bostock spent four years (1942–1945) in the U.S. Army. He re-joined the Barons in 1946, hitting .265 in his return to baseball.

His manager, Tommy Sampson, recalled that owner Tom Hayes wasn't impressed with Bostock when he returned from the army. Sampson argued to keep him. "He was kind of muscle-bound when he first came out and I kept him because he was a good ballplayer when he went in," Sampson said. "All he needed was to get hisself in condition."[7]

Bostock followed that with two years (1947 and 1949) for the Chicago American Giants, hitting .336 for the Giants in '49. During 1948, he played with the New York Cubans in the Mexican League and with Jackie Robinson's All-Star barnstorming team. He followed that with a stint in Canada's Mandak League, playing with the Winnipeg Buffalos (1950–51) and the Carman Cardinals (1952–53).[8]

Bostock also toiled in the minor leagues, playing five seasons, from 1950 to 1954.

After retiring from baseball, Bostock worked for the post office and carved handmade bats.[9] He died June 24, 2005.[10]

His son, Lyman Bostock, Jr., reached the majors in 1975 with the Minnesota Twins and batted .282 in his rookie season.[11] He followed that with a .323 average in 1976, including a game on July 24 when he hit for the cycle. He upped his average to .336 in 1977, a mark that was second in the league, behind teammate Rod Carew. He joined the California Angels for the 1978 season, but the younger Bostock's career was cut short when he was shot and killed September 28, 1978, while riding in the backseat of his uncle's car.[12]

EARL BUMPUS

Earl Bumpus was a native of Uniontown, Kentucky, and broke into the Negro Leagues in 1940 with the Kansas City Monarchs. He joined the Birmingham Black Barons during the season and stayed with the team through the 1946 campaign.

His first-year numbers were not impressive — a 1–8 record and a 6.50 ERA. Despite the poor stats, when the Barons won the Negro American League pennant, Bumpus was selected to start the first game of the Negro World Series against the Homestead Grays. Bumpus pitched a complete game, but the Barons lost the contest. The Grays eventually won the World Series in five games.

Bumpus improved to 4–2 with a 3.63 ERA in 1945, and then signed with the Chicago American Giants for 1947. He finished his career with the Giants in 1948, going 0–4 on the mound.

ERNEST "SPOON" CARTER

Spoon Carter spent 18 years as a pitcher in the Negro Leagues, playing for 12 different teams. He spent three seasons with the Black Barons — 1932, 1941, and 1949.

Born December 8, 1902, in Harpersville, Alabama, Carter broke into professional baseball in 1932, playing with the Louisville Black Caps, the Memphis Red Sox and the Black Barons. He finally settled down with the Pittsburgh Crawfords for four years (1933–1936), and then spent two years with the Philadelphia Stars (1938–39). After hopping around to a few other teams, he settled in again with the Homestead Grays from 1942 until 1945.

Carter didn't have a great fastball, but he had plenty of other pitches in his arsenal, including a curve, a screwball and a knuckleball. He was used sparingly, going 0–1 in 1935 with the Crawfords, the team still considered by many "to be the greatest black team of all time."[13]

His tenure with the Homestead Grays also paralleled their great years that included World Series championships in 1943 and 1944. Carter was the winning pitcher in one game of each of those series, defeating his former team, the Birmingham Black Barons. He returned to the Barons in 1949 to close out his career.

ALVIN "BUBBER" GIBSON

Bubber Gibson had a ten-year Negro League career (1941–1950) as a right-handed submarine pitcher. The bulk of his career came with the Birmingham Black Barons — seven seasons, from 1941 to 1947.

Born in Shreveport, Louisiana, Gibson broke into professional baseball with the Cincinnati Buckeyes in 1940. The next year he joined the Negro Leagues when he hooked up with the Birmingham Black Barons. He was winless in his first season, compiling an 0–7 record. He did little better in 1942, managing only to get his first Negro League win with a 1–4 mark.

Gibson improved to a 3–4 record in 1943 as the Black Barons won the Negro American League pennant. The Barons lost the following World Series matchup to the Homestead Grays, with Gibson making appearances in two of the games.

His best season came in 1944 when he went 10–6 and helped the Barons repeat as NAL pennant winners, but he dropped to 2–2 in 1945 and 5–6 in 1946. He left the Barons during the 1947 season, going to the Detroit Senators and then joining the Houston Eagles in 1949.

Napoleon "Nap" Gulley

Nap Gulley had a nine-year career as a pitcher in the Negro Leagues during the decade of the '40s (1941–1949). He spent two years with the Birmingham Black Barons, in 1941 and 1942.

Gulley was born August 29, 1924, in Huttig, Arkansas. He made his Negro League debut with the Kansas City Monarchs at the beginning of the 1941 campaign, then spent some time with the Chicago American Giants before joining the Barons later in the season. As a pitcher for the Barons, he was known for having a sharp-breaking overhand curveball, or "drop ball" that was his "out pitch."[14]

After leaving the Barons, Gulley shuttled between the Chicago American Giants, the Cleveland Buckeyes, and the Newark Eagles.. He spent one season (1948) in Canada and had six years in the minor leagues. He also tried one winter season (1945) of basketball with the Harlem Globetrotters, playing with Ted "Double Duty" Radcliffe.

Gulley was signed to a minor league contract by the Brooklyn Dodgers in 1950, but soon gave up on his pitching career. He switched to playing outfield at Visalia in the California League and stayed with the team for four seasons, from 1950 to 1954. His best season during that stretch featured a .333 average in 1952.

Gulley moved up to Spokane in the Northwest League in 1955. He hit for a .361 average in '55 — his best season as a hitter — and came back with a .316 average in 1956. A broken arm toward the end of the season ended his baseball career.

John Markham

John Markham's pitching career spanned 16 years, but he is most often remembered for his wartime years with the Birmingham Black Barons, from 1941 to 1945.

Born October 1, 1908, in Shreveport, Louisiana, Markham broke into the Negro Leagues with the Kansas City Monarchs in 1930 and was a regular on the team from 1937 to 1940. During this time, he also spent part of one season (1939) with the Satchel Paige All-Stars.

Markham signed with the Black Barons in 1941 and posted a 2–1 league record as a reliever. He had a 3–1 mark in 1942, also as a reliever. He moved into the starting rotation in 1943, putting together a 7–2 mark as the Barons won the Negro American

League pennant. Markham pitched in three of the subsequent World Series games, forcing a seventh game by winning the sixth with a 1–0 shutout of the Homestead Grays.

Markham posted a 4–2 record and a 3.39 ERA in '44 as the Black Barons repeated as NAL champions. He lost the only game he pitched in the World Series.

Markham ended his Negro League career with the Barons in 1945, posting a 2.94 ERA.

Felix McLaurin

Felix McLaurin was the center fielder and leadoff hitter for the Birmingham Black Barons during the team's back-to-back pennant-winning seasons in 1943 and '44. The Jacksonville, Florida, native began his career with the Jacksonville Red Caps in 1942, posting a .382 batting average before joining the Black Barons.

After McLaurin posted a .236 average in 1944, the Barons traded him to the New York Black Yankees in 1945. He became their leadoff hitter, putting up averages of .343 and .295 in his first two seasons. McLaurin stayed with the New York team through the 1948 season. He finished out his career by playing four years with the Chicago American Giants.

Leroy Morney

Leroy Morney spent three seasons as an infielder with the Birmingham Black Barons, 1942 through 1944. That tenure included back-to-back pennant-winning years in 1943 and '44.

Morney broke into professional baseball with the Monroe Monarchs in 1931. He played for ten other teams before joining the Black Barons, including the Homestead Grays, Pittsburgh Crawfords, Washington Elite Giants, New York Black Yankees, Philadelphia Stars, and the Chicago American Giants.

He played for three different teams in 1933, posting a .419 combined batting average and earning a starting role in the East-West All-Star Game as a member of the Cleveland Giants. Playing second base, he teamed with Willie Wells to turn the first All-Star double play. That was the first of three all-star appearances for the infielder. He also made the game in 1939 as a member of the Crawfords, and in 1940 with the Chicago American Giants.

Morney joined the Black Barons in 1942 after spending a year in the Mexican League. In his first season, he posted a .296 average from the cleanup position while playing second base and third base for the team. He closed out his career as a reserve player for the Barons in 1944.

Theodore Roosevelt "Double Duty" Radcliffe

The three most famous players ever associated with the Birmingham Black Barons were Willie Mays, Satchel Paige, and Charley Pride. But there is a fourth player who in his hey day may have been just as popular. Ted "Double Duty" Radcliffe was a flamboyant player who could challenge Satchel Paige for charisma. Had organized baseball been open to blacks, he would undoubtedly been a star in the major leagues.[15] He got his memorable nickname because of his versatility; he would occasionally catch the first game of a double-header and pitch nine innings in the second game.[16] His five-year tenure with the Birmingham Black Barons came in the pre–Robinson era (1942, 1944, 1945), but his career covered three decades and a total of 23 years—1928 to 1950.[17]

Born July 7, 1902, in Mobile, Alabama, Radcliffe made his Negro League debut in 1928 with the Detroit Stars. Over the next 20 years, he played with most of the major Negro League teams, including the Homestead Grays, the Pittsburgh Crawfords, the New York Black Yankees, the Chicago American Giants, the Memphis Red Sox, the Kansas City Monarchs, and the Louisville Buckeyes. In between, he also played in the Mexican League and—in his ultimate display of versatility—played basketball with the Harlem Globetrotters. And, as Riley noted, he was simply "one of the most colorful players in black baseball."[18] The only player who rivaled him in popularity was his friend, Satchel Paige, and the two often became partners in forming barnstorming exhibition teams.

At the plate, Radcliffe consistently hit in the .280-to-.350 range. As a pitcher, he consistently put together a winning record, including a 19–8 mark in 1932. He changed teams frequently because somebody else always seemed willing to pay him more money than his current employer, and he was always quite willing to accept it.

He played in six East-West All-Star Games, three as a catcher and three as a pitcher. He hit a home run in the 1944 game, contributing to a 7–4 victory for the West. He won his only decision as a pitcher.[19] As a catcher, the strong-armed Radcliffe warned opposing base runners by wearing a chest protector that read, "Thou Shalt Not Steal."

Although Radcliffe frequently would catch and pitch in back-to-back games, Damon Runyon gave him his "Double Duty" moniker after seeing him accomplish the feat in a double-header during the 1932 Negro World Series in New York. Radcliffe caught Satchel Paige in the first game and pitched a shutout in the second.

"He said I was the most versatile man he'd ever seen," Radcliffe told John Holway, referring to Runyon's comments. "He saw me and Satchel Paige pitch a double-header in Yankee Stadium. I caught Satchel in the first game and we won it, 5–0, then I pitched the second game and we won it, 4–0. The next day, Runyon wrote, 'It was worth the price of admission of two to see Double Duty out there in action.'"[20]

Radcliffe was the Negro American League MVP in 1943, playing for the Chicago American Giants. The Birmingham Black Barons won the NAL pennant that year, but lost their regular catcher to the military before the beginning of the World Series. Radcliffe was loaned to the Barons to play against the Homestead Grays in the championship series. The Barons lost the World Series, but they got to keep Radcliffe for the 1944 season.

Radcliffe was traded to the Kansas City Monarchs for the 1945 season. His roommate with the Monarchs was a youngster named Jackie Robinson.[21]

Later in his career, he became a player-manager for the Memphis Red Sox in 1937 and 1938, and then for the Chicago American Giants in 1943.

Radcliffe was 44 years old when Jackie Robinson broke the major league color barrier with the Brooklyn Dodgers in 1947. Radcliffe was too old to get his shot as a major league player. In the 1960s, though, he was hired as a scout by the Cleveland Indians.

"There have been better pitchers, better catchers, and better hitters, and there may have been a more colorful player, but there has never been another single player embued with the diverse talents he manifested during his baseball career. 'Double Duty' was unique in baseball annals."

Radcliffe retired to Chicago and became a regular visitor to the Chicago White Sox clubhouse. Umpire Bob Motley recalled meeting Radcliffe during this time. According to Motley, Radcliffe...

> ...had the gnarliest, ugliest, most deformed fingers I have ever seen. His catching hand had been bent and battered from — as he said — "catching Satchel's heat for over 20 years." Duty once told me, "Catching Satchel is like trying to catch a freight train barreling at you with the brakes gone bad!" And from what I saw, he was hardly exaggerating.[22]

Radcliffe made a publicity appearance in 1999 as a pitcher in a minor league game, becoming the oldest professional player in the history of organized baseball at the age of 97.[23] He was scheduled to throw out the first pitch at the July 27, 2005, Rickwood Classic, the retro game sponsored by the Birmingham Barons — the White Sox's Double A affiliate. A reception in his honor was also scheduled at the Alabama Sports Hall of Fame.[24] Illness and age interfered with both plans. Radcliffe was hospitalized in Chicago before making the trip to Birmingham. He died in August 11, 2005, at the age of 103.[25]

ULYSSES REDD

Redd broke into the Negro Leagues with the Black Barons in 1940 and remained with the team in 1941. After that, he changed sports, playing with the Harlem Globetrotters basketball team in the post-war era. He finished out his baseball career with a brief return to the Negro Leagues in 1951, playing with the Chicago American Giants.

ALFRED "GREYHOUND" SAYLOR

Greyhound Saylor was a pitcher for the Birmingham Black Barons from 1941 until 1945. That tenure included back-to-back pennant-winning seasons in 1943 and 1944, with Saylor playing a major role in both seasons. In 1943, he pitched in three playoff games, winning two and losing one. In 1944, he compiled a 14–5 record with a 2.74 ERA. He pitched in two of the subsequent post-season games, but lost both.

Saylor was a native of Cleveland who began his baseball career as a first baseman with the Cincinnati Buckeyes in 1940. He joined the Black Barons in 1941 as a pitcher. In 1945, he posted a 4–3 record in his last year with the Barons, which was also his last in the Negro Leagues.

QUINCY SMITH

Quincy Smith played only part of one year with the Birmingham Black Barons, hitting .284 during his half-season stay in 1945. During the second half of the season, he jumped to the Mexico City Reds in the Mexican League. Once the major leagues started signing Negro League talent, though, Smith received a shot at organized baseball. He spent six years in the minor leagues, all in the Mississippi-Ohio Valley League, compiling batting averages that ranged from .279 to .317, but never made it to the major leagues.

Joseph B. "J.B." Spencer

J.B. Turner had a six-year career in the Negro Leagues, from 1943 to 1948. Those years included a stop with the Birmingham Black Barons in their championship season of 1945. Spencer broke into pro ball with the Newark Eagles in 1943. A utility man who played every position except pitcher, Spencer also played with the Baltimore Elite Giants, the Homestead Grays, the New York Cubans, the New York Black Yankees, and the Pittsburgh Crawfords. With the Grays, Spencer was a member of two championship teams, in 1943 and 1944.

His one year with the Black Barons was undistinguished. He posted a .191 batting average, leaving the team after the '45 season to play a backup role for the New York Cubans. He left the Negro League after the 1948 season, but later played in Canada's Mandak League; he hit .239 with three home runs in 1951 with Elmwood, then put up a .288 average for Sweetwater in the Longhorn League.[26] Spencer also played with the Seattle Steelheads and the Harlem Globetrotters before retiring from baseball after the 1955 season. Spencer died May 17, 2003, in Gretna, Louisiana.[27]

Leroy Sutton

Leroy Sutton was a pitcher for the Birmingham Black Barons in 1943, posting a 5–3 record in his only season with the team. He debuted in the Negro Leagues with the New Orleans–St. Louis Stars in 1941 and played one season with the Chicago American Giants before joining the Barons. He returned to the Giants in 1944, and finished his career with the Indianapolis Clowns in 1945 and the Boston Blues in 1946.

Reese "Goose" Tatum

In the 1940s, Reese Tatum became popular in the game of baseball, playing center field for the Birmingham Black Barons. He became more famous, though, for his off-season job — playing basketball for the Harlem Globetrotters.[28] As "Goose" Tatum, he became arguably the most famous member of the Globetrotters during the 1940s and '50s. Green called him "the Clown Prince of Basketball, a talented and temperamental comic genius."[29]

Because of his basketball reputation, his skills on the baseball diamond were sometimes overlooked. Tatum was a first baseman for the Birmingham Black Barons before signing with the Globetrotters.[30]

Tatum broke in with the Black Barons in 1941, playing two seasons before shifting briefly to the Cincinnati Clowns in 1943. By then, he was also playing with the Globetrotters.

He was an instant hit with the Globetrotters, partly because of his unusual body and mannerisms. As Green noted, "He talked slow, walked funny and looked like a circus freak ... [and] ... did not look like an athlete. His body seemed all out of proportion, with arms so long."[31]

A tour of duty in World War II interrupted both careers. His departure nearly devastated the Globetrotters. As Green wrote, when Goose left the basketball team for the war, his "departure was almost a death knell for an already crippled Globe Trotters team."[32] But Tatum returned to the Globetrotters after the war to play basketball.

He also joined the Indianapolis Clowns to continue his comic antics on the baseball field.

Tatum was good enough that the Philadelphia Phillies offered him a minor league baseball contract.[33] Tatum turned down their $1,000-a-month offer to stay with the Globetrotters.

WILLIE YOUNG

Willie Young spent only one season with the Birmingham Black Barons, but there were those who were amazed that he even did that. Young was born with no right hand, yet became a pitcher for the Black Barons in 1945 at the age of 33. It was his only season, but it was a memorable one. As McClure noted, the pitcher "would climb the pitcher's mound and inspire spectators without even striking out a player."[34]

Young was born July 12, 1912, in Birmingham. He started by playing Little League baseball and, by the age of 19, was playing with the barnstorming Birmingham Black Foxes. He had moved to Birmingham's industrial league, playing for Stockham during the war years.

He joined the Barons in 1945 and quit the team at the end of the season to return to the Birmingham industrial league. "I left the Barons because I didn't like the way you had to do everything," he told Brent Kelley. "I came back to work."[35]

Whether Young was in the industrial league or with the Black Barons, fans were usually amazed to see the one-handed pitcher. "I could hit the ball and I could run," Young said. "I could put the glove on my hand and throw the ball, and before the ball would get to the batter, I could have the glove on, catch the ball, lay the ball down, and change the glove for the ball before he'd get to first base."[36]

"He was amazing to watch," former Black Baron Donnie Harris once said. "He had it down to an art."[37]

Young recalled a game for Kelley in which he faced Clyde Nelson of the Chicago American Giants. The catcher called for a fastball, but Young shook him off. The catcher went to the mound to tell Young that Nelson was a good curveball hitter. "He can't hit my curveball," Young replied, describing it as "a six-foot drop." He catcher conceded, Young threw the curve, and Nelson struck out.[38]

Despite being born with only one hand, Willie Young played several years with industrial teams in the Birmingham area. He joined the Barons for two months in 1945, quit because of the heavy traveling schedule, and returned to the industrial leagues.

Young's tenure with the Black Barons was brief—only two months. He resigned from the team after quickly growing tired of traveling and coping with a segregated society. "We'd get through playing at the Polo Grounds (in New York) at 11 o'clock at night and we'd get a hot dog and a piece of candy and go to Philadelphia," he once recalled. "About five miles from Philadelphia, we'd change clothes on the bus and get off and play ball."[39]

After Young retired from baseball, he coached softball and Little League. Young died August 9, 2002, at the age of 90.

PART II. THE BLACK BARONS AFTER INTEGRATION

Introduction

Their last shot at a world title came in 1948.[1] The '48 Black Barons were loaded with Negro League stars — manager Lorenzo "Piper" Davis, Bill Powell, Bill Barnes, Lyman Bostock, Joe Bankhead, and Ed Steele. They also had a young rookie who looked pretty good, a Fairfield kid named Willie Mays. The opponent was their old nemesis, the Homestead Grays. The outcome was predictable; the Grays again defeated the Barons, this time in seven games.

It was arguably the last real World Series for the Negro Leagues. Hauser's chronology of the Negro Leagues, in fact, ends with the 1948 World Series.[2] That was, after all, the final year of existence for the Negro National League. Some of the teams disbanded; those that were left joined with the Negro American League.

The precursor of the disbanding came the previous year. Jackie Robinson had joined the Brooklyn Dodgers and broken baseball's major league color barrier. It was a move that would eventually lead to the downfall of the Negro Leagues.[3] Other major league teams had started signing top talent in the Negro Leagues to minor league contracts, all with the intention of promoting these stars to the majors.

Harry Truman ordered the desegregation of the military following the end of World War II.[4] In 1946, four black players — Bob Willis, Marion Motley, Kenny Washington, and Woody Strode — would break the color barrier in professional football.[5] But such actions did not change attitudes and prejudices overnight. Negro League players still faced discrimination when they traveled, discrimination that mirrored what was happening across the South at the time.[6]

That discrimination was still prevalent in 1949 when Jackie Robinson brought an all-star team to Birmingham to play the Black Barons on October 19, 1949.[7] Five of the players on the field that day would later be enshrined in Cooperstown: Robinson, Cleveland's Larry Doby, and Brooklyn Dodgers teammate Roy Campanella played for the All-Stars. The Black Barons team included Willie Mays and a few players borrowed from other Negro League teams, including Buck Leonard. The All-Stars won the game, 9–3, with Robinson contributing a single and a double and Newcombe pitching two scoreless innings.[8]

The Black Barons continued to play home games in historic Rickwood Field, a classic structure that has been designated America's oldest baseball park; it is still the oldest ballpark in use today.[9] The park was built by A. H. "Rick" Woodward, who rented it out to the Black Barons and to white teams in the area. Seating was segregated, with a designated section for black fans when the white teams played.

When the Black Barons were playing, though, the roles were reversed; white fans used the segregated bleachers. That concession applied only to the stands, not the locker rooms. The visiting team was allowed to use the visitors' lockers, but the Barons either had to dress at home or share facilities with the opposing team. Blacks were not allowed in the home team locker room.

Black Baron managers during the 1950s included Vic Harris, Ted "Double Duty" Radcliffe, Hall-of-Famer Willie Wells, and Jim Canada.

After Jackie Robinson broke the major league color barrier, the Black Barons played baseball in a world of diminishing interest.[10] As Christopher Fullerton noted, "Negro League teams near big league cities soon found their attendance wilting, as fans drove hours to see 'their Jackie.' The wall that the Negro Leagues had pushed against for so long had fallen. Unfortunately, the Leagues fell with it."[11]

For a while, Birmingham resisted the trend, mainly because the strong roots of

Back, left to right: Charley Pride, Kelly Search, Will "Curley" Williams, Frank "Hoss" Thompson, Clarence "Pijo" King, Jessie Mitchell, Bill "Fireball" Bolden, Sidney Bunch, Willie Wells. Front, left to right: Jim Zapp, Danny Wright, Ralph Brown, Eddie Brooks, "Pee Wee" Jenkins, Otha Bailey, John Kennedy, Elliott "Junior" Coleman, Richard "Red" Wright.

segregation in the South continued to keep the races and their sports separated. Rickwood Field, which once boasted huge crowds for Negro League games, could still pack in fans but nothing comparable to its heydays.[12] But scouts continued to come to the games because the major leagues were still on the prowl for more players from this new pool of talent. Some of the Barons, most notably Willie Mays, got the attention of those scouts, becoming part of the African American contingent that helped the major leagues make the transition to that of a fully integrated sports organization.[13] Those successes were enough to fuel the hope of the others who kept playing at Rickwood.

They were playing between two eras — between the segregated decades of baseball and the years before full integration in the major leagues. "We were playing to get signed, to tell you the truth," Willie "Red" Harris said. "That was our goal, for some scout to see us and recommend us to the parent team and get a contract and see where we could go from there." It was a constant theme that showed up in these interviews. The scouts were so important that they could and did interrupt games, as they did when they stopped a game and asked Jessie Mitchell to make a few throws from the outfield. Or the time that six scouts visited Jake Sanders in the dugout. Willie Curry recalled a game in which he hit three home runs; he remembered thinking, "I didn't see any scouts but I knew some scouts were there."

They initially had a lot of success in getting the attention of the scouts. One former Black Baron, Dan Bankhead, was playing in the major leagues for the Brooklyn Dodgers before the end of the 1947 season.

Four players from the 1948 team reached the major leagues: Greason, Mays, Artie Wilson, and Jehosie Heard.[14] The older players received their chance, but they also knew that Mays — the youngest player on the team — had the best shot at a long major league career. They made a point to help him.

"What they did for me, I'll never forget," Mays has said of his Black Barons teammates. "Those ... guys knew I could play baseball, and even though they were older than I was, they would say to me, 'You have a better chance of getting to the big leagues than we do, and we want to make sure you get there.'"[15]

Many of those who did make it only had a brief stay, the proverbial "cup of coffee" in the major leagues, and had little chance to prove themselves.[16] Bill Greason pitched in only four innings at the major league level. John Irvin Kennedy, a shortstop for the Black Barons and Kansas City Monarchs, was the first African American player for the Philadelphia Phillies. But he only played in five games; the Phillies traded for another shortstop the day before Kennedy made his debut on April 22, 1957.

As the years passed, the scouts began signing young prospects at earlier ages, and the need for veteran talent diminished. Regardless, the players on the field were local heroes. Those on the team during the post–Robinson era played before smaller crowds, with less recognition than they deserved. They included outfielder Jessie Mitchell (1954–1958), his brother and fellow outfielder John Mitchell (1959), second baseman Tony Lloyd (1959), outfielder Ernest Harris (1959), outfielder Donnie Harris (1957), pitcher Willie Smith (1958–59), catcher Otha Bailey (1952–1959), first baseman Willie "Red" Harris (1958–1959), first baseman James "Sap" Ivory (1959), outfielder Willie Lee (1956), outfielder Jim Zapp (1954), and outfielder-manager Frank Evans (1955).

Their numbers included some of the greatest players the rest of the nation never heard about. In addition to those that reached the majors, others would sign minor league contracts. Jessie Mitchell went to spring training with the Baltimore Orioles. Pitcher Elliot Coleman, from the 1954 team, had a minor league contract with the Orioles and reached the Triple-A level before military duty and arm trouble ended his career. Tony Lloyd did the same thing with the St. Louis Cardinals. Jake Sanders got a shot with the Dodgers. Earnest Harris had two shots, one with the Detroit Tigers and one with the Philadelphia Phillies; he played in the minor league system with the latter. Cleophus Brown was invited to join the New York Yankees in training camp. Otha Bailey was scouted by the Boston Red Sox and had a tryout with the Dodgers.

Quite often, they faced major obstacles as African American players in the minor leagues. In some ways, they had it harder than Jackie Robinson because, as Fussman noted, "They didn't have Branch Rickey carefully managing all the details and easing their transition into what had until then been a white man's game."[17]

Back, left to right: unidentified trainer, Sammy Williams, William Greason, Pijo King, Bill Powell, Dick Watts, Ed Steele, Piper Davis, Vic Harris, Herman Bell, and bus driver Rudd. Front, left to right: Pepper Bassett, Hollin Ward, Jimmy Newberry, Norman Robinson, Johnny Cowan, Henry Baylis, and two unidentified players.

Making it to the majors was a long shot. Although the major leagues have denied any collusion, the Negro League players saw themselves fighting against an informal quota system that limited their access. "Baseball had a quota system," Red Harris recalled. "Baseball didn't have no more than two or three blacks on a [major league] team at the most. Most organizations had that policy. You never saw one black on a ball team ... always two or three so they would have some kind of companion out there. That quota went on for a while. Now the quota is what made us hustle."

Archie "Dropo" Young agreed. "There was a limitation as to how far you could go in baseball," Young said. "We just lived in a time frame when there was nothing you could do about it." That's one reason why most of the Negro League players never progressed very far. As Fullerton noted, "At the end of the season, no matter how well they did, they were released."[18] The result: The Negro Leagues were further depleted of talent while the players struggled fruitlessly to move up the chain.

During the final years, the players could make more money playing semi-pro ball or working out of baseball than they could for the Barons. They kept on playing in hopes of catching the interest of a scout. When that hope was gone, they had to retire. As Otha Bailey said, "In 1959, I knew I wasn't making no money and I knew I wasn't going to the majors. I had to get a job. I had a family, so that was it. I gave it up."

Bailey and the others didn't know it, but after 1956, they had no chance of making it to the majors from the Negro League. The last player to make that jump was John Irving Kennedy, the former Birmingham Black Baron who was signed by the

Back, left to right: Ben Adams, Jake Sanders, Bob Henon, Paul Gilbert, Tommy Taylor, Ira McKnight. Front, left to right: Willie Washington, Nate Dancy, Johnny Winston, Paul Palmer Hubbard, Jessie Mitchell, Garland Easly, Jr., Ozie Tilmore, Sugar Cane.

Philadelphia Phillies after the 1956 season. Kennedy's brief major league career (five games) would represent the last time a Negro League player moved up to the major leagues.[19] One other player, shortstop Ike Brown, played for the Kansas City Monarchs in 1960 when they were essentially a barnstorming team like the Black Barons of the time. Brown went through the minor league system before reaching the game's top level with the Detroit Tigers in 1969. He played six years with the Tigers, primarily as a pinch-hitter.[20]

Another came close. Willie Lee made it to the Detroit Tigers' spring training camp three times, from 1959 to 1961. In '59, he was apparently slotted for the Tigers' Opening Day roster until a spring training injury resulted in his returning to the minor leagues. He returned in 1960, was given another shot, but was injured again. He got another look in 1961, but was released and later signed with the Minnesota Twins organization but never made it to the majors.

By 1957, the scouting game was in transition. Some players were scouted on the Negro League teams and signed to minor league contracts, but none made it to the majors. More frequently, after 1957, the Black Barons became a fall-back option for those players who didn't make it with organized baseball.

After Robinson signed with the Dodgers, Peterson noted that Negro team owners made certain that they had signed contracts for all their players. That may the major leagues would have to pay the team for players they wanted to sign. Even then, most "sale prices were modest."[21]

Regardless, the major league organizations became less willing to pay the Negro League teams their asking price for a player's contracts. As Peterson wrote, they started "eliminating the middle man — the Negro clubs."[22] It was a shift that may have cost John Mitchell his shot at the majors. It definitely cost Raymond Haggins his chance; Haggins was a three-time all-star with the Memphis Red Sox. In 1954 he signed with the Chicago White Sox, but the White Sox had to send him back to Memphis because the Red Sox had a binding contract for him and wouldn't sell it to the major league team.[23]

Instead, the scouts and their clubs were more frequently signing talented athletes — or at least giving them tryouts — immediately out of high school. Carl Holden received a tryout with the Baltimore Orioles; when that didn't work out, he turned to the Negro Leagues. Similarly, Clifford DuBose got a tryout out of high school with the Brooklyn Dodgers, but ended up playing for the Memphis Red Sox and the Black Barons.

Still, some became local legends. There was Piper Davis (1942–49, 1959), an all-around athlete who played baseball for the Black Barons and basketball for the Harlem Globetrotters. Pitcher-outfielder Charley Pride (1954) had a distinguished baseball career, but became better known as a country music performer with hits that included "Kiss an Angel Good Morning" and "Is Anybody Going to San Antone?" William "Bill" Greason (1950–51) had a long career that included a brief appearance with the St. Louis Cardinals before retiring and devoting his time to the Christian ministry.

Similarly, pitcher Bill Powell (1946–1950, 1952), who led the Negro Leagues with 15 wins in 1950, also had a chance to pitch in the majors. Ted "Double Duty" Radcliffe (1942, 1944–45), the player-manager who got his unique nickname after playing as both catcher and pitcher in two separate games of a double-header, joined the Barons

"They Played through the Storm," commissioned by the Alabama Negro League Players Association and sold as a limited edition print as part of a fundraising project. All of the players depicted are from Alabama and many are former Black Barons, including Willie Mays and Satchel Paige. The title of the piece is from a sermon delivered by the Rev. William Greason, former Black Baron and St. Louis Cardinal, at his Birmingham church. (Artwork by Ronald McDowell, Ph.D.)

just before the Robinson era. Shortstop Artie Wilson (1945, 1947–48) was considered one of the best players to not succeed in the major leagues.

Regardless of the circumstances, they kept playing. Unfortunately, other teams were folding under the pressure of competition from the major leagues. By 1949, the decline of competitive teams forced the Negro National League and the Negro American League to merge into a single league. The Homestead Grays — the great rival that kept Birmingham from claiming so many World Series — suspended play in 1950.[24] Many players went back home to play in their local all-black leagues. A few went to Cuba[25] and some others headed north to Canada and its Mandak League.[26]

The Black Barons, though, continued to hold on. The segregation barriers within the South still limited their access to many baseball opportunities, but it helped to maintain fan interest. That, however, only delayed the inevitable.

In 1952, Black Baron pitcher Frank Thomson had a league-best record with 13 wins against only six losses. Thomson's 13 wins were more than half of the Black Barons' total for the year. Their 23–15 record was good enough to qualify for the Negro League Championship Series. Their opponent was the Indianapolis Clowns, who finished 26–18. The Clowns defeated the Black Barons in an extended series, seven games to five.

But Hayes had enough. He sold the Black Barons to "Sue" Bridgeworth. Bridgeworth, who also owned the Baltimore Elite Giants, shut down his Maryland-based team and used some of those players to help stock the Black Barons with talent. That, too, only delayed the inevitable. Two years later, in 1954, Bridgeworth sold the Barons too.

In 1956, the Black Barons' John Williams led the league in hitting with a .357 average. But by then, the Negro American League consisted of only four teams. In 1959, the Black Barons finally won the Negro League Championship. Ernie Harris became the only rookie to make the East-West All-Star Game, played in Chicago's Comiskey Park. The West won the game, 8–7 in 11 innings, with Earnest hitting an inside-the-park home run and scoring the winning run. The performance got the attention of major league scouts, and he was eventually signed to another minor league contract.

Meanwhile, more players left to join the minor leagues, to play in other countries, or to play locally in the industrial league. The industrial league remained the most feasible opportunity for those who wanted to stay in the local area. As Fullerton noted:

> The industrial leagues represented the most tangible link between the Black Barons and the community from which the team emerged. The significant, if undesirable, role of black workers in Birmingham's iron and steel industry granted them inclusion in the industrial paternalism that governed the lives of most workers. Developed as a form of welfare capitalism, industrialists' policies created league teams for both the black and the white workers of the city's massive iron industry, stimulated baseball in Birmingham generally, and provided talent for the Black Barons.[27]

By then, they had few other alternatives. At the end of the 1959 season, only five teams remained active in the Negro American League. Most were not doing well financially, but held on in hopes they might get a subsidy from the major leagues.

That didn't happen. The league opened the 1960 season with just four teams: the Birmingham Black Barons, the Kansas City Monarchs, the Raleigh Tigers, and the Detroit–New Orleans Stars. At the end of the year, the Negro Leagues were officially gone. The final death knell was the official demise of the Black Barons.[28]

By then, the Negro Leagues were no longer the fishing grounds of the major league scouts. The major leagues were adding more black athletes to their teams. Talented black athletes — like Huntsville's Carl Holden — were being signed out of high school and invited to major league tryout camps. If they failed to make the major league team, the remaining four Negro League teams or the industrial teams became a backup option for the players.

In Birmingham, other baseball opportunities were also disappearing. In 1962, local segregationist politician Bull Connor closed all of the local baseball fields, along with the city's golf courses and swimming pools (which were filled with dirt) rather than comply with a federal court order to desegregate the Birmingham parks system.[29] As Fullerton noted, it seemed that the "career of the Black Barons in the Negro Leagues not only mirrored the world of southern black baseball, but also of the southern black communities that supported it."[30]

"The Negro Leagues don't exist anymore," said former player Jessie Mitchell. "I hate that. That's why they're covering our pensions now. The major leagues broke up the Negro League. They got all the ballplayers. They got the players and the crowds."

"Instead of playing four times a week, it got to be only on weekends," Bob Veale recalled. "Then it wasn't at all. You know, the Negro Leagues meant money for a lot of people.... How many years did it take before the Negro Leagues folded for good? How many mouths weren't fed during that time."[31]

In May 1963, Jackie Robinson visited Birmingham.[32] It was an appropriate omen in that Robinson's visit corresponded with the demise of the team. The Black Barons disbanded following the close of the 1963 season. As Fullerton noted:

> For 43 years, the Black Barons had been a staple of the city's black community and part of the rich black culture that had grown up behind the walls of segregation.... The Black Barons provided the black community with heroes and heroics that renewed the belief of every mill hand and housemaid in his or her own ability and self-worth.... Their demise, however, was their triumph. Integration had always been the goal of the Negro Leagues; it simply had acquired a larger role in the black community over time. In the South, the teams became particularly important, restoring pride and dignity in the face of brutal dehumanization and degradation.[33]

By then, perhaps, the Black Barons and the Negro Leagues had served their purpose. "The Civil Rights workers who squared off against Bull Connor and his water cannons picked up where the Black Barons left off," Fullerton wrote, "inheriting a tradition of persistence and fortitude that served them well in the trying times to come."[34]

CHAPTER 4

Post–Robinson Era Black Barons

The history of the Birmingham Black Barons is rich with personalities and talented athletes. Many became "invisible players" who were lost to history, but some left an indelible mark on the game. Many of those were from the pre–Robinson era. One of the following chapters is devoted to them. By no means does it cover all those who should be remembered — just those with the highest profile. Still, many of them have gone unnoticed for their contributions.

The Birmingham Black Barons had an extensive number of players in the years from 1948 to 1963, too many to provide detail biographical information on all of them. Some of the players included in this selection are players who were available and willing to talk. Others were well-known players who have received attention from a number of sources. But there were others — players who made major contributions but for whom little information is available — who also deserve recognition.

Many were not around when interviews were conducted for this work, yet they have stories that are just as important as those more thoroughly discussed elsewhere. Much of the information is based on previous research done by James Riley and John Holway. Baseball historians should give them thanks for their valuable work in preserving the records and stories of these players. They, like the contributions of the Birmingham Black Barons, should not be overlooked.

After 1956, those playing for the Black Barons had little chance to make the major leagues. The major league scouts were looking to sign talented athletes immediately out of high school, placing them in the minor leagues, and letting them work their way up the system. Most of the Negro League teams had folded, or soon would. The Black Barons held on to the tradition longer than most, partly because the strong discrimination faced in Birmingham still encouraged segregated baseball, and partly because of the strong baseball tradition of the franchise. As the Negro League started to fade into history, several players continued to maintain the tradition.

JOE BANKHEAD

Joe Bankhead was the last of the Bankhead brothers to play in the Negro Leagues. Born September 8, 1926, in Empire, Alabama, Bankhead made his Negro League debut as a pitcher in 1948 with the Birmingham Black Barons. That would be his only season in the Negro Leagues. He played briefly with Grand Rapids in the Central League that same year. He died February 4, 1988, in his hometown of Empire.

LLOYD "PEPPER" BASSETT

Lloyd "Pepper" Bassett was best known as "the rocking chair" catcher, a title he earned while with the Indianapolis Clowns.[1] Still, he was an outstanding catcher for the Black Barons, playing with the team for nine seasons, from 1944 until 1952. That stretch included the Black Barons' pennant-winning seasons of 1944 and 1948. Bassett was a major contributor in both seasons, but particularly in 1948, when he put together a .350 batting average for the year. He finished out his Barons career with a .298 average in 1951 and a .271 norm in 1952.

Bassett was born August 5, 1919, in Baton Rouge, Louisiana. He had a 17-year career in baseball, playing for a number of teams that included the Homestead Grays, Toledo Crawfords, Chicago American Giants, Philadelphia Stars, Memphis Red Sox, and Indianapolis Clowns. He was a four-time all-star, earning the recognition once with the Pittsburgh Crawfords (1937), twice with the Chicago American Giants (1939, 1941), and once with the Black Barons (1950). His best year came with the Pittsburgh Crawfords in 1937 when he hit .395.[2] After leaving the Barons, he finished out his career with the Philadelphia Stars, Memphis Red Sox, and Detroit Stars. He retired from the game after the 1954 season.

Despite his high average and power-hitting ability, Bassett is best remembered as "the rocking chair catcher." He often entertained crowds by working from the catcher's position while sitting in a rocking chair. He developed the antic while playing with the Indianapolis Clowns in 1944, prior to joining the Black Barons. The ploy often fooled opposing runners, who assumed he couldn't throw them out while Bassett rested comfortably in his rocker. They were wrong. His strong arm was more than sufficient for cutting down most of the overly confident base runners at second base.[3]

Another former player, James Dudley, recalled that Bassett would sometimes lay down behind home plate "like a little child playing," telling the pitcher to "throw hard 'cause you can't throw bad." "It didn't make no difference where the ball went in the dirt," Dudley added, "he got it."[4]

HENRY J. "HANK" BAYLIS

Baylis was an infielder-catcher who played third base for the Barons in 1949 and 1950. The 5'9", 178-pound infielder was a slap hitter who hit .284 and .270 in his two seasons in Birmingham.

Born in 1927 in Topeka, Kansas, Baylis' first season in the Negro League was in 1948 with the Chicago American Giants. He hit for a .320 average that year before joining the Black Barons in 1949. He left Birmingham to play five years with the Kansas City Monarchs.

Baylis was a versatile athlete who would occasionally play catcher. Despite his 5'9" height, he was athletic enough that he spent some time playing basketball with the Harlem Globetrotters.

In 1956, Baylis received his shot at the major leagues, joining El Paso in the Southwestern League as a third baseman. He split his time in 1957 with El Paso, Tuscon (Arizona-Mexico League), Yakima (Northwest League), and Tuscon. That was as far as he went before he retired after the 1957 season.[5]

HERMAN BELL

Herman Bell was a star catcher for the Birmingham Black Barons. His career was only eight years in length but spanned two eras — before and after Jackie Robinson. He first joined the Black Barons in 1943 as a backup catcher, playing eight years, through 1950. He was a regular catcher on the 1948 pennant-winning team, hitting .261 for the year. In 1949, his average dropped to .196. He retired after the 1950 season. Former Black Baron Willie Young once described Bell as the best catcher he ever saw, saying, "He never missed a fly ball."[6]

WILLIAM "LEFTY" BELL, JR.

William Bell had a six-year career in the Negro Leagues as a left-handed pitcher. He began with the Kansas City Monarchs in 1949 and pitched with both the Monarchs and the Black Barons in 1950. After that, he returned to the Monarchs, finishing his career with Kansas City after the 1954 season.

WILLIAM "FIREBALL" BEVERLY

Bill Beverly concluded his Negro League career as a pitcher with the Birmingham Black Barons in 1954 and 1955. Born May 5, 1930, in Houston, Texas, he broke into the Negro Leagues with the Houston Eagles in 1950 and posted a 5–1 record. He described that record as "misleading" because "That 5-and-1 was league. We played every day, every night.... And on the way to play up in Winnipeg, every night we would schedule a stop ... and play a local team. We was probably 110, 120 games a year, maybe more."[7]

Beverly moved with the team to New Orleans in 1951 and finished the season with the Chicago American Giants. He stayed with the Giants through 1952.

For the 1953 season, Beverly signed with the Thetford Miners of the Provincial League in Canada and posted a 10–7 record. He returned to the Negro Leagues in 1954, joining the Black Barons and finishing his professional career the following year.

JIM "FIREBALL" BOLDEN

Jim "Fireball" Bolden had two stints with the Birmingham Black Barons — one season in the pre–Robinson era (1947) and one after Robinson broke into the majors (1952).

Bolden, born February 8, 1923, began his Negro League career with the Cleveland Buckeyes in 1946. He joined the Barons the following year for half a season. After that he played with a number of other teams — the Chattanooga Choo Choos in 1948, the New Orleans Creoles in 1949, the Brooklyn Cuban Giants in 1950, and the Elmwood Giants of the Mandak League.

Bolden got a brief shot in the minor leagues in 1951, but finished his career with the Black Barons in 1952. Bolden "was a masterful pitcher and had he not been hurt in a mining accident, there would be no telling what he may have achieved," former teammate Pat Patterson once said. "He could pitch, had a great variety of stuff, great control, and fierce talk for the batters he faced."

JOHNNY BRITTON

Johnny Britton played for the Black Barons for seven years, from 1943 until 1949. Born April 21, 1919, in Mt. Vernon, Georgia, Britton was a left-handed hitting third baseman who started for the Barons during their championship seasons in 1944 and 1948. He was more famous for his clowning antics, but also played a solid game at third base and hit for a high average. The combination of both skills made him a popular feature of Satchel Paige's All-Stars during the 1940s.

Britton broke into professional baseball in 1940 with a brief stay with the Minnesota Gophers. He joined the Ethiopian Clowns later in the season, staying with the team through the 1942 season. Britton became one of the top baseball comedians for the Clowns. His most popular routine involved him wearing a wig on his clean-shaven head, getting into an argument with the umpire, grabbing the ump's cap and slamming it to the ground, and then grabbing his own wig and slamming it to the ground too. He'd then pick both items off the ground and put both back on his own head.[8]

After a brief tenure with the Cincinnati Clowns at the beginning of the '43 season, Britton was traded to the Birmingham Black Barons for Hoss Walker. The Clowns gave up Britton because they wanted Walker to be their new manager.[9]

Britton was a part-time player during the 1943 season, but became a starter in 1944. He responded with a .324 batting average, playing a key role in the Baron's pennant-winning season. He followed with a .333 average in 1945, dropped to .262 in 1946, but then rebounded with his best season, a .336 average, in 1947. For the 1948 season, he was moved to the second spot in the batting order, hitting .289 as the Barons won their last pennant of the decade.

The Black Barons lost the Negro World Series to the Homestead Grays again in '48, and Britton may have indirectly contributed to their defeat. He played in only one game. He was injured in an automobile accident while traveling to the second game; the Barons lost his services for the rest of the series.

Britton dropped to a .242 average in 1949 and returned to the Indianapolis Clowns in 1950.[10] Britton left the Negro Leagues after that, playing for a year in the Mandak League. After that, he spent two years playing for the Hankyu Braves in Japan. That role made him one of the first two African Americans to play baseball in the Japanese leagues.

EDWARD "EDDIE" BROOKS

Eddie Brooks played second base for the Birmingham Black Barons from 1952 until 1955. He made his debut in the Negro Leagues in 1949 with the Houston Eagles. Except for a brief stint with the Memphis Red Sox in 1950, he played most of three seasons with the Eagles, staying with the team when it moved to New Orleans in 1951. His best season during this period was a .235 average with Houston in 1950.

Cleophus Brown

Had it not been for baseball, Cleophus Brown would likely have spent much of his life as a coal miner. After all, that was how his father and grandfather toiled to keep their families fed in the small Jefferson County, Alabama, mining town of Bradford, located about 20 miles north of Birmingham and near the town of Pinson.

Cleophus was born there November 25, 1933, the child of Thomas and Alberta Brown. He grew up in one of several mining towns in central Alabama that were company towns, many (like Bradford) owned by a company ABP (Alabama ByProducts) that mined the coal.

ABP earned its money by digging coal from the ground and transforming it into coke. The liquid byproduct could then be sold to companies in Birmingham or up north for making steel.

Jefferson County had a plentiful supply of coal for raw materials. And, during the 1930s, there were plenty of willing workers to dig the coal from beneath the Alabama soil. It was a hard job, hard on the body and hard on the spirit. Further, in a time when transportation was difficult and opportunities rare, most workers had limited access to any form of outside entertainment during their few hours away from work.

But they did have baseball. Cleophus' father occasionally played on one of the local teams. By the time he reached his early teens, Cleophus was playing the game too. He started out playing for one of several unofficial youth teams around Bradford. "We'd play in an old potato field that had been cleared out, or cornfield; that would be our ball field," Cleophus said. Getting up a game was no problem. "There were always a lot of kids around," he recalled.[11]

He was soon playing in the local junior league on teams composed of 13-to-15-year-old boys. His talent for the game soon became apparent, and the local coal mine recruited him for its industrial team.[12]

"They pulled me off the little boys team when I was fifteen, and I started playing with them. That's how I got started," he said. "When they'd go off to play another team, and they didn't have enough players to make a team, they'd come ask my mother if I could go."

The team played other coal-mining teams in such nearby towns as Adamsville and Parrish. Most of the teams they faced came from other communities anchored around the same company — Alabama ByProducts.

Those local games drew large and enthusiastic crowds, but the biggest crowds were for the Birmingham Black Barons. "People would be out there with big black pots selling fried fish," Cleophus said. "That was the only place they really had to go," he added. "They didn't have much to do except baseball. We'd play twice a week, on Saturday and Sunday."

Cleophus played in the coal-mining league until 1950 when, at the age of 17, he joined the army. He was stationed at Fort Polk, Louisiana, and soon found himself playing for the local military team. "I was in the military from 1950 to 1953, on special duty to play baseball. I pitched and played first base," Brown said.

In 1952, he was transferred to Munich, Germany, and joined another military team. "They had some good players," he recalled.

His military service ended in 1953, and Brown returned to Birmingham, where more baseball opportunities awaited. "Somehow word got around that I was home, and a scout from the Yankees approached me," he said.

Cleophus, though, turned down the Yankees' offer. "I just didn't see that baseball had much in it for me," he said.

Turns out, he was wrong. Soon afterwards, Cleophus was approached by James Bolin, a Negro League player who lived near Bradford. "He'd always been a good ballplayer," Cleophus remembered. "They called him 'Foul Ball' Bolin. He threw sidearm."

Bolin signed the young military veteran to a contract as a pitcher with the Louisville Clippers. That was the beginning of a Negro League career that included a year with Louisville (1955) and a stint with the Birmingham Black Barons. With both teams, he played as often as he was needed. "I loved to play the game. I could have played every day," he said.

"Back then there wasn't any of this pitching one day and getting four days rest," he added. "If they needed a pitcher, you'd get in there and throw. When I wasn't pitching, I played first base."

Brown relied on his arm to overpower hitters. "My main pitch was the fastball: I could always throw hard," he said. "I had a nice curve, but I could spot that fastball.

"I'd look at the way the man was standing at the plate and decide whether to throw it out or in. You've got some people who hug the plate — throw him one on the inside of the plate and he won't have a chance to get around on it. Somebody who backs off the plate, you can throw him a low outside pitch and he can't reach it. He'd have to go out to get it and that throws his power off.

"And you watch their swing," he added. "Some hitters like high pitches. And some loose swing hitters can hit a bad pitch. They might not hit a good pitch, but throw him a bad pitch and you might have all kinds of problems."

Some of the most memorable times came while traveling. "We had an old ragged bus, but it was all fun," he said. "You were with a bunch of fellows who wanted to play ball. We'd play cards on the bus, talk, and sing."

Still, an all-black team faced a number of obstacles. "We couldn't get into none of the white hotels. We'd go into a town that had a little black hotel, or people would furnish us a place at their house.

"Some guys would sleep on the bus," he added. "We'd get money to pay for a room, but they'd rather sleep on the bus and save the money for beer. You know, they're gonna drink that beer."

The Clippers, like most barnstorming Negro League teams, frequently ran into other teams on the road. Those meetings often turned into an opportunity for a temporary exchange of players. "We was always swapping good players," Cleophus recalled. "We'd flip-flop them. We might pick up a Birmingham Baron in Mississippi after they'd just returned from Detroit, and he might go with us to play a team in Arkansas."

Cleophus' most memorable road trip was the infamous southern swing into Yazoo City, Mississippi, that led to the Charley Pride trade. The Clippers were in Yazoo City when their bus broke down.

"It was a raggedy old bus, it tore up, and some of us had to lay back," he said. "There were about seven or eight of us who got hemmed up down there in Yazoo, Mississippi. We stayed down there about a week. James Bolin made sure we were fed. I don't know how he did it, but he made sure we were fed down there. We stayed there with John and Jessie Mitchell, and Charley Pride. Finally, we got another bus to come get us."

Despite such discomforts, Cleophus enjoyed barnstorming with the Clippers. "We had some good times, playing in Arkansas, Oklahoma. It was good traveling. We had Charley Pride for entertainment. He had a little old three-string guitar: he didn't even have a good guitar."

The other players liked Charley but not necessarily his music. "He'd be back there singing a lot of hillbilly songs," Otha Bailey recalled. And Bailey recalled the advice he gave Pride. "Man, you ain't gonna do nothing with that kind of music."

Cleophus Brown turned down a contract offer from the New York Yankees because he didn't think much of baseball's career potential. He ended up playing with both the Louisville Clippers and the Birmingham Black Barons, and still gets autograph requests.

"He'd keep going until we made him stop playing. We'd tell him to cut it out. 'Don't be singing that country music,'" Cleophus said. "But look at him now. He's a millionaire now, because he kept singing that country-western music."

Cleophus' tenure in the Negro League was cut short by arm trouble. The problem developed while on a road trip in Musovee, Michigan. "It was on a Sunday, and I had my worst game on the trip," he recalled. "My arm hurt, and I couldn't get nobody out that day."

Cleophus left the team and returned to Birmingham to see a doctor and get some treatment. "That's when I left the team," Cleophus said. "That was my bad time. But the other times with the team were good times."

The trip back home ended Brown's career as a pitcher with the Negro League, but he stayed in the game as a first baseman for a local industrial team. "Mr. Woodward heard I was in town. He got me to come out and pitch a game for them. Woodward Iron," Brown said.

Rick Woodward owned several

companies in the Birmingham area. He built the local ballpark, Rickwood Field, which is named after him. "He's the one who hired me to play with them," Cleophus said. "I threw about three or four innings for him, and he told me he was going to hire me for the steel mill. I got into that steel mill and I didn't go back on the road."

Cleophus found that playing in the Walter Horn industrial league provided a more stable paycheck than the Negro Leagues. "We really weren't getting all our money on the road," he said. "We'd make a little here, a little there. We get a little eating money. We were having a good time — we just weren't making a lot money."

The industrial league gave Brown a chance to concentrate on his hitting. "I was always a good hitter," he said. "I got a regular chance to hit when I played first base. So, when my arm went down, I just played first base."

Brown's one regret is that he didn't start out as a hitter in the Negro Leagues. "I was a good hitter," he said. "I wish I'd started that earlier. One game I hit four triples. That was the first time that had happened in our league."

Another memorable game was at Roosevelt on a diamond that didn't have an outfield fence. "I hit one so hard that the fellow chasing it just stopped and came on back."

Cleophus was also a fast runner. "I didn't run that much when I was in the Negro League. My playing there was limited, because I was pitching. But I ran a lot in industrial baseball. They'd run me to death."

Brown played in the industrial league for 40 years. "They called me 'Hard Hittin' Brown,'" he said. "I still led the league in hitting even late in my career. I didn't quit until I was 62."

The secret to hitting, he said, was watching the ball. "It's keeping your eye on the ball," he said. "A lot of people talk about the stance, but you want to hit the ball. They've got that free swing now, all the way around, with no follow through.

"I didn't do that," he said. "I always believed in watching that ball. I was a hard man to strike out."

Brown is now a member of the Negro League Legends Hall of Fame in Baltimore. He received the honor in recognition of his year of service with the Louisville Clippers and Birmingham Barons.

Brown now spends most of his time as a truck driver for the U.S. Postal Service, an organization he joined in 1980, but still follows baseball. He watches televised games and frequently visits the local industrial leagues on the weekend.

"I go to one of the local leagues most every Saturday and Sunday," he said. "I talk with them fellows. They'll say, 'Bet you could still hit it hard.'"

And he has no regrets about his baseball career. "I'd do it again," he said. "You'd meet different people and visit different towns. It was fun."

JOSE BURGOS

Jose Burgos was a rarity for the Birmingham Black Barons in that he was a star player who didn't come from the Birmingham area and who did not get his start in the local industrial league. Burgos was a native of Puerto Rico, born in 1928, who played shortstop for the team during two seasons, 1949 and 1950. Riley described him as "a light-hitting shortstop," and his numbers support the label.[13] Burgos hit .224 for the 1949 season, and hit .243 in 1950.

Despite the poor hitting, Burgos' defensive skills earned him a contract with organized baseball. He moved to the minor leagues in 1951, playing in the Florida International League for Leesburg and Lakeland. He batted .263 with Leesburg and .221 at Lakeland before moving to Richmond in the Piedmont League for the 1952 season. He batted .243 at Richmond during his final season in the minor leagues.

TOMMY "PEE WEE" BUTTS

Butts was an outstanding defensive shortstop whose career spanned the two eras. His tenure with the Birmingham Black Barons came in the post–Robinson era, in 1952 and 1953.

Born in 1919 in Sparta, Georgia, Butts broke into professional baseball with the Atlanta Black Crackers in 1938. He is best remembered for his years with the Baltimore Elite Giants, where he spent 12 season (1939–42, 1944–51).

Butts was playing in Cuba in 1947 after Robinson broke into the major leagues. The Dodgers were scouting the Cuban winter leagues, and they signed Butts' double-play partner, Junior Gilliam, to a contract.

Butts, though, didn't move out of the Negro League until late in the 1951 season. He played for Winnipeg in the Mandak League, hitting for a .286 average. He started the 1952 season with Lincoln in the Western League, but could only manage a .170 average. He returned to the Negro League, joining the Barons at midseason in 1952. He stayed with the Barons in 1953, hitting .240, and then signed with the Memphis Red Sox in 1954.

ELIJAH "ELI" CHISM

Eli Chism first broke into the Negro Leagues in 1937 with the St. Louis Stars. But the outfielder was out of baseball for eight years before returning to the league with the Cleveland Buckeyes in 1946, hitting for a .210 average. In 1947, he joined the Birmingham Black Barons as their starting left fielder and posted a .287 average. He was out of the league from 1948 through 1950, but returned to the Barons in 1951 for one season. By then, the top talent on the Barons had been signed to contracts by organized baseball.

ELLIOT "JUNIOR" COLEMAN

Elliot "Junior" Coleman made his Negro League debut in 1954 as a pitcher for the Black Barons. Coleman was part of a pitching duo with Kelly Searcy that made the Barons a tough team to beat in 1954 and '55. Coleman put together a 12–5 record for the Barons in 1954, and was 16–6 in 1955.

Brent Kelly noted that Coleman "was moving up the minor league ladder when Uncle Sam summoned him for military duty."[14] Coleman made the East-West All-Star Game in 1955 and was signed by the Baltimore Orioles. He was also being scouted by the Brooklyn Dodgers and the New York Yankees at the time.

His first stop in the minors was Aberdeen, South Dakota, where he spent two years. He had a 14–8 record and a 1.56 ERA in 1956, a record that warranted a promotion. After joining the major league team for spring training, he was assigned to Double-A San Antonio in the Texas League for the 1957 season, putting together a 12–15 record and a 2.56 ERA.

In 1958, the military interrupted his move up the minor leagues, but Coleman returned to the Baltimore organization in 1960 after completing his duty. He quickly moved up to Triple-A Vancouver in the Pacific Coast League and put together a 3–4 record, but a high 5.75 ERA. The problem was an arm injury in a game against San Diego that eventually ended his baseball career. He stayed in the minor leagues with other teams until 1964, but as he later said, "From '60 to '64, I couldn't get anybody out."

JOHNNIE COWAN

Born May 31, 1913, in Birmingham, Johnnie Cowan broke into the Negro Leagues with the Black Barons in 1934 when the team was part of the Negro Southern League. He finished his career with the Barons in 1950. In between, the infielder played for the Detroit Stars (1939), Cincinnati Buckeyes (1942), the Cleveland Buckeyes (1944–47) and the Memphis Red Sox (1948–49). His heyday came with Cleveland, batting eighth in the lineup and posting marks that ranged from .210 to a high of .247.

Cowan's career also included a stint in the Mandak league, playing for the Elmwood Giants. That tenure included one game in which he hit three doubles.

The highlight of his career came in 1945 when the Buckeyes won the Negro American League pennant and swept the Homestead Grays in the Negro World Series. Cowan got the first hit in game one of the series. He also knocked in a key run with a deep sacrifice fly to right field in the seventh inning of the Gray's 2–1 win. He capped the series with the game-winning hit in the final contest.

In 1950, Cowan briefly joined the Black Barons again, but left in midseason to play with the Elmwood Giants of the Mandak League. He returned to Birmingham after the season, and finished his career playing for Stockham in the Birmingham industrial league.

During his career, Cowan was consistently considered one of the best infielders who ever played the game. Former baseball commissioner A. B. "Happy" Chandler is reported to have seen Cowan in an all-star game and commented, "Johnnie Cowan is one of the best ground ball men I've ever seen."[15]

Part of his success in the field was due to his large hands, a physical trait that made it easier to snag hot grounders. Those hands also earned him his nickname "J-Hands." Piper Davis, who played against Cowan, described him as "just a good, all-around player. Not too much power, but a real good glove man."[16]

"He could play anywhere in the infield," said former Black Baron Sam Hairston, "but was one of the best second basemen I've seen in baseball. He could have played in any league."[17]

Cowan was 35 by the time Jackie Robinson broke baseball's color barrier. That was too late for Cowan to make it to the majors. "I don't think he was ever bitter," said his son, Charles, after Cowan's death. "That's just the way it was back then."[18]

After retiring as a player, Cowan returned to Birmingham and became manager of the Stockham team in the industrial league. Later, in 1991, Cowan was part of a delegation of former Negro League players who were honored at a ceremony in Cooperstown. His family recalled that was a highlight for their father.

"Dad started getting recognition and went to card shows toward the end of his life," said Charles. "I'm happy he got to experience that."[19]

Cowan died October 24, 1993, in Birmingham.

JOHN WILLIAM "JIMMIE" CRUTCHFIELD

Jimmie Crutchfield had a 16-year career in the Negro Leagues, beginning in 1930 and ending in 1945. Crutchfield was an acrobatic athlete who would sometimes make behind-the-back catches of fly balls. He is best known for his years with the Pittsburgh Crawfords (1931–36), but the outfielder started his professional baseball career as a member of the Birmingham Black Barons.

Born May 25, 1910 in Ardmore, Missouri, Crutchfield was an all-around player who was sometimes called "the black Lloyd Waner."[20] He joined the Black Barons in 1930 for $80 a month, making his debut in center field on a day when Satchel Paige was pitching for Birmingham. Crutchfield hit a home run to give Paige the victory and finished his rookie season with a .286 batting average.

He joined the Crawfords in 1932 and stayed five seasons, posting batting averages that ranged from .267 to .308. He was a starting outfielder for three consecutive East-West All-Star Games during this stint, making the game in 1934, '35, and '36. He made his fourth all-star appearance in 1941 as a member of the Chicago American Giants.

WILLIE "BOO JACK" CURRY

Willie "Boo Jack" Curry was born September 3, 1934, in Johns, Alabama, in 1934. His family moved to the Birmingham area when he was five. His father worked in the nearby coal mines, and his mother was a housewife. His first memories of playing baseball as a child was in a place called Rock Slope, a coal-mining camp near the Tennessee Carolina Railroad Company.

The family moved from Rock Slope to Docena, another coal-mining camp, when Willie was twelve. He was soon playing baseball with others in the Docena area. "I was a pretty good ball player and the manager [Ed Steele] of the Black Barons heard about me and he sent and got me," Curry said. "I was a catcher and a pitcher."[21]

Mostly a catcher. "I don't know why I was a good catcher, I just was," Curry said. "A catcher had to be a big enough fool [to handle] people swinging a stick. I loved to catch. I didn't want to play any other position but catcher.

"When I played with Docena, I would get down there on third base and shag a few, but catcher was my position," he added. "We didn't have but one catcher and that was me. I played every game."

Curry said it was easy for him to be a catcher. "I liked catching because I didn't have to jump up and be running every time somebody hit a ball," he said. " I could just squat back there and wait on them to throw me the ball and I would throw it back to the pitcher. We had some pitchers you wasn't going to hit. They were just that good."

Curry was proud of his skills as a catcher. "Any time of the day, I don't care who you put in there, I would catch," he said. "I didn't have a certain pitcher for them to put in for me to catch.

"I called the pitch and if he didn't throw what I called, he wished he had because I would throw the ball back so hard, I would knock his glove off," he added. "He would know better than not to throw what I tell him."

He also enjoyed throwing out runners attempting to steal second base. He would bait them into making the attempt by getting on his knees behind the batter. Runners would take off, thinking he couldn't throw them out from that position. They were wrong. "I would be squatting back there and didn't have to get up to throw you out," he said. "I hardly ever stood up to throw anybody out."

Curry was a good hitter. "If a pitch came to me, I would hit it," he said. "You better put it in your hip pocket and make a motion when you throw it up there. I would hit it.

"I was hitting about 350, close to 400," he added. "I didn't have just one season I hit good. I hit good in every season until I went to play with the Birmingham Black Barons."

He joined the Black Barons in 1953 and stayed four years while playing under two managers, Steele and Jim Canada. Again, he was mostly a catcher, serving as the back stop for a group of talented pitchers that included Frank McCullum, Charley Pride, and Fred Clark.

Catching in the Negro League was also somewhat dangerous. Curry didn't care. He just wanted to play. "I have gotten bumped back there many a days from a double swing," he said. "We didn't have hard hats back in those days; I wore the same hat that I used to pitch. Sometimes I got hit so hard, I had to come out of the game. But that was the love of the game that I played."

He also had to deal with the equipment of the day, including the mitt, glove, chest protector and mask. "The masks were as heavy as a piece of iron. It was made out of steel and some were made out of aluminum."

Curry was also considered one of the toughest catchers of his day. He was known for sometimes catching outside pitches with his bare hand.

Occasionally, because of his strong arm, he would fill in as a pitcher. "I wasn't a slouch pitching with the Barons," he said.

Hitting against Negro League pitching, he discovered, was a bit tougher than the competition he had faced before. "The difference in the players at Sand Lot and the Barons, they had something they called the forkball. That was something I couldn't hardly hit," he said. "Then there was something called a knuckleball. The fastball, the curve, I could hit. But when I got to playing with the Birmingham Black Barons, they were pitching their pitch but I was still hitting good."

One of his most memorable hits was a home run, a blast to right field in Memphis that he thought had earned him a five hundred dollar prize. "They had a tire out on the right field [fence], just about halfway between center field and right field. If you hit a ball through that tire, they were supposed to give you five hundred dollars," he said. "I hit one through there. I was looking at it when it went through there and he [the advertiser] said it didn't go through.

"He was doing that because if you hit a ball through the tire, that would draw crowds," he added. "The stands were full that Sunday, but he didn't give me my five hundred dollars."

One of Curry's best friends on the team was his roommate, a young player named Frank McCullum. McCullum eventually left professional baseball and became a physical education teacher in a Mississippi high school. McCullum was killed in a automobile accident, but Curry believes he was a victim of anti-black violence so prevalent in Mississippi at the time. "I believe they killed Frank and ran his car into the bridge," Curry said. "I will always believe that they killed him."

Curry's complaints regarding his time with the Barons were those common to many players of the era—travel. The problems intensified if their bus quit running. "We would have to sit until the mechanic came and fixed it," he said. "Then we would get hungry. They gave you two dollars a day for what they called eatery. You had to eat off of that two dollars for two meals.

"They would give it to you that night and you had to eat supper that night and breakfast the next morning," he added. "You wouldn't get another two dollars until over in the next evening, so you had to save some of that two dollars to eat three meals out of it."

And, of course, they had to deal with the instilled discrimination of the day. "We would be going along and see a café and we would have to go in the side door or back door to get what we wanted," he said. "You couldn't stay in the café and eat, you had to come back out. If you wanted to eat, you had to either eat on the bus or sit on the ground."

Most of the time they slept on the bus. Occasionally, the team's owner would pay for a hotel or find boarding rooms with local baseball fans. "I think we stayed at one hotel, but they'd find people who had rooms to rent out," he said. " There would be someone with about three beds to rent and the other houses that had some beds until they got all of us placed.

"The team paid for that—we didn't have to pay for it. How are you gonna pay for that and when you didn't get but two dollars for eatery?"

After the 1956 season, he joined the Louisville Clippers. With Louisville, Curry would have the best game of his career when he hit three home runs in the same contest. "I was down in Arkansas, and I hit three: one to right, one to left and one to center. We won the game.

"I didn't see any scouts, but I knew some scouts were there," he added. He was right. After the game, one scout came down to the dugout and tried to purchase Curry's contract for $5,000. Curry gave the team his opinion: "Sell me." Instead, the Clippers gave him a ten dollar bonus for the game.

That move was a signal to Curry that it was time to give up on professional baseball. In the off-season, he had been getting another job with Birmingham Slag, a company that later became Vulcan Materials. "I was making more money working for Vulcan

Materials than I was playing baseball," he said. "I decided it was time to quit playing baseball when I wasn't getting any money and I got a better job digging a ditch.

"My father had a fractured spine and he couldn't work," he added. "When we traveled and played baseball, I would get a little taste of change, but it wasn't enough to take care of my father and mother, and I was still living with them."

He retired from baseball and settled in Detroit, Michigan, where his brother-in-law said he could get a construction job. "I went back to Detroit with him," he said. "He got me a job and I was making $12 and $14 per hour up there. I wasn't making but $2 here. So you know I stayed."

He remained in Detroit for 34 years. When he finally retired in 2001, he returned to his hometown of Birmingham, the locale of his baseball background.

"If I had to do it over again, I would play baseball again," he said. "I would play for the love of the game.

"I love baseball," he added. "Right now, if I could, I would get out there and catch right now. But I know if I get down there, they got to get a block and tackle to pick me up!"

Willie Curry died December 18, 2007.[22]

Lloyd "Ducky" Davenport

Lloyd Davenport had a 16-year career in black baseball as an outfielder and manager, beginning in 1935 and ending in 1949. He played for a dozen different teams, including two years with the Birmingham Black Barons, in 1941 and 1942.

Born October 28, 1911, in New Orleans, his best season came in '42 with the Barons. He put up a .360 batting average and made the East-West All-Star Game. For his career, Davenport was a five-time all-star. His notched the recognition in 1937 as a member of the Cincinnati Tigers. He also made received the honor in 1943 and '44 when he was with the Chicago American Giants, and in 1945 with the Cincinnati Buckeyes. He completed his Negro League Career in 1949 with the Chicago American Giants, batting .248 for the season. His final season in baseball came in 1951 with Elmwood of the Mandak League.

Wesley "Doc" Dennis

Wesley "Doc" Dennis was a multi-positional utility player for the Black Barons for five seasons. He first joined the team in 1950 for one season. He returned in 1952 and stayed with the Black Barons until 1955.

Born February 10, 1918, in Nashville, Dennis broke into the Negro Leagues with the Baltimore Elite Giants in 1942. He became a starter for the team in 1944, batting .285. He moved to the Philadelphia Stars in 1945, spent one year back home with the Nashville Stars, and then joined the Black Barons.

Jesse Douglas

Jesse Douglas had a 22-year career in baseball as an infielder, with 14 of those in the Negro League. He played with the Black Barons for two seasons (1941–42) before moving on to the Mexican League and the minor leagues of organized baseball.

Douglas was born March 27, 1920, in Longview, Texas. He joined the Negro Leagues with the Kansas City Monarchs in 1937 and played with the New York Black Yankees in 1938. He and the Satchel Paige All-Stars in 1939. He spent his two years with the Barons as an outfielder, and then moved to the Chicago American Giants and to the Mexican League.

Douglas made it into the minor leagues in 1951 with Colorado Springs in the Western League, hitting .262.[23] It was the closest he ever came to making the major leagues. He moved from there to the Mandak League in Canada. He returned to Mexico in 1956 and finished his career with Yakima in the Northwest League in 1958.

CLIFFORD "POP" DUBOSE

Clifford DuBose had a three-year career, from 1957 until 1959, as an outfielder-third baseman with the Memphis Red Sox and Birmingham Black Barons. Born July 16, 1937, in Montevallo, Alabama, DuBose graduated from high school in 1957. He was immediately invited to a tryout camp in Vero Beach by the Brooklyn Dodgers. That shot didn't work out. "I wasn't in shape, I hurt my leg, and I came back home," he told Brent Kelley.[24]

But he didn't give up on baseball. Negro League veteran Raymond Haggins got DuBose a shot with the Memphis Red Sox. DuBose joined the team as an outfielder and third baseman. His tenure with the team included a game in Spartandale, Mississippi, in which he went 4-for-4.

He was still a youngster, only 19 years old, and he looked to older players for guidance. "I didn't know too much," he said. "I sat around and listened to the baseball players that was older than I was — how they came out and how they'd go in restaurants."[25] The older players generally accepted the youngster. "Lots of 'em were teaching me how to hit and everything like that," he said. "They were pretty good to me."

Much of the guidance came from roommate Raymond Haggins and his friend, Eddie Lee Reed. "Those were two that helped me," he said. "I would be with them most all the time." DuBose stayed with the team for three months, when he was one of six players cut from the squad during a road trip to Birmingham. He briefly joined the Black Barons, but was soon cut from that team as well.

He shifted to the industrial league, playing for Stockham. The industrial league provided a training ground for improving his game. "I started hittin' the curveball when I came back and started playing in the industrial league," he told Kelley.[26]

He returned to the Barons in 1958, hitting .270 for the season. DuBose finished his Negro League career in 1959 with the Black Barons. He played for several more years in the industrial league before retiring as a player. He continued to stay close to the game, though by serving as a coach for sandlot teams.

HENRY ELMORE

Henry Elmore was born December 2, 1941, the son of Willie and Josephine Elmore. His birthday is important — particularly the year. Elmore is currently the youngest of the surviving members of the Negro League players.

He grew up in Kingston, off Tenth Avenue, right down the street from Stockham —

the valve and fitting company that financed one of the most successful teams in Birmingham's industrial league. Most of his early days in baseball were spent on the sandlots and streets of Kingston. "When I was a kid, we made a baseball field," he said. "We'd cleaned off an area like the baseball diamond now and cut the infield out, make the outfield round, and make some bases. That's where we played in Kingston."[27]

"Everybody in my neighborhood could play ball," he said. "We enjoyed playing just like we enjoyed cleaning off the diamond."

When he got a little older, Elmore attended Ullman High School in Birmingham, in a historic building that is now part of the University of Alabama at Birmingham campus. He continued to play baseball, hoping for his own chance to become a professional. With a little luck, he was hoping to follow in the footsteps of his hero, Frank Evans. "He was my idol," Elmore said. "He was older than me and he went off and played with the Cleveland Buckeyes and some other teams."

Another idol was his uncle, James West, who played with the Cleveland Buckeyes and the Philadelphia Stars. "They called him 'Shifter'; he played first base," Elmore said. "They say he was one of the greatest first basemen in the world.

"I never saw him play, but they used to always tell me about him," he said. "Me and my daddy tried to play like him, but he couldn't play."

Elmore wanted to emulate his uncle. He got his chance. "When I got big enough, they asked me if I wanted to leave home and I said, 'Yes.'" He was only 16 years old at the time, and the invitation came from the Philadelphia Stars. The opportunity came as a result of an exhibition game in Birmingham between the Stars and the Indianapolis Clowns.

He joined the team in 1958 as a left-handed-hitting third baseman, occasionally moving over to second. His first contract was $150 a month plus two dollars a day for meals, or "eating money," as Elmore called it.

The Stars took a look at him because of a recommendation from his idol, Frank Evans. "He told them to find me and take me with them," Elmore said. "I played my first day out at Rickwood, the same day they hired me.

"I played third base against the Clowns and did good because I could hit good," he added. "I couldn't throw that hard but I knew how to cheat. I could get two or three hits a game."

That Sunday evening after the game, the Stars put him on the bus and drove to his grandfather's house. Elmore got off the bus, went inside, and started packing his clothes. When his grandfather saw him packing, he asked where his grandson was going. Nodding toward the bus, Henry replied, "I'm leaving with them to go and play ball."

"You're my grandboy," the older man replied. "I might not let you go."

"You can't stop me. I'm going," Elmore said.

"Go ahead," his grandfather said. "If you get in any trouble or if you need me, call me. You're big enough to take care of yourself."

Elmore stayed with Philadelphia for two full seasons, in 1959 and 1960. His teammates included first baseman Gideon Javier and catcher Harry Barnes. Fred Banks was the manager.

His most memorable teammate during that time was Charlie "Bulldog" Drummond, a big player who had a brief stint in the major leagues with the Baltimore Orioles. Drummond, Elmore said, "could throw the ball through a brick wall. He played with the Baltimore Orioles and when he got out of the army, he played with Philadelphia because Baltimore cut him a loose."

Another memorable teammate was Mel Robinson. "Mel was a big giant," Elmore said. "He could have been 6' 8". If he picked the ball up when you were going to another base, you were out, because he was going to throw you slap out!"

Elmore has good memories of his years with the Stars, particularly when Philadelphia returned to play the Black Barons at Rickwood. "We had a center fielder name Mel Robinson," he recalled of the game. "He picked up the ball in the center field and threw to home plate and threw a man out that was running the bases."

One of his teammates — a man named Cast — did the unthinkable by hitting a home run over Rickwood's centerfield fence. "He hit a line drive," Elmore said. "When it got to that clock, it went over the top of the clock. A line drive!"

He was still a teenager, only 18 years old, during his final year with Philadelphia. "I couldn't go anywhere," Elmore recalled. "The managers would make you go to bed."

After two years with the Stars, Elmore returned to Birmingham to play two years for the Barons and his idol, Frank Evans, who was the manager of the Black Barons by then.

He played alongside Satchel Paige and Goose Tatum.

There was a bonus in returning to Birmingham, namely a little more freedom. "There was a boy on the team named Phil who lived in the airport area," he said. "Phil was older than me and really liked me. When I couldn't go anywhere he would give me his identification.

"Back then there were no pictures on the IDs," he added. "You just had a straight ID. So I would take his ID every summer and keep it all summer. Then I could go anywhere they went because I had an ID in my pocket."

He stayed with the Black Barons for two years, hitting at the top of the order. "Usually, I led off in the lineup because I could hit," he said. "I never hit down in the fifth position. I always hit in the top. They knew I was going to get on base."

In a game against either Chattanooga or Nashville — he wasn't sure which — Elmore had a game in which he went 4-for-4. "I remember we were up in some part of Tennessee," he said. "The third baseman came in on me. I hit that ball down that line and cut the whole shirt off of him! The buttons jumped off the shirt, I hit it so hard!"

Even though the Negro Leagues were in their final years, the Black Barons still attracted fans to Rickwood. "We could draw crowds like flies," he said. "It was nothing to fill up Rickwood because people didn't have anything else to do. Fans would drink and have fun. Eat, drink and have fun. They brought their liquor with them.

"They dressed real nice and would come to the game on Sundays with their suits on," he added. "They would go to church and leave church and come straight to the ballpark. Whatever he wore to church, he wore it to the ball field. It was a big deal. *Big deal!* That's all people had to do was come to a ball game."

The players were local heroes. "The role that the Negro Baseball League played in the black community in the 50s was nice," he said. "It was always somebody you could look up to. There was always a black ball player that you could look up to and respect."

On the road, the team continued to face discrimination. "If you didn't like pressure, being on the road was rough," he said. "Because you knew what was going to come up before you got there.

"You knew you could not go in the front to eat," he added. "You knew you were going in the back, so it was no problem. You just go in the back, eat, and go on about your business."

Sometimes they would spend the night in a hotel that catered to blacks. "We would play one night, ride all night, then you're in another town, so you're mostly sleeping on the bus," he said. "We went to Champagne (Illinois) sometimes and stayed in a hotel. We went to Kansas City and stayed in a hotel. But usually we stayed on the bus because we weren't doing anything but traveling."

Eating on the road required a little budgeting. "Two dollars a day was plenty for us to have for food," he said. "It had to be plenty enough because that was all you were going to get! There was nobody you could ask for money.

"We made it off of that," he added. "A burger was just a quarter. Lunch didn't cost that much. Dinner didn't cost that much. You had an extra quarter to put in the jukebox."

He recalled one trip to South Dakota that required a return route through Mississippi. Their bus was stopped by a policeman about ten at night.

"When y'all came through here two weeks ago, y'all was speeding," the policeman said. The charge was spurious. The team kept a log for their schedule and travels; the report showed they were not near Mississippi at that time.

That didn't matter. The policeman had the team return to its bus, then he led the players to the home of a local judge and knocked on the door. When the judge came to the door, the policeman repeated the charge.

The judge instructed the policeman to lock the team up in the local ballpark. "I'm going to bed," the judge added. "I'll talk to them in the morning."

"They left us out there and turned the lights out," Elmore recalled. "They had a nice big ballpark. They made us drive the bus in there.

"Mosquitoes ate us up," he added. "You couldn't do anything about the mosquitoes. We had to open the windows or we would suffocate. We couldn't go anywhere. They turned the lights off and left us out there all night long and went on about their business."

The next morning, the judge met with the players, fined the team $500, and sent them on their way with some advice. "Y'all go on back to Birmingham when y'all come back through here and don't be speeding in my town."

Professional baseball for Elmore came to an end when the Barons folded in 1963. "The Barons shut down because they integrated," he said. "When you integrate, people start going to see blacks and whites, and the blacks just had to fade out."

Elmore and most of his teammates moved to Birmingham's industrial league. "When the league folded, the whole ball team went to Stockholm because Stockholm had lights," Elmore said. "They played three to four times a week."

The nucleus of the group stayed at Stockholm for ten years. "We beat everybody in the city," Elmore recalled. "Beat everybody! We had Jessie Higgins, Dubose, Jim Zapp, Walter Stoles, Pete Mumford, Jesse Bass, Melvin Stoll, and Carl Lewis. We had a dynamite team."

He stayed in the industrial league for ten years before easing out of the game. In 1965, he led his team to the league championship, pacing the club in batting with a .500 average.[28] In one documented game, a Sunday, August 7 meeting against Moore-Handley, "Henry Elmore led the attack" with two hits in the Stockham 12–6 win.[29]

He didn't quit entirely, though, switching instead to softball. "I played softball about five years and then my eyesight started getting bad and my reflexes started leaving me," he said, "so I came on home before somebody hit me in my head and killed me."

"I just gave it up," he added. "I wasn't mad at anybody. I just quit playing and got my glove and went on home and put it behind the couch."

He continued to work at Stockham. He moved up to the position of supervisor and stayed with the company for more than 35 years. He still tries to instill a love of baseball into a new generation of young athletes.

"I've got the best neighborhood in the world," he said. "The kids come around me, talk to me, and I take them out in the yard and up to the school ground to teach them how to play. I throw and catch with them."

But he sees less interest in the game among today's young African Americans. "I go by parks now and don't see anybody in them," he said. "It's because they got too much—too many games in the house.

"They got a basketball in their hands," he added. "They got a football in their hands. Nobody has got a baseball glove in their hand. Nobody! You go to a baseball diamond now and it's an empty field out there. People have gone away from the real entertainment."

But Elmore has no regrets about his own baseball career and his time in the Negro Leagues. "During all the traveling, I met a bunch of new friends and enjoyed all of the players I played with," he said. "If I could do it all over again, I would."

Felix "Chin" Evans

Felix "Chin" Evans had a 16-year career in baseball, playing from 1934 until 1949. Only one year of that—his last one—was with the Black Barons. Still, he was a memorable player in the league.

Born October 3, 1911, in Atlanta, Evans was a college star at Morehouse College. He broke into professional baseball as a pitcher with the Atlanta Athletics in 1934 while he was still playing football at Morehouse. He moved up to the Negro Leagues and the Atlanta Black Crackers in 1935 and stayed with Atlanta through 1939, when the team broke up.

Evans spent the 1940 season with the Indianapolis Clowns, playing under the clown name of "Kalihari." His pitching was no joke, however, as he was credited with a 26–4 record for the Indianapolis team.

Evans began to make a name for himself after joining the Memphis Red Sox in 1940. He stayed with Memphis for nine seasons, with his best year coming in 1946.

Evans had a 15–1 record at the all-star break and was selected as the starting pitcher for the West. He picked up the win, throwing three shutout innings and allowing only one hit.

After retiring from professional baseball, Evans used his college degree to become a teacher and coach. He died August 21, 1993, in Pompano Beach, Florida.

Elijah Gilliam

Elijah Gilliam was born July 4, 1934, in Gordonville, Alabama, a small town in Lowdnes County that Gilliam described as being "across the bridge from Selma. I started playing ball down there," he said.[30]

When he got a little older, Gilliam's family moved to Birmingham, where Gilliam attended W.C. Davis Elementary. He later graduated from Ullman High School. By then, he was playing on his first organized baseball team, toiling as a pitcher on a sandlot team called the Birmingham Browns that played in the industrial league. "We did pretty good," Gilliam said.

After graduating from high school, Gilliam traveled to New York to attend his sister's wedding. The trip would give him a chance to move up in his baseball career. On a visit to Central Park, Gilliam stopped to watch a game with a local team, the Central Park Pearls. When invited to participate, the 6'7" hurler grabbed a baseball and threw some fastballs over the plate. The team signed him to the club that day.

The Pearls became Gilliam's shot at a major league career. Soon after joining the team, he was spotted and signed by the Brooklyn Dodgers. He signed a contract with the team in 1955, but it didn't work out. "I developed a sore arm and got an unconditional release," he said.

With his baseball career apparently over, Gilliam returned to Birmingham. Once his arm started to feel better, he returned to the diamond and signed with the Birmingham Black Barons. The Barons would occasionally use Gilliam as a hitter. "I was pretty good with the bat," he said. "They used to use me for a pitch-hitter."

He stayed with the Barons for half of the season, and then joined the Raleigh Tigers in North Carolina. "I did real well up there, and I came back and gave the Birmingham Black Barons the blues," he said. "They came to Raleigh, and I almost shut them out one night. We beat them 3–2."

In 1958, following a brief stint with the New Orleans Bears, Gilliam returned to the Barons. He wore jersey number 17, and kept it on his back for three seasons.

In 1961, he changed teams by returning to Raleigh and donning number 19 for his final season in the Negro Leagues. It was a good finish, with Gilliam playing in the 1961 East-West All-Star Game in Yankee Stadium.

Gilliam was the starting pitcher for the West. The opposing pitcher for the East was the legendary Satchel Paige. Both hurlers tossed the first three innings of the game, with Satchel coming out ahead. "I couldn't beat Satchel," Gilliam said. "We didn't pitch but three innings but I wanted to…. That was my biggest moment in baseball."

"I got a thrill and kick out of it although I didn't get the money I was suppose to have gotten," he said. "Still, I did all I could do. I gave it all I had."

Elijah Gilliam died July 2, 2004.[31]

LOUIS "SEA BOY" GILLIS

Louis "Sea Boy" Gillis played right field and catcher for the Black Barons for three seasons, 1950–1952. He was born August 8, 1924, in Birmingham. Prior to joining the Barons, he played with the Atlanta Black Crackers for two seasons—1946 and '47—and the House of David for another two—1948 and '49. The House of David was a team of barnstormers formed by a religious colony in.[32] Gillis was an only child whose first athletic interest was football, but he started playing more baseball as a teenager.

After graduating from Parker High School in 1943, he was drafted into the U.S. Marines. He served as a gun captain of an anti-aircraft in the South Pacific while also playing baseball.

He returned to Alabama after completing his military duty in 1946, but quickly signed to play for the Atlanta Black Crackers for two years. That stint was followed by two years in Michigan to play for a House of David team. He returned home to Birmingham in 1950 to become the Black Barons' catcher. He played with the team through 1952 while spending more time in the outfield during the latter part of his career.

Gillis once noted that travel in the Negro Leagues and eating meals in a climate of discrimination was a constant problem. "That's why I don't care anything about hamburgers, hot dogs, or sardines anymore," he once said.[33]

Gillis' tenure behind the plate with the Barons included catching for James "Fireball" Bolden. "Catching for James Bolden was like eating ice cream," he once said.

Gillis died February 3, 2005.[34]

ACIE "SKEET" GRIGGS

Acie "Skeet" Griggs was born September 13, 1924, in Union Springs, Alabama, and grew up in Birmingham. He began playing baseball as a teenager in 1938, but World War II delayed his entry into professional baseball. After graduating from Parker High School, Griggs served in the navy for two years (1942–1944).

When he returned from the military, Griggs returned to baseball, first playing for the New York Cubans for two seasons—1947 and 1948. In 1949, he joined the Birmingham Black Barons as an outfielder and stayed with the team through the 1950 season. The 1950 season effectively ended his Negro League career. He played some in Canada during the 1950s, but never returned to the Negro Leagues, perhaps because the fans of Canadian baseball were more accommodating to black players than were the fans in the South. Griggs later became a high school teacher, working in math and coaching athletics.

WILEY LEE "DIAMOND JIM" GRIGGS

Wiley Griggs was a third baseman who played for the Birmingham Black Barons for 11 seasons, from 1948 until 1958. His tenure with the Barons was occasionally interrupted by brief stints with other Negro League teams including the Cleveland Buckeyes and Houston Eagles in 1950 and the New Orleans Eagles in 1951, but most of his career was with the Barons.

Griggs was born May 24, 1925, in Birmingham. He started playing in Birmingham's city league as a teenager and continued into the 1940s. He jumped from the city league to the Birmingham Black Barons in 1948. After retiring from baseball, he worked with the Birmingham Water Works for 28 years before retiring in 1987.

WILLIE "RED" HARRIS

Willie "Red" Harris was born December 12, 1932, in Birmingham, Alabama, to Ed and Florence Harris. Willie grew up as one of seven children (three boys, four girls) in a one-bedroom house. His father supported the family as a coal miner. Willie began playing baseball in elementary school and continued in the game when he went to high school at Ullman High and Parker High.

He was soon playing semi-pro baseball in Birmingham, first for the 24th Street Red Sox, from 1947 until 1949. He joined the Moore-Handley team in the industrial league in 1950, staying with them through 1951. He played briefly with the Birmingham Black Barons and the 24th Street Red Sox again in 1952.

Harris became a member of the Negro Leagues in 1953 when he joined the Louisville Clippers as a first baseman. He made the East-West All-Star Game in Chicago as a rookie.[35] "My first year, I hit fifteen home runs," he said. "That wasn't bad. I faced some pretty good pitchers too. I guess it might have been from A to Triple-A pitching we got."[36]

In 1954, Harris joined the Memphis Red Sox as a first baseman and outfielder. He again made the East-West All-Star Game. He stayed with the Red Sox through the 1956 season until his baseball career was temporarily interrupted by service in the military.

It was a short stay in the army. He completed basic training at Fort Jackson, South Carolina, and was then stationed at Fort Hood, Texas. Later in the year, he was released from the military, and he returned to Birmingham.

Harris hooked up with the Birmingham Black Barons, finishing the 1957 campaign with them and returning for a full season at first base in 1958. All the time, he was hoping to get spotted by a major league scout. He knew his chances were weak because of the informal quota system that seemed to dominate the major leagues at the time.

"Baseball didn't have no more than two or three blacks on a [major league] team at the most," Harris recalled. "Most organizations had that policy. You never saw one black on a ball team ... always two or three so they would have some kind of companion out there. That quota went on for a while. Now the quota is what made us hustle."

There wasn't much money in playing for the Black Barons by then. Their best hope was getting a shot at the majors. "We weren't getting any money so we would try to put ourselves in a position to be on our best behavior and play our best baseball because we knew guys were watching us," Harris said. "We were playing to get signed, to tell you the truth. That was our goal, for some scout to see us and recommend us to the parent team and get a contract and see where we could go from there."

Occasionally the players could pool their resources and save a little from their food money. "We got two dollars a day to eat," he said. "How could you eat off of two dollars? We could and had some left, believe it or not. Seventy-five cents for a hamburger steak dinner was not bad. We ate a lot of sardines, though, and Vienna sausage, bologna, pork and beans."

Harris sometimes helped the team get food from local restaurants. Because of his light complexion, he was sometimes not recognized as an African American. "When we wanted to get some food, we'd send Red in," the Rev. Bill Greason recalled.

Jessie Mitchell recalled another incident during a game in Louisville when Harris' light-hued skin became an issue. Harris hit a home run early in the contest. As he rounded the bases, a white fan in the stands shouted, "They've only got one white boy on the team, but he's the best player out there."

Two innings later, Harris came to the plate again and hit a second home run, this one a mammoth shot to deep center field. "Can't that white boy hit that ball," the fan yelled.

Harris came up for his third at-bat and slammed another home run, this one to right field. "I told y'all, I told y'all," the white fan shouted. "That white boy is the best ball player on the field." Finally, in Harris's last at-bat, he hit a line drive between two outfielders. He raced around first, trying to get a double out of the hit. As he rounded first base, though, his cap flew off and his African American heritage became obvious.

The white fan who had been yelling for him stood up and said, disappointedly, "Lord have mercy, he's a nigger too."

During his six seasons in the Negro Leagues, Harris made the all-star team one time. He played for the East team in the 1960 game.

Harris received one shot at the major leagues. He was invited to the St. Louis Cardinals' minor league camp in Peoria, Illinois. He lost his chance when the team cut him in the middle of spring training. "They said I couldn't throw," Harris recalled. "I told them Stan Musial couldn't throw either — and he couldn't — but he could do everything else pretty good. He could hit."

It didn't matter. Harris was out of the major leagues and out of the minor leagues. He would never get a second shot. He retired from baseball, but continued living and working in Birmingham. He was one of the players who attended the opening of the Negro League Museum in Kansas City in 1997.[37] He lived out his life as a Birmingham Black Baron, dying on January 4, 2006, after a long illness.[38]

CURTIS HOLLINGSWORTH

Curtis Hollingsworth was a pitcher for the Black Barons from 1946 to 1950. He made only a brief appearance in 1946, but posted a 4–0 record in 1947, his best season. He finished his career with one appearance on the mound in 1950.

HENRY F. "HEN" HOWELL

Henry F. "Hen" Howell had a brief career with the Birmingham Black Barons during the 1950s. Howell was born July 11, 1937, in Birmingham, the eighth child to Arthur and Mollie Howell. He first broke into professional baseball with the Detroit Stars, and then had a brief tenure with the Black Barons. Howell died May 1, 1999. Another former Black Baron, the Rev. William Greason, said a prayer at his funeral.[39]

JAMES "SAPP" IVORY

James "Sapp" Ivory was born September 1, 1939, in Birmingham and grew up in the area. He played for the Birmingham Black Barons from 1957 through 1960. Although he would spend a little time playing for Mexico City in the Mexican League, the right-handed-hitting first baseman spent his entire Negro League career with Birmingham.

Ivory started playing semi-pro ball in the industrial league with Stockham while still a young teenager. He also got into professional baseball at an early age, joining the Birmingham Black Barons at the age of 16, when he started traveling with the team during the summer months.

His teammates included fellow Negro League legends Jessie Mitchell, "Dropo" Young, and Willie Smith. His manager for two of those years was Piper Davis. "He was a good manager," Ivory recalled. "You had to be on time. Whenever he said the bus was going to leave at a certain time, you had to be there, 'cause he wasn't gonna wait on you."[40]

His most memorable game was a contest in Meridian, Mississippi, against the Detroit Stars, a team that included his older brother. The game was going well, but the two teams had hit so many home runs and foul balls out of the park that they were running out of baseballs to use in the game.

All the balls on the field were eventually exhausted, but the manager of the Detroit team knew of one remaining ball on the team bus. He ran to the bus and retrieved it. "But when he came back, we still didn't have no balls, because I hit that one over the school," Ivory said. "That was the best thing that ever happened to me." The fact that his brother was on the opposing team only made the achievement sweeter.

Ivory retired from the Barons following the 1960 season. He returned to Stockham in the industrial league and played for a few years. In a game on August 21, 1965, Ivory went 2-for-3 as Stockham won, 9–6.[41] He finished with a .408 average that year, second best on the team to fellow Negro League veteran Henry Elmore.[42]

He eventually quit the industrial league "Me and the manager didn't get along, so I just pulled and left," he said.

But Ivory has no regrets about his years with the Barons. "I loved it, loved traveling," he said. "You got to see a lot of people you didn't know and different towns. I really loved that."

And the game. He really loved playing the game. "Just the playing, getting involved in the game, and winning," he said. "I loved winning. I was a pretty good hitter. I was a helluva first baseman.

"It's a good game," he added. "We didn't make no money, but just the enjoyment of playing, traveling, meeting different people, I really enjoyed it."

JAMES EDWARD "PEE WEE" JENKINS

Pee Wee Jenkins was a pitcher for the Birmingham Black Barons during part of the 1952 season. He also played with the Indianapolis Clowns for part of '52. He began his professional career in 1944 with the Cincinnati-Indianapolis Clowns. He followed that stint with four years with the New York Cubans, from 1946 until 1950, his longest tenure with any team. During the 1947 season, Jenkins compiled a 2–2 record as the

Cubans won the Negro National League pennant and defeated the Cleveland Buckeyes in the Negro World Series.[43] He then played in Canada's Mandak League for a season before joining the Black Barons. Jenkins also had a brief stint in the minor leagues, playing in 1951 with Three Rivers and with Brandon during the 1953 season, both members of the Provincial League.

Leroy Johnson

Leroy Johnson had a brief two-year career with the Black Barons as a pitcher. He broke into the league with the team in 1950, completing his career the following year.

Ralph Johnson

Ralph Johnson had a five-year career as an infielder in the post–Robinson Negro Leagues. A native of Lakeland, Florida, born in 1924, Johnson broke into the Negro Leagues as a shortstop with the Black Barons in 1950. Later in the season he joined the Indianapolis Clowns, becoming a teammate of Hank Aaron. Johnson stayed with the Clowns into the 1952 season. He joined the Kansas City Monarchs during the '52 season and stayed with the team until the end of his Negro League career in 1954, hitting .296 in his final season.

Fate Jones

Fate Jones was an outfielder for the Black Barons in 1950, but little data is available regarding how much he played for the team that season. He was born in Tarrant, Alabama, on May 28, 1923, graduated from Hooper City High School, and attended Daniel Payne College in Birmingham. Jones served in the U.S. Army in the 761st Tank Battalion during World War II and was awarded the Purple Heart. Jones died in 1999.[44]

Henry "Kimmie" Kimbro

Henry Kimbro was an outfielder who made his reputation as a player with the Baltimore Elite Giants in the 1930s and '40s. He was part of the Barons during the post–Robinson years, serving as the team's manager in 1952 and 1953.

Born February 19, 1912, Kimbro broke into the Negro Leagues in 1937 with the Washington Elite Giants. He joined Baltimore the following the year and was with the team for 13 of the next 14 seasons. His one excursion from Baltimore came in 1941, when he was traded to the New York Black Yankees for Charley Biot. He quickly returned to Baltimore in 1942.

He left Baltimore after the 1951 season and took over the helm of the Black Barons. He stayed on the job for two seasons before retiring from the game.

Riley describes Kimbro as "the best center fielder in the Negro National League in his prime."[45] He appeared in six all-star games, but his best season came in 1944 when he hit .329 and led the league in stolen bases. He also fell only one dinger short of tying for the league lead in home runs with Josh Gibson and Buck Leonard.

Kimbro had several other good years. In 1946, he hit .371 while leading the league in runs scored. In 1947, he posted a .353 average, again led the league in runs, and tied for the lead in doubles.

After Kimbro retired from baseball, he drove a cab in Nashville, Tennessee.[46]

CLARENCE "PIJO" KING

Pijo King was an outfielder and catcher for the Birmingham Black Barons from 1947 until 1950. After a respite from the team, he returned for two more seasons, 1952 and 1954, before finishing his career with the Detroit Stars in 1958. Former Black Barons teammate Junior Coleman described King as "probably the best player that we had and probably the highest paid."[47] Prior to beginning his baseball career, King served in the army during World War II.

JIMMY NEWBERRY

Jimmy Lee Newberry pitched for the Birmingham Black Barons for nine seasons, from 1942–1950. His stint with the team included a 14–5 record and a 2.18 ERA in the 1948 pennant-winning season. His record led the league in wins and tied for the league lead in strikeouts. He pitched in three games in the Negro World Series against the Homestead Grays, losing his only decision. After leaving the Black Barons, he continued to pursue a baseball career in the minor leagues and also played one season (1952) in Japan.

Newberry was born in 1922 in Birmingham. He started playing with the L&N Stars of Birmingham before joining the Black Barons in 1942. He had a 1–3 record in his first full season of 1943. He improved to 4–5 with a 3.22 ERA in 1944, then to 5–3 with a 3.06 ERA in 1945. He seemed to reach his full potential in 1946 when he put together an 11–6 record.

Newberry's fondness for alcohol reportedly kept him from reaching his full potential. Riley reported that Newberry's drinking habits prompted manager Piper Davis to make sure the pitcher and the team's youngster, Willie Mays, were kept apart after all ball games.[48] He left the Barons during the 1950 season to play in the Mandak League, where he went 7–7. In 1952, he traveled to Japan to join the Hankyu Braves and put up an 11–10 record and a 3.22 ERA. He finished his professional career in the minor leagues, playing for five different teams — Abilene, Amarillo, Big Springs, Port Arthur, and El Paso. He never again achieved the success that came his way with the Black Barons in the 1940s.

ELMER KNOX

Elmer Knox was born April 26, 1919, in Griffin, Georgia, and grew up in the Birmingham area. He first went to school at Westfield, and then attended high school on the campus of Miles College. "Everybody thought I was going to college," he said. "I wasn't going to college; I was just going to high school. They had a high school part and then they built the high school at Westfield."[49]

Knox remembers attending games at Rickwood when he was twelve years old with the help of a Red Finley, the bat boy for the Birmingham Barons in 1931. Finley let youngsters in the game in exchange for returning balls knocked out of the park.

Knox's family moved to Atlanta and he furthered his education at Booker T. Washington Aircraft School. From there he entered the navy, getting some training at the U. S. Naval Academy of Physical Education. Eventually, he completed his college work at Howard University, graduating with a degree in labor management relations.

Along the way, Knox began playing semi-pro ball in 1937 with the Steel Plant, the Atlantic Steel Company in Anniston, Alabama. "Don't let nobody fool you now," Knox said. "The steel industry has developed more baseball players than any other industry in this country.... They say it's amateur baseball, but how in the world are you going to play amateur baseball when you hire a man to play?"

Knox noted that the coal mines sponsored a number of semi-pro teams, including teams at Wylam, Edgewater, Bay View, Docena, and Westfield. "That's where Mays came from and many other ball players, like Piper Davis and Bozo Jackson, played at Westfield — just to name a few.

"At Wylam, they had Soc Collins, A. B. Easley, James Easley, Andrew Cephus — who played for the Black Barons — Rich Wilder, Joe Blaylock, Cliff Hood, J. D. Hubbard, and a pitcher they call 'Chalk Eye,'" he added. "He could throw it just like they said, on that chalk."

Many of those players were of major league caliber. "Playing black baseball, you would find major league ball players playing in the cow pasture," he said. "Any small town you went to, you would find a major league ball player playing there. Because of the circumstances, beyond their control and my control, they didn't leave."

Becoming a true professional for a black athlete required a willingness to travel. "The only way you can make it is when you go on the road," he said. "You go in some towns, you had some baseball players, that's all they did during the summer. They play from one town to the other with a promise of five dollars."

The key word is "promise." "We played 'promise baseball' in those days," Knox said. "We were promised some money by promoters. But if it rained, we got nothing."[50]

Knox noted that the teams often relied on the kindness of strangers for lodging while on the road. Local fans "would say to us, 'I'll take two players at my house,'" he said. "Someone else would say, 'I'll take three of 'em.' And we slept like that, house to house."[51]

On one trip, some of the players couldn't get a taxi to take them to the game. Instead, they had to hitch a ride in the hearse of a black mortician.[52]

After leaving Anniston, Knox moved up to the Atlanta Black Crackers. That began a career that included stops with the Chicago Giants, St. Louis Stars, Knoxville Grays, Harrisburg Giants, and the Grand Rapids Athletics. At each stop, he played the same position.

"I played outfield center from 1937 to 1949," he said. "I didn't play anywhere but in the outfield and I played center field. That was my specialty. Every team I played on, I played center field. I was a pretty good outfielder; I robbed a few fellas of some flies that they hit."

Knox was proud of the baseball tradition around his adopted home of Atlanta. Atlanta had a number of baseball leagues, including the Branch Rickey League, the George Gibson League, the Georgia State League, and the Peach State League. "All of those leagues operated from North Georgia all the way down to the borders down in Sylvester, Georgia," Knox said. "They had 168 teams in those leagues. Out of that league we had about six or seven boys who got forty thousand dollars for signing the contract."

One noted major leaguer who got his start in the Georgia leagues was John "Blue Moon" Odom. Odom had a 13-year major league career as a pitcher, mostly with the Kansas City/Oakland Athletics. He was an all-star in 1968 and 1969, and helped Oakland win a World Series championship in 1972. He also teamed with a relief pitcher to throw a no-hitter for the Chicago White Sox in 1976.[53]

Knox said Odom was initially offered $40,000 to sign with a major league team. "I told him not to sign it," Knox recalled. "It's a hard thing for a man that has never had more than ten dollars in his pocket to turn down that kind of money. But I said, 'If you're worth forty thousand now, you'll be worth eighty next spring.'"

The following spring, the person who turned up with an offer for Odom turned out to be Knox's old childhood friend, former Black Barons bat boy Red Finley. When Finley showed up, Knox told Odom, "Now, you're going to get the money. He is going to offer you eighty thousand."

"There ain't no way in hell a poor man who ain't got ten dollars in his pocket will turn down eighty thousand," Knox said, "so he signed with the Athletics."

Knox's most memorable game came in Tampa, Florida, in 1942. The opponent was the Pepsi Cola Giants from Port Tampa. The baseball diamond had been built on a former parade ground used as a staging area in the Spanish-American War by the 9th and 10th Calvary units. The two units used the area prior to shipping out for the war in Cuba.

Knox's team won the game, but that wasn't what made the game memorable. Instead, it was a mysterious character named "Old Joe." Prior to the game, the visiting players were told to be careful around "Old Joe." "Everybody was talking about Old Joe," Joe said. "I was wondering, 'Who was Old Joe?'"

Knox was playing center field on a ball field with no fence. Instead, center field was bordered by a lagoon, its edges marked by a palm tree. There were no problems until a player for the Giants known as "Tobacco John" hit a towering fly ball to center. "I was fortunate enough to run under it, and I caught the ball out there at the lagoon," Knox said. "And guess what. There was an alligator laying up under the tree. That was Old Joe.

"I found out who Old Joe was," he added. "From then on, every time a ball was hit, I would jump."

Fortunately for Knox, Old Joe was merely sunbathing. Still, he would have appreciated some warning from the other team. "I saw all the tracks around the concession stand; it didn't mean nothing to me," he said. "Some of the ballplayers knew it, but I didn't. I'm the visiting team; they knew everything and I didn't know anything.

"Of all the places I have played and all the ballparks I have seen — and I have seen some pretty baseball parks — that ballpark in Tampa is the one I'll always remember," he added.

Old Joe's presence on the field was a byproduct of a new war. That game was played during World War II. Plant Field, the usual site of baseball games, had been taken over for military use. The staging area near Port Tampa had been converted to a baseball diamond, but few efforts had been taken to keep alligators away. "Joe never got after me," Knox said. "I could run a hundred in under ten seconds."

Knox has fond memories of his baseball years, even though he didn't make a lot of money as a pro. "The economics of Negro League baseball worked against the players. The Negro team did not have the three [financial] elements that go with the game — the fence, the gate and the concession," Knox said. "The Negro League only got the gate. But if you owned the park, you got all three of them. You sell the fence [advertisements] and you got enough money to operate the ball club for two months, plus what you made on the gate and the concessions."

The importance of black fans to the game became apparent to Knox in 1950 when he became commissioner for the Georgia championship baseball tournament, a competition associated with the National Baseball Congress. The winner of the Georgia championship participated in a national championship competition in Wichita, Kansas, with the winning team claiming a prize of ten thousand dollars.

The first competition was held in 1935 and was won by a team that included Satchel Paige. "Here's the catch to it," Knox said. "They didn't guarantee that a black team would participate in it. When the gate started falling, they made a way to guarantee that a black team be one of the 32 teams in the bracket."

Despite the small financial rewards, Knox said, "Baseball has been good to me and I have seen many great baseball players." But he acknowledges that the best players didn't come from his adopted home of Atlanta. "We had some good baseball players," he said, "but the great baseball players came out of the city of Birmingham."

Elmer Knox died November 13, 2007, in Atlanta.

LEROY "SATCHEL PAIGE, JR." MILLER

Leroy Miller, a native of Leeds, Alabama, starting playing sandlot ball in Leeds under the direction of coach Elbert M. Daniels. He took the foundations that Daniels taught him and turned them into a solid career with the Philadelphia Stars and Birmingham Black Barons in the early 1960s. He had winning seasons for the Barons and developed a reputation as a strikeout pitcher. He routinely had double-digit totals for strikeouts in a game, but his most memorable moment came when he had to substitute for Satchel Paige. "That's the game that sticks in my mind, the game when they had me as Satchel Paige, Jr.," he said.[54]

The year was 1963, and the game was an exhibition contest in Seattle, Washington, on the campus of Washington State College.[55] Miller was surprised at the size of the crowd. "More people than I had ever seen at a ball game," he said. "That's one thing that scared me. I had never seen that many people at a ball game. I found out later that they were coming to see Satchel Paige."

Paige was indeed supposed to be at the game, scheduled to pitch three innings. He was late arriving, though, and the crowd grew impatient. The others on the team turned to Miller, who was thin like Satchel and somewhat resembled him. "Miller, you have to be Satchel Paige, Junior," someone said.

Miller found he was nervous, facing the double stress of playing before a large crowd and impersonating Satchel Paige, Jr. "I'd never really pitched in front of a crowd like that."

He started off by giving up back-to-back doubles, which made the crowd uneasy. The crowd was booing and calling him a fake. "I got mad, and said, 'Those guys were hitting Satchel Paige, Jr. Now I'm going to see them hit me.'"

He settled down and struck out the next three batters to end the inning. He returned to the mound for two more innings, striking out all six batters. That gave him a streak of nine consecutive strikeouts.

After the game, he was besieged by fans wanting his autograph. "That's the first time I ever signed any autographs," he said. "I signed Leroy S. Paige, Jr.; I couldn't spell Satchel."

On the road, Miller ran into the typical discrimination of the day. "When you went to a restaurant, you had to go to the back, especially in the South," he said. "But in Leeds, we were going to the back door then. So it was really just a way of life. We really didn't think too much of it."

Left: Leroy Miller was a pitcher with the Black Barons in the early 1960s. In 1963, while playing in Seattle, Miller was recruited to appear as "Satchel Paige, Jr." for a crowd that expected Satchel to pitch that day. Right: After retiring as a player, Miller started a community center program in his hometown of Leeds, Alabama, offering boys and girls the chance to play baseball and softball. He's pictured here in a visit to Birmingham's Rickwood Field.

The first place that allowed him to eat in the front of the restaurant was in Danville, Illinois. Even that became a problem when he discovered that his pie was contaminated with broken glass. "I don't know if it was a mistake or intentional," he said. "When I spit it out, it was two pieces of glass."

Another team member said he should sue, saying, "Man, you can own this place."

Miller didn't think that was likely, not for an African American. "Back in the 60s, what could you own," he said. Instead, he took it to the manager.

"What do you want us to do about it?" the manager said. "We can give you your money back or another slice of pie."

Miller took the refund. "I never did think no more about it," he said. "But it showed me why, when you were on the road traveling, that you have to be careful about what you do."

Other problems were also treated routinely. "People would call you names, but nobody ever threw anything at the bus or did anything out of the way," he said.

A bigger problem was saving money, given the financial problems faced by the team. Some players were still only getting two dollars a day for meal money, the standard used in the 1950s. Miller was getting three dollars a day for meals and seven dollars per game. They averaged playing three games a week, meaning his weekly income was only $42.

How did the players get by on that budget? "You always had a roommate, and we always put a dollar up for baloney and bread, pitched in together and bought things," he said. "We made it. Nobody went hungry, because food didn't cost that much at the time."

Pooling their resources allowed them to save a little money. "Wherever we went, we had a refrigerator," he said. "Maybe just be in one room, but we had access to a refrigerator."

Sometimes they didn't get to spend much time in any city. "Sometimes, you'd get through playing, you'd have to ride all night," he said. "You'd probably get there the next morning, get a nap or two and then you'd have to play that night.

"It was mostly tiring, but whatever town we'd get to, they [the crowds] were waiting," he added.

Most of the other Negro League teams were gone by them. The Barons' opponents were usually a team from a local industrial league. "A lot of times, when we'd get to those towns, they'd be done stacked the teams," Miller said.

The Barons' visit was advertised weeks in advance, giving the local team time to recruit other players from nearby towns — sometimes former Negro League players. "I was wondering why they'd be so hard to beat, but they had stacked the team," he said. "Anywhere you go back then, within a 10-to-15-mile radius, somebody had a team. If somebody like the Philadelphia Stars come to town, all you have to do is borrow two or three players and put them in key positions where you were weak.

"And they'd be hard to beat," he added. "You had a ball game when you went into a town to play them."

The Barons' road schedule also worked to the local team's advantage. "It was rough to travel all night and play the next day," he said. "Sometimes we had to travel and then play a double-header. I can't say we won every game, but all in all, the strength that we had, it didn't faze us too much."

The Black Barons also had to play well without modern conditioning techniques. "Now people lift weights and have exercise rooms, but most of the people back then just played on their own strength," he said. "All we had was running. You'd make five or six laps around the field to loosen your legs up. Now they have a whole lot more things in the game. If your legs give out, that's it. That's why we built up the leg muscles."

The Black Barons closed down after the 1963 season. Miller turned to semi-pro baseball. "After the Barons folded, we just went to the industrial league and kept on playing," he said. "I played there until I had a team of my own, still in the industrial league. It was the team that Jake Sanders was running. That's what most everybody played in."

When he retired from baseball, he was working at a cement plant in Leeds. He got married and had a son — now a deputy sheriff in Jefferson County, Alabama — who went to college on a basketball scholarship. "I showed him some of my moves," Miller said.

While his son was in school, the college's baseball coach tried to recruit the young Miller to join the team. The younger Miller didn't realize how good his father was until Leroy was honored as a Negro League Living Legend. "Dad, if I'd known you were that good a player, I wouldn't have played basketball. I would have played baseball," he said. Leroy said his son would have been a good pitcher. "He threw way harder than I did."

He has continued to work in the Leeds community, starting the community center program for boys baseball and girls softball. "I felt like I could be a big influence on the kids," he said. "Now, on Christmas and special days, I'll get cards from some of the kids. As I look back, I was teaching them more than baseball."

But baseball was his way of reaching them. "I saw young guys who didn't have a team, so I tried to give something back," he said. "I took a team of guys, about 11 or 12. Now they're grown and got kids. When I see them now, they put the handle on my name — 'Mister Leroy.'

"I see them today, see someone that I started out when they were 12, the same way Elbert May Daniels did me," he added. "It's like they owe you one. That was the biggest moment of my life, just seeing the young kids who grew up. Some went to the army, some are gone, some come back. But they always remember 'Mister Leroy.'"

He rarely watches baseball. "After I quit playing, it just seemed hard to go see a whole ball game," he said. "It's hard to watch one for nine innings. I'll go to Atlanta to watch one. I'll stay about four or five innings, and I'll be ready to go.

"Once you go to see a game, and there's something inside of you saying you can't play, it's hard to watch it," he added.

But the Black Barons remain a major part of his memories. "I'd do it again, because I really enjoyed it," he said. "I went places where I probably never would go back no more.

Back then, that was the only thing there was to do, was to play ball. That was an experience I'll never forget."

WILLIE "PAT" PATTERSON

Willie "Pat" Patterson was born April 1, 1919, in Americus, Georgia, the oldest of six children of Willie Lee and Hallie Pickett Patterson. Patterson broke into the Negro Leagues with the Birmingham Black Barons in 1946. The third baseman/catcher played three other seasons with the Barons — 1947, 1951, and 1955. In between, he also had some years with the Memphis Red Sox (1948, 1953), Chattanooga Choo Choos (1948), Chicago American Giants (1949, 1951–52), New York Cubans (1950), Philadelphia Stars (1952), and Louisville Clippers (1954). His career also included a brief period in the Canadian Provincial League.

Patterson had a brief stint of playing weekend baseball for industrial teams, but had his athletic career interrupted by World War II. After the war, Patterson joined the Birmingham Black Barons in 1946 as a catcher and third baseman. His manager was Tommy Sampson; Sampson also played second base for the team. He stayed with the team through the 1947 season before joining the Memphis Red Sox in 1948. Later in the year, he also played for the Chattanooga Choo Choos.

Patterson signed with the Chicago American Giants in 1949. He stayed with them for the complete season, but frequently packed his luggage after that. He spent the 1950 season with the New York Cubans, and returned to Birmingham for part of the 1951 season.

Late in the year, he was back in Chicago, staying there through the 1952 season. The 1952 season with the American Giants was arguably his best in the Negro Leagues, good enough to get him named to the East-West All-Star Game. He also got an invitation from Abe Saperstein to join the Harlem Globetrotters for an exhibition tour to Japan, but turned down the offer.

In 1954, Patterson joined the Louisville Clippers. He was one of several former Barons who played with the Clippers that year. In 1955, Patterson returned to Birmingham and finished his baseball career with the Black Barons.

After retiring from baseball, Patterson became a longshoreman in Mobile. He retired from there in 1981.[56]

Pat Patterson died in Mobile on August 20, 2004.[57] Prior to his death, he was inducted into the Black Baseball Hall of Fame in Milwaukee.

ROBERT PHILLIPS

Robert Phillips was a pitcher and outfielder for the Birmingham Black Barons in the late 1940s who became better known as a jazz musician.[58] His baseball career began at the age of 14 in 1942 when he pitched against a barnstorming professional team. The pros beat Phillips' local team, but he struck out 22 of their batters. "The next day they came by my home, wanted my father to let me go with 'em, but he said I was too young."[59] Two weeks later, the team made another offer — $100 a month — and his father agreed to let him go. Phillips stayed with the Clowns for three years before signing with the Black Barons for $275 every two weeks. Phillips reportedly played on the 1948 Black Barons as a teammate of Willie Mays. Phillips also claimed that Mays' famous World Series catch, where he chased down the ball in deep center with his back to home plate, was a technique that he taught the youngster when both were in Birmingham.⁶⁰ Phillips also remembered playing against Ernie Banks, once saying that he "used to strike out ol' Ernie all the time."⁶¹ After retiring from baseball in the early 1950s, Phillips became a tenor saxophonist in the Bowling Green, Kentucky, area.

NATHANIEL "NAT" POLLARD

Nat Pollard had a six-year career as a pitcher with the Birmingham Black Barons. He played with the Barons from 1943 until 1950, but lost two seasons (1944–45) to military service in the army during World War II. Pollard is one of the few players whose entire career in the Negro Leagues was with the Black Barons.

Born January 19, 1915, in Alabama City, Pollard attended school in Piper, Alabama. He worked in the mines near Piper before moving to Birmingham to play in the industrial league. He played on the two biggest teams in the league — ACIPCO and Stockham — before being recruited by the Black Barons.⁶²

The curveball pitcher made his debut with the Black Barons in 1943. His best year came after he returned from the war, posting a 5–2 record in 1946. He was 2–3 in the Barons' 1948 championship season. He finished his career with a 7–3 record in 1950.

CHARLEY PRIDE

Willie Mays may be the most famous alumnus of the post–Robinson Birmingham Black Barons, but Charley Pride is a close second. Pride played in the Negro Leagues with the Louisville Clippers, the Black Barons and the Memphis Red Sox. But he became world famous in the field of country music, hitting the top of the charts with tunes such as "Kiss an Angel Good Morning" and "Is Anybody Going to San Antone?"

In some ways, Charley says that baseball was easier. "I was more nervous about singing than I was about playing ball," he said. "I started singing later [in life]. I started playing baseball when I was 14, but I didn't start singing until I was a young man. I still get a little nervous when I go out to sing, a few jitters until I sing that first song, but I need that so I can give it a hundred and ten percent."⁶³

Charley Pride began his professional baseball career with the Memphis Red Sox. "I played with the Red Sox first, and then I joined the Louisville Clippers," Pride said. "And they needed a bus, so they sold Jessie [Mitchell] and me to the Barons in 1954 so they could buy a bus."

The Black Barons owner approached Mitchell about the trade when Louisville was in Nashville. Louisville was in need of a new touring bus; their old one had broken down during a trip to Mississippi. The Barons owner took advantage of that situation to get Pride and Mitchell on his team. He offered to buy the Clippers a bus in exchange for the contracts of the two players.

The Clippers accepted the swap. "They sold me and Charley that night," Mitchell recalled. "Charley stayed about a month and they sent him to Memphis to play with the Memphis Red Sox, but I stayed with Birmingham."

Still, Pride had an impact on the team. He was signed as a pitcher, but he was so good with the bat that they put him in the lineup as an outfielder on his off days.

Pride faced the normal problems of traveling in the Negro League, but he had one advantage. He could spend some traveling time singing and entertaining his teammates.

When Charley Pride first visited Birmingham's Rickwood Field, he was a member of the 1954 Birmingham Black Barons. Pride went on to become a Grammy-winning country music singer. His most recent return to Rickwood was to sing the National Anthem for an ESPN-sponsored retro game.

As former Baron Cleophus Brown recalled, "We had Charley Pride for entertainment. He had a little old three-string guitar — he didn't even have a good guitar."

The other players liked Charley, but not necessarily his music. "He'd keep going until we made him stop playing," Brown added. "We'd tell him to cut it out. 'Don't be singing that country music.' But look at him now. He's a millionaire now, because he kept singing that country-western music."

Pride was the pitcher in an exhibition game for a team of Negro League players against a team of major leaguers at Austin, Texas. "Charley had a knuckleball, and he beat them, 4–2," Mitchell recalled.

Pride retired from the Negro Leagues and started singing in local clubs. He eventually became one of the top country music singers in the nation. As Casey Jones, one of his teammates on the Red Sox, noted, "Charley Pride was a good man. He didn't stay in the league long enough to play the way he'd like to. He was in there for a good little while, but he ran off with his career — singin.'"[64]

As a singer, Pride became the Jackie Robinson of country music — the first black performer to become a star in Nashville after he was signed by RCA. "The slight difference between me and Jackie is that nobody sat me down and said, 'Sit down, n-word, we're gonna have you sing country music.'"[65]

RCA released his first record to radio without providing a photo of its new singer. "Early on, I'd shock a few people walking onstage in small venues," he recalled.[66]

He first faced an arena-size crowd of 10,000 as one of five acts for a major concert in Detroit. The emcee introduced him as a singer with three songs on the charts.

> I went out to all this applause, and then all of a sudden it was like someone turning down the volume so you could hear a pin drop.
>
> But I had seen how it worked in the little venues, so I said, "Ladies and gentlemen, I realize it's unique me coming out on a country music show wearing these burgundy pants."
>
> When I said that, there was some laughter, and then a big round of applause, and I just hit it. From that matinee show to the 8 o'clock show that night I signed autographs. They had to assign a team of ushers to hold people back. And it's been that way for 40 years.
>
> I'm sure that Jackie Robinson had something to do with that moment.[67]

Buck O'Neil had a theory that might explain why Pride was so successful in country music. "Music can't be racist," he said. "I don't care what. It's like baseball. Baseball is not racist. Were there racist ballplayers? Of course.... But we never had any trouble with the real baseball players. The great players. No, to them it was all about one thing. Can he play?"[68]

Unknown to most fans, there was a point in his career when he almost lost his singing career too. Pride was singing in Branson, Missouri, when he noticed that he was only singing with one side of his vocal chords.

He was referred to a doctor in Little Rock who specialized in eyes, nose and throat problems, a physician who also treated then president Bill Clinton. "I figured that if he was good enough for the president, he was good enough for me," Pride said.

Because Pride's condition required a biopsy, his wife, a former medical lab technician, insisted on going with him since the procedure required anesthesia. When he awoke from the surgery, he noted that he was extremely thirsty ("I wanted to drink a lot of water," he said.), but little else seemed out of the ordinary.

He started teasing the nurses and others in the room, including his wife, asking them what the doctor had found, but nobody said anything. Eventually, the surgeon came in and told him that they had done an entire operation — not just a biopsy.

The growth on his vocal chords was precancerous, and Pride's wife had given permission to operate. He removed part of the left vocal chord and did a laser process on the right one. Pride was monitored for six years afterwards to make sure cancer did not develop again.

The surgery had a minor impact on his singing career. "I lost the ability to hit some low notes," Pride said, "but it had no effect on my high range."

Jessie Mitchell still stays in touch with his former teammate. He considers Charley Pride to be one of the best people he knows. "He's not a snooty person to be a celebrity," Mitchell said. "Some people when they make it don't look back at the other guys."

Pride has a similar opinion of his former teammates. He loves to attend reunions with the players. "I love getting around the guys," he said at the Birmingham Negro League Banquet in 2006. "The last time I saw them was in Kansas City five years ago.

A buddy I played with years ago has passed away, Red Harris. Jim Zapp and I played together too."

Meanwhile, Charley Pride has become a country music legend. He is enshrined in the Country Music Hall of Fame in Nashville. "I'm in the Hall of Fame," Pride said. "It's just not the Baseball Hall of Fame."

LAYMON RAMSEY

Laymon Ramsey was a submarine-style pitcher whose cross-fire delivery intimidated hitters. After playing with the Black Barons, Ramsey used the Barons-Globetrotters connection to pitch for the Harlem Globe Trotters baseball team. He pitched for the Globe Trotters when the team was an independent entry in the Western Canada League in 1949. On June 24 of that year, he tossed a seven-hitter against the touring House of David team in a 9–1 win at Taylor Field in Regina, Canada.

NORMAN ROBINSON

Norman Robinson was an outfielder-infielder for the Birmingham Black Barons from 1947 until 1952, all in the post–Robinson era. He is best known as the Barons' center fielder in 1947, i.e., the person who played the position before Willie Mays joined the team. Robinson injured his leg, allowing Mays to become a Baron and the starter. After recovering, the speedy Robinson returned to the Barons' starting lineup, but moved to left field.

Most of his career was spent in the pre–Robinson years. He started by playing with Satchell Paige's All-Stars in 1939, and spent six seasons with the Baltimore Elite Giants in the 1940s before joining the Barons.

Two famous former Black Barons, Charley Pride and Willie Mays, made a 2007 joint appearance at Birmingham's Rickwood Field as part of ESPN Classic's broadcast of a retro Black Barons game.

Robinson was born April 1, 1918, in Oklahoma City. The outfielder first broke into professional baseball with the San Angelo Black Sheepherders. From there he was picked up to play center field for Satchel Paige's All-Stars.

He signed with the Baltimore Elite Giants in 1940, but was used mostly as a backup. He spent the 1941 and '42 seasons playing for local teams in the Baltimore area before returning to the Elite Giants in 1943.

Again, he was mainly a backup player. In 1945, he moved into the starter's position in right field. He held the job through 1946, batting .361 and .321 in the two seasons, before joining the Barons in 1947 as a center fielder under manager Tommy Sampson.

Piper Davis took over as manager in 1948, but Robinson held on to his starting position. He compiled a .299 batting average in the Barons' championship season. He had two more excellent seasons, batting .323 in 1949 and .309 in 1950. He stayed with the Barons for two more years, retiring after the 1952 campaign.

TOMMY SAMPSON

Tommy Sampson started his career has a slick-fielding infielder with the Birmingham Black Barons and eventually took over the dual roles of player and manager for the team.[69] He was a four-time all-star (1940–43) as a player and stayed with the Barons for eight seasons (1940–47).

Sampson was born August 31, 1914, in Calhoun, Alabama. His family moved to Majestic, Alabama, (near Birmingham) when he was 12 and then to West Virginia when he was 15. He quit school at the age of 17 to play semi-pro baseball and work in the West Virginia coal mines. "My mother told me if I wasn't going to school, I had to go to work, so I went to work," he once said.[70] He stayed in the coal mines for eight years, during which time he loss his right index finger while working as a brakeman on a coal car.

Sampson eventually moved up to semi-pro baseball in Portsmouth, Virginia, playing third base for a team that barnstormed around Virginia and North Carolina. One game in 1937 was against the Homestead Grays, and Sampson hit two home runs against the well-known Negro League team. "When this happened, my name kind of flourished out a little bit," he said.[71]

The attention was enough that he signed with the Bellville Grays, Portsmouth's pro team, in 1939. Their barnstorming tour included a game in Birmingham against the Birmingham Stars. He was signed by the Birmingham Black Barons after a game in Atlanta in early 1940. He later recalled his introduction to the team for Brent Kelley:

> Jim Taylor was the manager. You remember Candy Jim Taylor? We made up a team and after spring training he was still trying out guys; they was going and coming. I never saw so many ball players; they'd bring a carload this week and next week they're shipping out a carload. I didn't know whether I was gonna make it or not.[72]

The Barons moved him to second base, partly to compensate for an arm injury and partly to give him a shorter throw to first base. His missing index finger created a natural curving action that made long throws more difficult to execute. "I caught myself helping my arm out, so I switched over to second," he said. "That was a harder position, but it was closer to first base."[73] The move worked and Sampson made the all-star team in his rookie season and repeated the all-star honor in 1941 and again in 1943. Sampson considered the 1943 East-West All-Star Game to be the highlight of his career.

He had a hit and the only RBI for the West as they defeated the East, 2–1, in a game that he played with his mother in the stands. Defensively, he made a sterling play that kept the hitter, Jerry Benjamin who was the potential tying run, from reaching base. "I went in behind second base and threw him out," Sampson recalled. "It was one of those bang-bang plays. The next guy was Buck Leonard ... and he hit a home run. That's the only run they got."[74]

Sampson's best season came in 1942 when he hit .354, but the team's best season in the decade may have come the following year. The Barons won their first Negro American League pennant. They repeated the championship performance with another pennant in 1944. Sampson hit .272 and fell two short of the stolen base title with 16.

Sampson's career as a player abruptly ended during the 1944 World Series, when he was severely injured in an automobile accident. He was in critical condition for several days and missed the rest of the series. Riley cites his absence from the remaining games as one reason the Barons lost the series to the Homestead Grays.[75]

Sampson returned to the team in 1945 and became a player-manager in 1946. His average dropped to .205 in '46. "I enjoyed managing," he said. "It was a headache at first. See, I had too many guys from Birmingham on the team, the hometown boys, and they were hard to handle."[76]

He returned to the team in 1947, and improved his batting to .272, but that was his last season with the Barons. "Me and [Birmingham owner] Tom Hayes had a falling out at the end of '47," he explained.[77]

Sampson played for the Chicago American Giants in 1948, batting .252. He ended his career with the New York Cubans in 1949.

Sampson made one other major contribution to baseball. Riley noted that after he left the Barons, he spotted a talented young player in Birmingham. He recommended the young player to the Black Barons' new manager, Piper Davis. The new rookie became a Hall of Fame player in the major leagues, an outfielder named Willie Mays.[78]

GEORGE "TUBBY" SCALES

Tubby Scales was the manager for the Birmingham Black Barons in 1952, his final year in professional baseball. Scales was born August 16, 1900, in Talladega, Alabama. He broke into the pros as an infielder with the Montgomery Grey Sox in 1919. He subsequently played for a number of teams, but is best remembered for his years with the New York Lincoln Giants (1923–29) and the Baltimore Elite Giants (1938, 1940–44, 1946–48).

He also played two seasons with the Homestead Grays (1930–31), batting fifth in the lineup, between Judy Johnson and Josh Gibson. He posted a .303 average in 1930, and upped that to .393 in 1931.

Scales increased his responsibilities to managing in the 1940s. He is credited with grooming Junior Gilliam, who later became a star in the major leagues with the Brooklyn Dodgers.

Scales died in 1976 in Los Angeles.

JOE SCOTT

Joseph "Joe" Scott had a three-year career as a first baseman-outfielder with the Birmingham Black Barons. Scott was one of the fastest players on the Barons, but never developed the necessary hitting skills to stay with the team for long. Regardless, he was part of the team that won the pennant in 1948.

Scott was born June 15, 1918, in Shreveport, Louisiana. He started playing semi-pro ball in Louisiana after graduating from Central High School in Shreveport. He played for the Shreveport Black Sports in 1938, and jumped to the Texas Black Spiders in 1939. The barnstorming Spiders disbanded in mid-season while in Wichita, Kansas, and Scott hooked on with the Dunsiath Giants, a semi-pro team from North Dakota. He returned to Shreveport for the 1940 season.

Scott joined the U.S. Army in 1941, becoming part of World War II. He served with the 350th Field Artillery and saw major action on the European front. Scott's unit entered France only six days after D-Day, moving through the country and into Belgium when the war ended. He was discharged in November 1945, having risen to the rank of staff sergeant.

Scott moved to the West Coast after his discharge, playing winter baseball in the Los Angeles area before joining the Detroit Senators for the 1946 season.

Scott became a Black Baron in 1947, playing mostly as a backup. He returned to the team in 1948, but the battle for the outfield positions became more competitive when Willie Mays joined the club. He dropped to a .196 batting average.

In 1948 he saw some time at first base, and his average improved to .249. But his days with the Black Barons, however, were numbered. He joined the Chicago American Giants for the 1950 season, but hit for only a .226 average. He retired from baseball at the end of the season and moved back to Los Angeles to work in the railroad industry. He retired from Amtrak in 1979.

EUGENE SCRUGGS

Eugene Scruggs was born May 17, 1938, in Madison County, Alabama. He and his six brothers grew up in the town of Meridianville, a rural community near Huntsville, and attended a one-room schoolhouse called Meridianville Bottom. The school was near a church where the students played baseball six days a week. Scruggs developed his skills as a pitcher and a switch-hitting batter. By the age of 14, he was playing for a sandlot team called the Moore's Mill Red Sox.[79]

At the age of 16, still playing for the Red Sox, he started impressing observers by consistently reaching double figures in strikeouts during games. "I can remember I was on the average of 17 or 18 strikeouts per game at the age of 16," he told Brent Kelley. "I had a curveball and a pretty good fastball. I struck out 20 once in a game."[80]

Jim Tally, a local scout for semi-pro and pro teams, noticed Scruggs. Talley's assessment was that Scruggs had a good curveball, but his fastball needed improvement, and he needed more weight and size. "He stated by the time I turned 17 or 18 years old, he would like to take a look at me again," Scruggs said.[81]

As he approached graduation, the scouting assessment had given Scruggs hopes of playing baseball professionally. "There were few opportunities for a black kid growing up on a sharecropper's farm in Alabama," he said. "Baseball offered a path out."[82]

In 1955, when he was seventeen years old, he received a tryout with the Birmingham Black Barons, but a dislocated shoulder kept Scruggs out of action for a season.

Instead, he worked at a local farm while healing his injured arm. He eventually got the attention of R. E. Nelms, the local funeral home director who booked Negro League games in Huntsville. Nelms "came into my life after the death of my mother," Scruggs said. "He became a father figure to me and offered me sound advice."[83]

Nelms got Scruggs a tryout with Ted Rasberry's Detroit Stars. Scruggs won a spot on the team a month into the 1956 season. He made his Negro League debut on Sunday, May 17, 1956, his 18th birthday.

It was a memorable outing, with Scruggs going five innings against the Memphis Red Sox. He struck out nine, surrendered only five hits, and won his first game, 6–3. It was also his last game, at least for a while. Manager Ed Steele pulled Scruggs from the rotation despite the fine performance. Steele "did not want me to pitch more until I got in shape," Scruggs said.[84]

"I won that game against Memphis," he said. "However, I really didn't know the fundamentals of baseball like the other players on the team, who were trained through the ranks of baseball."[85]

He was transferred to another Rasberry-owned team, the Grand Rapids Black Sox. He was signed to a salary of $250 a month and moved to Grand Rapids. "I never moved to Detroit," he said. "I didn't spend enough time there."

Rasberry used him sparingly at first. "I played with the team for two months because I was too shy for the large crowds and the noise from the fans," he said.[86]

Scruggs credits Rasberry with teaching him how to be a professional player. "I went through training and learning the fundamentals of baseball and getting used to large crowds and the noise of the fans," Scruggs said. "He made me feel good about myself."[87]

There he met two other Negro League players who lived in Alabama, Willie Lee and James Ivory. "We played with the Black Sox team where we all were rehabbing to get back on the road," he said.

His roommate would later become a manager for the Black Barons. "Frank Evans used to be my roommate my first year," Scruggs said. "He was older than I was. He was a man who could help young people choose the right way in life."

When Scruggs returned to the Stars' lineup, he responded with a complete-game shutout. He wasn't short on confidence going into the game. "I knew I had the speed it would take and my curveball was one of the best in the league," he said.[88]

Another game still haunts him — a 3–2 loss in North Carolina against an independent military team. "I gave up a home run with two outs in the ninth inning to lose a game," he said.

> I had struck the player out like two or three times. I remember shaking the catcher off and he hit the home run. [Ed] Steele, the manager, told me that night, the longest day I live, never shake the catcher. I knew I had made a mistake because he hit a fastball. Since I was small, I got weak in the last inning.[89]

Regardless, he finished the 1956 season with an 8–4 record for the Stars and won five other games with Grand Rapids.

One memory of traveling with the Stars was a trip to Raleigh, North Carolina. The memorable event occurred off the field. He and teammate Abdul Johnson had a chance to see rock 'n' roll singer Little Richard performing at a local nightclub.

Sometimes the traveling wasn't much fun, like the time in Virginia when a teammate loaded his clothes too close to the motor of the bus. The clothes caught fire, and the team had to "get in there and put the fire out," Scruggs said. No problem, though. "We got that fire put out and we just journeyed on," he added.

Scruggs stayed with the Stars through the 1957 season, posted an 8–5 record, and then joined the Kansas City Monarchs — another Ted Rasbury team — for the '58 season. It was a different team, but the traveling was the same.

"Most of the time we were just traveling a hundred or two miles at a time," he said. "We'd be in Decatur and that night we'd travel to Birmingham or Memphis. There were no hotels in most places that we could live in. We'd either have to go to Birmingham, Memphis, Nashville or Chattanooga.

"Sometimes we'd have a long jump," he added. "The longest ride I ever had was from El Paso, Texas, to Durham, North Carolina. One time I left Michigan to join the team in Miami, Florida. We drove with Ted Rasbury, and it took a couple of days. There were no interstates back then, and very few four lanes."

Scruggs retired from the game after the 1958 season, when he split time with Detroit and the Kansas City Monarchs. "Mr. Rasbury owned both teams and sometimes they would get unbalanced and we would transfer to the other team," he said.[90] He finished the season with a combined record of seven wins and four losses.

By then, Martin Luther King, Jr., was leading a series of civil rights protests. Racial unrest was spreading, particularly in the South. He recalled an event in 1957 that influenced his decision to quit the road.

"I was either in Birmingham or Mobile and this man was pushed or made to jump off a bridge between Montgomery and Birmingham," he told Kelley. "I started thinking that I should be at home.[91]

"I made the hardest decision of my life when I decided not to return to the team because of all that was going on in this time period for African Americans riding on buses in the South," he told Brent Kelly. "By this time I was married and my wife had just given birth to our first child."[92]

When the team's bus was scheduled to stop by his house to pick him up for the 1959 season, Scruggs simply made sure he wasn't home. "I knew I would go if I stayed there and I needed to be home to take care of my family," he said.

Unfortunately, staying home didn't prevent him from getting caught up in the racial violence of the day. On his way home from work, he was stopped and hit in the head by a state trooper who thought he was participating in a King-led rally at the First Baptist Church in town.

Today Scruggs is pleased at the progress he has seen in modern times, particularly in terms of racial equality. As he told Brent Kelley:

> As I reflect back to a time when the South was segregated, my wish then was to see all children playing together as a team. Now you can see in these pictures the different races of children are getting ready for opening day ceremonies for the Little League games.[93]

The changes came too late for Scruggs' baseball career, but he has no regrets. "I enjoyed it," he said. "Back then, for what I was doing, you couldn't beat it."

WILLIE SCRUGGS

Willie Scruggs was a pitcher for the Birmingham Black Barons during three different seasons — 1949, 1952, and 1958. He broke in with the Black Barons in '49, but left to join the Louisville Buckeyes in mid-season. He split time with the Cleveland Buckeyes and Houston Eagles in 1950, and played for the New Orleans Eagles in 1951 before returning to the Black Barons for 1952. After a time out of the Negro Leagues, he returned to the Barons in 1958.

KELLY "LEFTY" SEARCY

Brent Kelly described Searcy as "one of the best pitchers of the latter days of the Negro Leagues." Elliot Coleman described Searcy as the best player he ever saw in the Negro Leagues. Similarly, Bill "Fireball" Beverly said Searcy was "the best pitcher I went up against," adding, "He wasn't what you would call a flamboyant guy ... but he could pitch."[94]

Searcy began his career in 1950 with the Baltimore Elite Giants. He also played with the Memphis Red Sox and Birmingham Black Barons that year before settling in with the Black Barons in 1953. The left-hander pitched for three years with the Barons before hanging up his glove after the 1955 season.[95]

TAYLOR SMITH

Taylor Smith was a pitcher for the Birmingham Black Barons during two seasons in the post–Robinson era, in 1952 and 1958. He spent two seasons with the Chicago American Giants (1948–49) before joining the Black Barons.

ED "STAINLESS" STEELE

Ed Steele had a ten-year career with the Birmingham Black Barons, playing from 1942 until 1951. After he left the Barons, he had a brief minor league career, became the manager of the Detroit Stars, and helped to discover another Black Baron — John Mitchell.

Steele was born August 28, 1915 in Selma, Alabama. He started playing semi-pro baseball with ACIPCO in Birmingham's industrial league.

Steele broke into the Negro Leagues in 1942 as a reserve outfielder for the Black Barons. He left the team for most of the '43 season, but returned at the end of the year when he, Gentry Jessup, and Ted "Double Duty" Radcliffe were added to the roster for the 1943 World Series against the Homestead Grays.

Steele stayed with the Barons for the 1944 season as the starting right fielder. He batted .303 and had a .491 slugging percentage as the Barons repeated as NAL pennant winners. Birmingham again lost the World Series to the Grays, but Steele did his part, batting .368 in the series.

Steele had an even better season in 1945, hitting .352 as the number five batter in the Barons' lineup. An injury in 1946 cost him playing time and batting points, as he dropped to .277, but he rebounded with a .300 average in 1948. Again the Barons won the pennant, and again they lost the series to the Grays. During three of these seasons — 1946–48 — Steele also barnstormed with Satchel Paige's All-Stars in the off-season.[96]

Steele continued to play well after the 1948 season. He batted .316 in 1949 and .306 in 1950. Despite his consistently high averages, the 1950 season was also his only appearance in an East-West All-Star Game.

Steele received his shot at the minor leagues in 1952, joining Hollywood in the Pacific Coast League. He batted only .213, though, and was demoted to Denver in the Western League. He upped his average to .254, but was released after a mid-season injury.

He tried playing two seasons in Canada and then finished his career with a three-year tenure as manager for the Detroit Stars. During this time, while the Stars were in Birmingham, he spotted John Mitchell and convinced Mitchell's mother to let the youngster travel with the Stars.

During his playing days, Steele was a powerful hitter. Fireball Beverly considered Steele the toughest batter he ever faced. "He didn't only hit me, he hit other pitchers," Beverly said. "I don't mean Texas leaguers — bloopers — a line! Everything he hit you could hang clothes on it."[97]

WALTER THOMAS

Walter Thomas was an outfielder-pitcher with the Birmingham Black Barons in 1947. He broke into baseball with the Kansas City Monarchs in 1936 and spent three years with the team. He also played with the Detroit Stars, St. Louis Stars, Memphis Red Sox and Chicago American Giants before joining the Barons. Despite a mediocre batting average in the Negro Leagues, ranging from .220 to .279, Thomas got a brief shot in organized baseball. He played in 12 games with Wilkes-Barre in 1948, posting a .268 average.

FRANK "GROUNDHOG" THOMPSON

Frank Thompson was a left-handed pitcher for the Black Barons who had two different stints with the team — his 1945 rookie season in the Negro Leagues and three years in the post–Robinson era (1952–54). He joined the Homestead Grays in 1946, playing with them through the '48 season, and was a key player in defeating the Barons in the 1948 World Series.

Thompson broke into professional baseball with the New Orleans Black Pelicans in 1945. He made the jump to the Negro Leagues later in the year when he joined the Black Barons. He compiled a 2–3 record in his rookie season, but left the Barons in 1946 to join the Grays. His best season came with the Grays in 1947, when he put together a 7–3 record. He was also a major player on the Grays pitching staff during their championship season in 1948.

The Negro National League folded after the 1948 season, and Thompson moved to the Memphis Red Sox in 1949. His best season with the Red Sox came in 1950, when he posted a 7–7 record. He finished his career with three seasons with the Black Barons that ended in 1944.

The 5'2" Thompson was a bit eccentric who once stopped a game to search for a gold crown that had fallen off a tooth. He was considerably smaller than the average baseball player which sometimes made him an object of ridicule. Riley reported that Josh Gibson was a major antagonist, claiming that Thompson should be on the Negro

League's "all-ugly" team.[98] Thompson also reportedly had a bulldog-like "won't-back-down" attitude. When one of his teammates on the Grays threatened to kill him after an argument over a card game, Thompson reportedly took out a knife and told the attacker that he would "cut you down to my size."[99]

TED TURNER

Turner was a pitcher for the Birmingham Black Barons on the 1948 team. He was a member of the club that won the Negro American League pennant but lost the World Series to the Homestead Grays.

ROBERT UNDERWOOD

Robert Lee Underwood was born December 24, 1934, in Birmingham. He started playing for community teams when he was about 13 years old. His sandlot team didn't get much publicity, but they played against some of the more notable teams in the industrial league — ACIPCO, Stockham, and the 24th Street Red Sox.

Underwood joined the Barons in 1955 at the age of 20. "I was in prime playing age," he said. "I stayed in shape because all I did was play baseball and basketball."[100]

He joined the Barons as a shortstop. "I could throw," he said. "I had a strong arm, and I had footwork."

Underwood was recruited for the team by the legendary Baron, manager Lorenzo "Piper" Davis. "He and I lived in the same hometown, a place called Westfield, where Willie Mays came from," Underwood recalled. "He knew I could play."

His tenure with the Barons included a lot of travel to play such teams as the Memphis Red Sox, Louisville Clippers, and Detroit Stars. He had to adjust to the perils of traveling, which included riding a bus. "I messed around once and took my shoes off and my feet swelled up," he said. "I knew not to do that no more, not riding a bus."

Underwood finally quit the Barons in 1957. "I got tired of playing for nothing," he said. "I loved the game, but if I was going to play for free, I figured I might as well stay at home and play."

He went to work for Connor Steel and played for their team in the industrial league. "I had a job, and if you wanted to play ball, you could still play," he said. "And you made more money than on the road."

Connor Steel had a good team, once winning 18 straight games during the 1957 season. His most memorable game came with this industrial league team, not the Barons.

In fact, it was two games, and he was playing against his former team. "We played against the Barons in Rickwood and in Montevallo," he said. "They've yet to win one."

"I didn't get too many hits [against them]," he added, "but they didn't get no hits down either."

Underwood finally retired fully from the game in 1966. "It's a great game," he said. "I loved it, loved to play. I wish I could still play it."

JESSE "HOSS" WALKER

Hoss Walker had two stints as a shortstop with the Black Barons. His first three seasons came from 1941–43, playing with the team during the wartime years. Later, he returned to the Barons in 1953, in the post–Robinson era, and stayed through the 1954 season.

Walker posted a .231 average for the Barons in 1941. He was used sparingly after that, sometimes filling in at second base. He left the Barons to become player-manager of the Indianapolis Clowns. He returned to the Barons in 1953 in a managerial role.

ANDY WATTS

Andy Watts was a third baseman for the Birmingham Black Barons in 1950. He posted a .299 average for the Barons, but was off the team the following year. He finished his career with a season for the Indianapolis Clowns in 1952.

RICHARD "DICK" WATTS

Dick Watts had a two-year career as a pitcher with the Birmingham Black Barons. He played for the team in 1949 and 1950.

WILLIE WELLS

Willie Wells was a star with the St. Louis Stars in the 1920s and the Newark Eagles in the 1930s, but he spent one season—1954—as the manager of the Birmingham Black Barons in the post–Robinson era. As a player, Wells was considered the "best shortstop in black baseball during the 1930s and early 1940s."[101] Donald Dewey and Nicholas Acocella described him as the "successor to John Henry Lloyd as the Negro leagues' greatest shortstop."[102] Negro League veterans picked him as the all-time shortstop from the Negro Leagues.[103] Wells sometimes was referred to as the "Shakespeare of Shortstops," but Pat Patterson went further, calling him "the greatest shortstop that ever played the game."

Wells won two batting titles, topping the .400 mark with one of them, and was a member of three pennant-winning teams. And he was a defensive master. "He didn't have a strong arm, but he could always get that man at first," Hall of Famer Buck Leonard recalled. "He would toss you out, the boys used to say."[104]

Born August 10, 1905, in Austin, Texas, Wells broke into professional baseball with the San Antonio Black Aces in 1923. The next year, he moved into the Negro League by signing with the St. Louis Stars. He became a regular player for the team in 1926, posting a .378 batting average and setting a season record by hitting 27 home runs in 88 games.[105]

His fielding prowess was also evident, as he became the Negro League equivalent of a Gold Glove defensive player. Wells was known for playing with a fielder's glove that had a hole in the middle of it, a technique that he said improved his defensive play.

Initially, Wells had trouble hitting the curveball. He cured that after working with Hurley McNair, considered by some to be the best two-strike hitter in the Negro Leagues. Hurley taught Wells to stand in on the pitch by tying his foot to home plate.[106]

Wells posted a .346 average in 1927. In 1929, Wells upped his average to .368 and won the Negro National League batting title. He repeated the batting title in 1930 with a .404 norm as he led the Stars to the Negro League championship. The Stars repeated the championship title in 1931, with Wells again leading the way.

The Stars folded after the 1931 season, and Wells played for the Detroit Wolves [107] and three different teams over the next four years before hooking up with the Chicago American Giants in 1933.[108] He batted for a .300 average and was part of the team that claimed a pennant for the Negro National League that season. He also played in the first East-West All-Star Game that year, providing two hits as his contribution to the win by the West team. It was the first of eight all-star appearances for Wells.

In 1936, Wells left the Giants to join the Newark Eagles and posted a .357 batting average.[109] During this time, Wells became the first person to play with a batting helmet. The breakthrough came in a game against the Baltimore Elite Giants, when he was hit in the head by pitcher Bill Byrd.[110] Wells was advised to sit out the rest of the series. Instead, he borrowed a miner's hard hat and modified it for baseball.

Wells added a .386 average to his resume in 1937, and then posted a .396 average in 1938. After registering a .346 average in 1939, Wells jumped to the Mexican League for two seasons. There he became known as "El Diablo" while playing with Vera Cruz.[111] That was translated to "Devil" when he played in the U.S., a tribute to his "relentless playing style"[112] and because "he played with white-hot intensity."[113]

Wells returned to the U.S. to serve as player-manager of Newark in 1942. By then, talk was beginning to circulate that the major leagues might soon add a Negro League player to the roster. Wells' reputation, plus his .361 average in '42, made him listed as one of the top five players under consideration.[114] Supporters for the move activated a "Wells-for-Reese" program to pressure the Brooklyn Dodgers to sign Wells and use him to replace new signee Pee Wee Reese.[115]

By 1943, though, he was back in the Mexican League. He stayed there through the '44 season. He returned to the U.S. late in the '44 season, playing for the American Giants, the Memphis Red Sox, the Elite Giants, and Indianapolis Clowns.[116] He finished out his playing career with three years in Canada before retiring in 1951.

By then, Wells had compiled a .358 career batting average and 111 career home runs in league play. In the various exhibition games in which he faced major league pitching, Wells had a documented average of .392.

Wells came out of retirement in 1954 to take the dugout helm of the Birmingham Black Barons. Even then, he was highly respected among his fellow players. Negro League shortstop Ulysses Redd called Wells "the best all-around ball player I ever saw. I saw Marty Marion, Pee Wee Reese — I saw quite a few of 'em — but he was the one I admired the most."[117]

Wells' reputation stands up well, although statistical analysis puts a small caveat on it. After reviewing his career, statistical guru Bill James concluded that Wells "did everything outstanding except throw."[118] Regardless, as Connors noted, he remained "one of the best shortstops in the Negro League."[119]

Wells was elected to the National Baseball Hall of Fame in 1997.[120] It was a long overdue honor.[121] He died January 22, 1989, in Austin.[122]

Ernest "Tennessee Ernie" Westfield

Ernie Westfield was a pitcher for the Birmingham Black Barons in the latter years of the organization, beginning in 1959. He was the starting pitcher in the August 21, 1960, East-West All-Star Game in Comiskey Park, the last official all-star game for the Negro Leagues. Born November 30, 1939, in Cleveland, Tennessee, Westfield was signed by the Chicago Cubs in 1958 and assigned to their minor league team in Carlsbad. He was released at the end of the season and signed with the Black Barons in 1959. After leaving the Barons, Westfield moved to the Kansas City Royals. After his baseball career, Westfield earned a college degree from Eastern Illinois University and had a 30-plus career as a civil servant in Illinois. He retired in 1999.

Archie "Dropo" Young

Archie "Dropo" Young was born September 29, 1930, in Livingston, Alabama, and spent his early childhood years in a mining camp. The family moved to Birmingham in December of 1941, and young Archie attended Mulga Elementary and Junior High School. He dropped out of school to take a job—first at Fairfield Steel and then in the coal mines.

As he grew older, he started playing baseball on a sandlot team called the Red Caps. "I played baseball there until I went into the army," he said.[123]

While still with the team, Young got his nickname in 1948 when the Southern League Birmingham Barons had a power-hitting first baseman named Walt Dropo. "With me being a long ball hitter, too, and a first baseman, they started calling me Dropo."

In 1950, Young was drafted to fight in the Korean War. He was sent to Fort Campbell, Kentucky, for basic training and then assigned to the 710 Tank Battalion. Later he was transferred to Fort Drum for training in field artillery. The military gave him another chance to play baseball. "When I went into the army, I got a chance to play on a post team in 1951 and in 1952," he said.

He was one of only two black players on the military team, but the army turned out to be his ticket to the Negro Leagues. Until then, he had not played in any professional or semi-pro leagues. The military gave him a chance to meet some players with Negro League experience and to showcase his talents to some scouts.

One scout who showed some interest was Bing Devine of the St. Louis Cardinals. Devine offered Young a tryout with the Cardinals, but an injury prevented that from happening. "I had several chances when I was in the army and I was scouted all around," he said. "But I just didn't have a feel for it."

The Negro Leagues offered a better option. "I met one of the fellas that played ball in the Negro League that I played with in the army," Young said. "He told me when I got out to see some of the fellas to get a tryout with one of the Negro League teams."

That didn't happen immediately. When he was released from the military in 1952, he returned to Birmingham and went back to school, attending Parker High School, to complete his high school degree. He also got married, wedding wife Alice on December 20, 1952.

Meanwhile, he worked in the coal mines to support a growing family that would eventually include four girls and three boys. "I love the game, but after I got out of the army, I just didn't see where I could make a career out of playing baseball," he said. "So I just chose to spend my time in the coal mine."

That changed in late 1953 when he got laid off from the mines. He left Birmingham, moved to Avon Park, Florida, and started playing baseball with the Lou Haney Stars in 1954. "I played winter baseball until I hurt my arm," he said.

After the injury, Young returned to Birmingham. In the meantime, some scouts had spotted him in Florida. The Philadelphia Phillies offered him a contract in their minor league system. "I wasn't working then. The mine had closed down and I had a chance to play some," he said, "but I decided not to take that. It would have been $175 a month to play up around Minnesota somewhere."

He instead hooked up with the Negro League. In 1955 when the Louisville Clippers came to town for a game with Birmingham, he got a tryout and joined the team on a part-time basis for the 1956 season. "I didn't pursue a career or play regularly in the Negro League because I had two children and a family. I didn't play for a full season because I had other options," he said, "but I did play part of '55, '56, and '57."

Although he started his baseball career as a first baseman, he also played as a catcher for the Barons. "I started catching when we were playing ball in Westfield," he said. "The [regular] catcher got his finger broken and they couldn't get anybody to go behind the plate. So I told them I would try it.... I pitched in the league some too — about four or five games."

His most memorable game came when the Barons played an all-star team in Aliceville, Alabama. He had been to bat twice and made an out both times. When he came up for his third and final plate appearance, the manager called time out for a discussion. Knowing that Young was using a 36-ounce bat, he said, "Dropo, you're on the ball but the man is throwing it by you. You can't get around on it. Take this 33 and I believe you'll get around on it."

Young changed bats and returned to the batter's box. The opposing pitcher wound up and threw a chest-high fastball. Young swung and hit the horsehide. "When I hit the ball, I thought I had popped it up," he recalled, "but the second baseman jumped up at it. It was just out of reach. The center fielder went back and couldn't get it either.

"There were six or seven white boys that came in the park who were sitting up on a hill way back behind the ballpark," he added. "They saw that ball coming and got up, and the ball went between them."

Young said that team officials walked back to the spot where the boys had been sitting to locate the baseball. The boys told the team that "the last time they saw the ball, it was still rising." As a result, Young added, the team estimated the total distance of his home run "to be around 700 feet."

After 1957, like many other former players, he continued his baseball career in the industrial leagues,[124] but it was mostly a hobby by then. His major income came from working in Alabama's coal mines, something he did for more than 40 years. "I played on up until the latter part of 1960 off and on," he said. "The league had started folding. I played a couple of games with a team and a couple of games with the all-star teams, but not much else."

Young said that he quickly recognized that despite progress in the post–Robinson era, the odds of a baseball career were still stacked against most black athletes. "They had what they called the quota system set up," he said. "They weren't going to take but so many ball players. I don't care how good you were, each team was going to take only so many ball players.

"A lot of us got caught up in the quota system, but I did learn how to deal with all of that," he said. "I had already decided that I wasn't going to leave home no more. I would go as far as Louisville, but as far as quitting my job and depending on baseball for a living, I decided I wasn't going to do that."

Young has no hard feelings over not getting a solid shot at a major league career. "I don't hold any resentment of what happened, because that was just the time that I came along when those things were in effect," he said.

"There was a limitation as to how far you could go in baseball," he added. "We just lived in a time frame when there was nothing you could do about it."[125]

He has no regrets. "I really enjoyed the game of baseball and I learned a whole lot through playing in the Negro League," he said, adding that today's youngsters could also learn from the game.

As an example, youngsters could learn to follow the rules. "We have rules and regulations; they are everywhere you go," he said. "There are so many youngsters now who break the rules — if not on the field, it's off of the field. My advice to them is to learn the rules and regulations and abide by them."

Another lesson: the importance of teamwork. "Always try to play for the team with the name on the front of your uniform, not the one on the back," he said. "Nine times out of ten, the one on the back is going to be your name. The one on the front represents the whole team."

That mantra includes a willingness to accept the position on the team where you're most needed. "You can't have a negative idea about playing the outfield if you're a pitcher," he said. "If the manager tells you that his right fielder has gotten hurt and he wants you to go out there, tell him, 'I'll try it.'"

Young said the player should make the move, even if it's just a different outfield position. "If you can play one outfield, you can play the other one, but you got to catch the ball differently," he said. " It's different, but don't ever tell a man you can't play. I don't care what kind of sport it is. Always tell him, 'I'll try it.' Then you'll have confidence in yourself and the man will have confidence in you.

"Always keep a positive idea," he added. "That's why I got a chance to pitch, a chance to play first base, to catch and to play a little third base. I would play anywhere they would ask me to fill in and would give them my best, and it paid off for me."

And, he added, there was one final lesson that he learned from the managers he played for in the Negro League. It was a simple one: "They didn't fool with no sorry ballplayers."

Chapter 5

Players and Tryout Camps

By the mid–1950s, the major leagues were sapping an increasingly larger number of players from the Negro Leagues. Scouts continued to come to the games at Rickwood, in search of prospects, but the contract offers became fewer. Instead, the scouts increasingly relied on inviting prospects to tryout camps. There the players were evaluated by a team of observers and, if lucky, signed to a minor league contract. Most were sent back to the Black Barons with little or no explanation as to why they were not signed. The rest of this chapter is devoted to those who made it to those camps, but were never signed to major league or minor league contracts. The fact that they received a look from organized baseball, though, speaks well of the talent on the Birmingham Black Barons and the other teams in the Negro Leagues.

OTHA S. "BILL" BAILEY

Otha S. "Bill" Bailey was born June 30, 1930, in Huntsville, Alabama. He started out playing sandlot ball, but quickly made the move to semi-pro and Negro League baseball by playing a position sometimes considered the quickest way into the pros — catcher. The 5'6", 150-pound Bailey was small compared to most catchers, so small that one of his nicknames was "Little Catch."[1] But he was still competitive. One source described him thusly: "The scrappy little catcher had an accurate arm and was quick behind the plate, often beating the runner to first base while backing up the play." As teammate Jessie Mitchell later said, "He was one fine little catcher."[2]

At the age of 18, he received his first shot at joining the Black Barons. It didn't last. "I started in 1948 with the Black Barons, but they let me loose that year," he said.

What followed next was a series of short stays with a variety of teams. Bailey described that period, saying, "I shuttled through 1949 on up to 1950." He first returned to Huntsville, playing for the Huntsville Pirates and Huntsville Stars in 1949. After completing the season in Huntsville, Bailey received his second tryout with the Birmingham Black Barons, but was released from the team in the spring of 1950.

He quickly hitched on with Jim Canada and the Chattanooga Choo Choos, but only for a short stay. That was followed by a short one-season tenure with the Cleveland Buckeyes before that team folded.

The Newark Eagles offered another opportunity. When they moved to Houston, becoming the Houston Eagles, he had reached his final stop for the season.

In 1951, the Eagles again moved, this time to Louisiana, and became the New Orleans Eagles. Bailey made the move with them.

In 1952, he finally returned to the Birmingham Black Barons. He would stay with the team through the championship season of 1959. During this stint, Bailey had a memorable game in which he was catching for renowned Black Baron pitcher Bill Powell. Powell, for some reason, had trouble throwing strikes that day. Finally, after a couple of innings of wild pitches, Bailey walked out to the mound, leaned back to look up at the taller Powell, and said, "If you don't start throwing the ball over the plate, I'm going to kick you from one side of this park to the other."[3] Bailey returned to his position behind home plate, and Powell started throwing strikes.

Bailey later recalled the incident for Joe Posnanski, looking "a bit sheepish," but added, "Baseball turned me into a madman, but I wasn't scared of nobody."[4]

Bailey retired from baseball following the 1959 season and took a job with Connor Steel. "In 1959, I knew I wasn't making no money and I knew I wasn't going to the majors," he said. "I had to get a job. I had a family, so that was it. I gave it up."

During those years, Bailey received two shots at the major leagues. The Boston Red Sox took a serious look at him in 1950. They were impressed by his catching skills, once described as being as good as those of the Dodgers' Roy Campanella.[5] But the Red Sox decided not to sign him because of his size. "The scout told me if I was two inches taller, they would've signed me," he said.

His only other shot, a tryout with the Dodgers in 1951, was foiled when he overslept. Hall-of-Famer Roy Campanella gave him the invitation when Bailey was in Miami and the Dodgers were in Florida for spring training. "I overslept," Bailey said. "I woke up and it was too late. They were gone."

Bailey ran into Campanella again two weeks later. Campy chided him for not showing up, telling him that he didn't want to play ball. Bailey insisted that he did. "I figure I might have missed a chance there," he said. "I might have at least gotten farmed out."

Bailey spent his entire baseball career as a catcher. "I was brought up among the catchers, among the best," he said. "I knew Buck O'Neil when I was about 18 years old; I used to go down and talk with him all the time. I've been taught be several ballplayers."

"I was a hustling catcher," he told Brent Kelley. "I played like I was really after it. I just loved the game. I played hard."[6]

Bailey was also known for his ability to call a game. "A good catcher has got to know the players, know the batters, know what they can hit and what they can't," he said. "I learned the hitters. When I saw a guy hit the ball out of the ballpark, I'm watching it. He won't get that pitch again."

Bailey believes the comparison to Campanella were realistic, particularly in terms of defensive skills. "The only thing [Campanella] had on me was some weight and some hitting," he said. "As far as the rest of it, I didn't think so."[7]

"I figure I was good enough to go to the majors," he added. "I look at the catchers nowadays, they couldn't carry my glove. The balls gettin' off by 'em and between the legs. I didn't let none get by me hardly. I used to catch the knuckleball and all those trick pitches and I loved to do all that."[8]

His most memorable game was catching the legendary Satchel Paige. "He was the best pitcher I ever caught," Bailey said. "He was tough. I was about 26, he was about 49 or 50, but he could still throw the ball. He'd stand there and pose and once you let your bat down, he was going to throw the ball. You can't get up there to hit it. That was it."

He remains happy that he had some years in the Negro League. "I was young. I liked playing the game," he said.

He also enjoyed the travel. "I'd sit on the keg looking in the curves to let them know if they had a steep curve," he said. "We'd drive all night. We drove to Minnesota one night. When we got to the ballpark, we laid out in the bleachers until about four or five o'clock, then we started to take batting practice."

And, given the chance, he'd do it again. "If I could get in shape, I think I'd play," he said. "I'd need about three weeks."

CARL HOLDEN

Carl Holden was born August 22, 1941, in Madison, Alabama, the son of Thorton and Mattie Holden. Carl was one of nine children in the family — four boys and five girls. He started playing baseball at an early age. "We were playing stick ball as kids," he said. "When I'd go to visit my grandparents, all my cousins and us would play ball. I started like that, so I started pretty early."[9]

How early? "We actually started throwing a hard ball when I was about 10 or 11 years old," he told Brent Kelley.[10]

His education began at West Huntsville Elementary School and moved to West Huntsville Junior High in 1953. By 1955, while still in the eighth grade, he started playing sandlot ball with the Huntsville Giants under manager Ed Kennimore. Holden described his sandlot team as "a bunch of young kids."

Holden attended William H. Council High School and continued his baseball training by joining the Rocket City Dodgers. "That was a semi-pro team that played in the big park [Optimist Park]," Holden said. "I played with the adults. We played against stiffer competitions."

In 1958, he joined another semi-pro team, the Huntsville Braves, as a catcher. "I started catching when I started filling out," Holden said. "They noticed that I was getting a little size on me. I caught some, but I played infield and outfield before that. They were just looking for somebody chunky who had a good arm on them, I guess."

Later, while he was still on the team, they changed their names to the Huntsville Hawks. "They got some new uniforms and took on a new name," he said, "but it started as the Huntsville Braves."

Holden stayed with the Hawks for two years, leaving to attend Alabama A&M University in the fall of 1959 and to play football. A knee injury playing sandlot baseball that summer ruined his plan. "I stepped in a hole running out a ball I hit in the gap," he said. "It came back to haunt me a couple of times.

"That's what really got me out of college," he added. "I was getting ready to start college my freshman year, but my knee messed me up."

With his football career over, Holden returned to baseball. He wrote a letter to scout Fred Hoffman requesting a tryout with the Baltimore Orioles. Holden was one of four players Hoffman invited to a tryout in Pensacola, Florida. The four men spent an hour and a half trying to impress the scouts. "They timed us, we ran, (we) threw, they let us field," Holden said. "It was in the middle of winter."

"They had some guys they called 'bird watchers,' who would recommend you," Holden added. "Mr. Hoffman was the head scout, but they had scouts in different areas and they'd send you to this guy. He would look at you and determine whether he wanted you to go to the camp or not."

Holden soon discovered that he was pretty fast ... for a catcher. "A friend of mine from Southern University was also a catcher," he said, "and we ran off and left all the catchers, so they made us run with the outfielders."[11]

Hoffman wanted Holden. He was invited to attend the Orioles' minor league camp in Thomasville, Georgia.[7] Unfortunately, his knee started acting up again. The Orioles suggested he have an operation and work with the rookie league in Bluefield, West Virginia.

Holden turned down the offer and returned home to enroll in Drake College while rehabilitating his knee. That didn't last long, though, because he was contacted by local businessman and promoter R. E. Nelms, a funeral home director who dabbled in sports. "He was a guy who would pick guys out of the area and send them to the Negro Leagues," Holden said.

Nelms knew Holden and watched him play in a practice game against Alabama A&M. "He called me over to the side," Holden recalled. "Otha Bailey was getting ready to quit, and [Nelms] was telling me that I could go down and try out with Birmingham. Or if I'd wait a little later on, I could try out with Kansas City."

Nelms set up the tryout with the Birmingham Black Barons. He signed for $300 a month, but didn't always see his money. "They could've told me $500 a month knowing they weren't gonna pay," he said.[12]

He opened the 1960 season as a catcher for the Barons. "My first game, I played at Hattiesburg, about a week after I got down there," he said. "It was the first game where I had a chance to bat. I got base hits the first two times that I faced a pitcher, my first two at-bats."

By then, the Black Barons were playing the other three teams in the league and barnstorming for exhibition games around the Southeast. "We would travel, go stay a few weeks out, then come back and play at Rickwood," he said. "Then we'd go back out."

Some of the parks on the road lacked the facilities that were available at Rickwood. "The lights were a little bad, especially those stadiums in Mississippi," he said. "A lot of those lights weren't high enough. The ball would go out of the lights and you had to trail that ball until it came back into the lights. That was the hard part for a catcher. You had to wait until the ball started coming down to pick it up."

A lack of money caused the team to cut the 1960 season short. "The funds for the team dried up," Holden said. "Most of the team disbanded before the season was over. I left about a week before the season was over."

That ended Holden's brief career in the Negro League, but not his baseball career. In 1961, he returned to Huntsville and rejoined the Hawks as a semi-pro player. He stayed with the team for two years until most of the players shifted over to an American Legion team. "In 1963, we started playing for the American Legion Post 351," he said. "They sponsored us, so we went by that name.

"It wasn't American Legion ball; it was a semi-pro team," he added. "We played for them for four or five years. We won quite a few championships there."

During the 1963 season, the team went 33–1, losing only one game to Redstone Arsenal. "We beat them three or four times that year," Holden said, "but we lost one to them."

Holden stayed with American Legion Post 351 until 1968, rising to the rank of team captain and playing a number of positions in the infield and outfield and, occasionally, pitcher.

Holden retired from baseball, driven from the game by the decline of the Negro League. "It was breaking down. I came back home and got a job," he said. "Out there on the road some days you didn't get your meal money. The money started drying up."[13]

He worked as a civil servant for the federal government for 10 years and had a 32-year career as a small businessman. Still, Holden reflects on his time in the Negro League with fond memories. "I enjoyed it," he said. "It was an opportunity for an 18-year-old to get out and travel and meet a lot of people."

Would you do it over again? "Oh, yeah," he said. "I'd probably start playing at three instead of five. And if my health was good, I'd probably still try to play."

Tony Lloyd

Anthony "Tony" Lloyd spent only one year in the Negro Leagues, playing second base for the Birmingham Barons in 1959. But his year was a memorable one, as the team won the Negro League championship that season.

Lloyd was born in Fairfield, Alabama, a suburb of Birmingham, on April 27, 1936, one of six children (four brothers, two sisters). His father was a local steel mill worker, while his mother worked in the school cafeteria. "Birmingham ... was a steel mill town," he said. "My father worked in the steel mills for 46 years, and my uncles all worked in the steel mills."[14]

He grew up under the Jim Crow laws of the state, playing baseball at Robinson Elementary in Fairfield and then at Fairfield Industrial High.[15] "There was a ballpark down by the post office that was nice and manicured, but only white kids could play there," he said. "We black kids had to play on the black side of town on a field that was rocky and weedy, but we did the best we could because we enjoyed playing baseball."

Baseball was a welcomed form of recreation for the youth in his community. "My mother would have to call me in at night, because I'd be playing baseball," he said. "If you didn't play baseball, you weren't hanging out with me. I didn't date, I didn't do a lot of other things. It was baseball, baseball, baseball."

Getting a group of kids together for a game was no problem because the community had plenty of youngsters interested in the game. "In those days, there were a lot of kids around. Families had a lot of kids," he said. "It wasn't unheard of for a couple to have ten kids. Eight and nine were common.

"There were six of us, and I was somewhere in the middle," he added. "There were two boys and a girl above me and a boy and a girl below me."

Finding competition was also easy. "On our street, we had enough players to have a team playing for our block, and we'd play a team from another block."

Lloyd's favorite position as a youngster was shortstop, but he eventually switched to second base. "As I got a little bigger I found out that I didn't have that strong arm to throw the ball to first base [from shortstop] when you went in the hole, so I switched to second base," he said. "That was my natural position. I didn't have to throw it far, and I was nimble so I could turn the double play."

With few coaches available, Lloyd learned the game by watching older players, including Willie Mays, Papa Luke and local coaching legend Cap Brown. "I was really just raw talent, learning from older guys," he said. "I watched them and try to emulate them. I'd watch what they did wrong and what they did right, and went from there."

Lloyd finished high school in 1954, the same year the U.S. Supreme Court struck down segregation in the public school system with is famous *Brown v. the Board of Education* decision. "I was really elated [at the decision]," he said. "I thought that, being an Alabama guy, I could go to the University of Alabama or Auburn. I figured I was good enough at playing baseball that I could win a scholarship and my parents wouldn't have to pay my way.

"It just wasn't so. Times just weren't right then," he added. "It took years later before black people would enter into any of the so-called white colleges in Alabama."

Instead, Lloyd wound up on the baseball team at Tuskegee Institute while majoring in commercial industries with a minor in English. "I played four years of college ball, and I started every game there."

But, he might have added, he played only against other black collegiate teams. "Tuskegee is only about 40 miles from Auburn," he said. "We couldn't compete with them in football, but we had a pretty good baseball team. I just wondered how we would have done against their baseball team."

Lloyd believes his Tuskegee team had an edge in speed over the white university teams in the state. "One thing about black baseball is speed," he said. "You can't teach speed. We could hit and run and all that stuff. But we couldn't even play against them."

Nor could it happen in any other Alabama town at the time; the state's Jim Crow laws banned whites and blacks from playing together. "I always wanted to test my skills against the best — black, white, green or whatever color. But it just didn't happen.

"You know how times were back then," he added. "I grew up in an all-black section of town, I went to an all-black school, an all-black church, etc. I was never able to intermingle with whites except when you'd see them downtown."

After graduating from Tuskegee, Lloyd played for the Gray Sox in the industrial league. Later he was invited to a tryout camp with the St. Louis Cardinals in St. Petersburg, Florida, in 1959. The two-week camp, run by Cardinals veteran catcher Hal Smith and third baseman Ken Boyer, was held just prior to spring training. The Cardinals used the camp to identify players who might be invited to spring training.

"It was all of us young guys at the tryout camp who were just trying to maybe get a chance to go to spring training and then maybe get started in the minor leagues," Lloyd said. "Even there, it was segregated. It was set up like a military complex, but all the white guys stayed on the complex and all the black guys stayed in black neighborhoods. I stayed about two or three miles from the ballpark, in a black family's house. They were nice people, but we had to walk to the ballpark in the rain or get there the best way we could."

Lloyd was one of the last players cut from the camp. "It came down to between me and a guy from Brooklyn. An Italian guy. His name was also Anthony, and he won out.

"I thought I was better, and he thought he was better. But it was close."

Lloyd believes he might have made the cut had he not contracted the neuromuscular disease Bell's palsy during tryout. "My right eye would not close. When I went to bed at night, I'd have to push the eyelid down."

Lloyd's doctor didn't have a name for the disorder at the time, but told him it would go away. "Since I was young, he said it would leave in two or three months. That's been 45 years ago, and I still suffer with it."

Regardless, Lloyd was cut by the Cardinals. "We had to be heads and shoulders above any white guy [to make the team]," he said. "You had 24 or 25 guys on the team. You couldn't be the 24th or 25th guy and be on the team. You had to be good enough to start.

"I knew that I had to be almost ready to go to Triple-A to make the team. There would be no use to go to the rookie league to get ready to play. I had to be ready for at least Double-A to have a chance. That's the way it was back then."

Lloyd left St. Petersburg and returned to Birmingham. "I came back home wondering what to do," he said. "Then I heard that the Barons were having a tryout for the Negro League team."

He made the team, joining the Birmingham Black Barons for the 1959 season at the age of 23. "I played the whole year with the Birmingham Black Barons. We won the championship and I started every game at second base," he said.

"No one else played second base for the Birmingham Black Barons that year except Tony Lloyd," he added. "You can check the records, and any lineup you see with the Birmingham Black Barons in 1959, there'll be Tony Lloyd at second base."

His first game was a Sunday home game at Rickwood Field before a typical full house. "In those days, we packed the stadium. People would come out in their Sunday best to watch us play ball," he said.

"I had a couple of hits and stole a couple of bases, but the thing I remember most is that we won the game," he added. "I don't remember what the score was, but we won the game."

Lloyd had several other multi-hit games in his career, but few home runs. "I never hit many home runs, but I hit singles, doubles and triples, and I had a golden glove," he said. "I was a little guy. If I got a home run, it was usually inside the park."

His most memorable home run came during a game in Nashville against the Memphis Red Sox. "That was something for me. I don't know how it happened. A guy threw me a fastball and I connected just right, and the ball flew over the left field wall."

Lloyd's manager for the season was the legendary Lorenzo "Piper" Davis. "I learned more baseball from him than I did in four years of college," Lloyd said. "I learned how the pros played from Piper Davis — what position to be in when the ball was hit to the outfield, how to cover a base, how to tag, how to slide. I was a hot-shot ball player, and I thought I knew it all. But when I got with the Barons, I found out [how to play]."

Lloyd's teammates included one future major leaguer. Willie "Wonderful Willie" Smith played in the majors with the California Angels and hit 35 home runs in his rookie year. "He pitched and played first base for us in 1959. A couple of the other guys I played with went to the minors, but he was the only [one] who went to the major leagues."

Some players on the opposing teams were also memorable, particularly Memphis Red Sox outfielder and left-handed hitter Frank Williams. Williams was the brother of Chicago Cubs Hall of Famer Billy Williams. "He hit the ball the hardest I've ever seen," Lloyd said. "Playing second base, I always had to play in short right field — a real deep second base — because he hit that ball real hard and I had to be ready for him.

"That's one guy I thought was going to the major leagues, but he didn't," Lloyd added. "I don't really know what happened."

His most memorable road trip was a game against the Newark Eagles in Ebbets Field. "I was playing second base at Ebbets Field, in Brooklyn. I kept thinking that I was playing the same spot, on the same ground, where Jackie Robinson played.

"I also played in Yankee Stadium that year," Lloyd added. "But I remember the Brooklyn game more because [of] Jackie Robinson. All the black kids during my time, when Jackie Robinson went to the major leagues, we said, 'Man, we've got a chance now. They've opened the doors for the blacks to go to the major leagues.'"

That trip also provided Lloyd with a chance to meet Dodger great Roy Campanella. The wheel-chair-bound Campanella had been seriously injured in an automobile accident the year before. "We went to his liquor store in New York. That was such a sad thing to see. He had such a promising career."

Lloyd's tenure with the Barons also gave him his first chance to play against whites. "The first time I remember playing against white guys was when I went above the Mason-Dixon line in places like Chicago, New York, and Louisville. We played some semi-pro teams. Some were all white, and some were mixed — black and white players.

The year culminated with the Black Barons winning the Negro League championship at the end of the 1959 season. Lloyd hit a triple and stole home for the winning run as Birmingham defeated the Memphis Red Sox, 3–2.

Lloyd remembers the year fondly, even though he didn't make much money. "I was promised $300 a month; I was lucky to get $150 or $200," he said.

"They'd pay you according to the gate. You'd get $25 one week, $30 the next, and hope that it would add up to your salary. And we played a lot of games. We'd play maybe six days a week, with a lot of double-headers.

"We had some owners — some white owners and some black owners — who weren't that great as financial whizzes. They took the money. You could have 10,000 people [in the stands] and they'd report that we had only three or four thousand, so we'd have to take less. But we loved to play."

Despite the glory of winning the championship, Lloyd also remembers the inequities that black athletes faced at the time. Discrimination was apparent even in the name of the local baseball team. "The [white] team that played in Birmingham was called the Birmingham Barons. We were called the Black Barons because we were black, and they were white. I always said when I was a kid that they should have been called the Birmingham White Barons."

Black players had to cope with poor and often inadequate facilities. "There were times, especially in Mississippi, [that] they'd let us play in the ballpark, but we couldn't use the showers. So we'd have to get on our bus and ride another fifty or sixty miles to the next town before we could take a shower.

"And during those times, the buses didn't have air conditioners or bathrooms. So we all sweated. You can imagine how it was."

Fullerton wrote that "Negro League teams realized that southern tours were an important leg of any barnstorming circuit because of the density of the South's black population; but players dreaded the tours, anticipating the possibility of racial violence."[16] Lloyd has some vivid memories of the discrimination faced by the team.

"A lot of times we'd stop by the side of the road to relieve ourselves and go from there. There were places that would sell us gas, but wouldn't let us use their bathrooms. There were places that we could buy food, if we paid for it up front and go to the back to pick it up.

"You'd order 20 to 25 hamburgers," he added. "They'd want their money first, and you'd go to the back to collect the hamburgers. Suppose you have only 13. You pay for 20 or 25, but you may get only 13 to 15 hamburgers. You had to accept that and go on."

Despite the problems, Lloyd knew the Birmingham Black Barons were a source of pride for the community. "It was something that was good for the black community. Most of the people back then were hard-working. After church, especially on Sundays, they'd come out to Rickwood. The entire neighborhood came out when I was a kid. There'd be no place to sit. They loved baseball and loved the home team.

"Remember," he added, "there were very few TVs. When I was in high school, there was only one guy who had a little TV. Now, everybody's got a TV and video games, computers, and all that stuff. They've got more outlets [for entertainment] than when I came up. It was a sense of pride and joy for people to pull for the home team and watch baseball."

Lloyd left Birmingham, the Black Barons, and baseball after the 1959 season and moved to Cleveland, Ohio, to take a job with the post office. "We ended our season in September. I started at the post office in October 1959."

He decided not to return to the Barons when spring training for the 1960 season was approaching. "I went to personnel and tried to get a leave of absence so I could go play ball. I wanted to give it one more try and maybe make it to the majors. But I was told that I would have to quit and then take my chance on getting re-hired again. I hadn't been there long enough to get a leave of absence, so I weighed my options and decided, 'I'd better keep this job.'"

He didn't miss much. The Negro League, which had prospered for nearly 40 years, was on its final full season in 1960. "What happened was that the guys were going to the major leagues, and the fans went to watch the guys in the major leagues, so attendance dropped in the Negro Leagues," he noted. "There was not enough [fan] support to support many teams."

The quality of play also suffered, as the major league teams signed many of the better black players. "The best players were going to the minors and on to the major leagues, as it should have been," he said. "If you think about it, there should never been a Negro League from the start. Everything being equal, no matter what color you are, if you were good enough to play, you should have been able to play in the major leagues."

Lloyd stayed with the U.S. Postal Service for 33 years. He retired in 1993 after transferring to Detroit and moved back to Fairfield. "I got married at sixty-two to a young lady from Fairfield," he said. "I bought a house and I'm living the good life."

He has no regrets on missing a career in the major leagues. "In my case, I believe I wasn't good enough to make the major leagues," he said. "In 1959, if I was that good, I would have been signed. So I don't hold any grudge about that.

"I played in the Negro League, and there were some injustices done toward me. And maybe I would have made the major leagues, but I wasn't signed and I don't cry about. I just accept life the way it is."

Lloyd also has a second career as a dealer in Negro League merchandise, frequently setting up shop to sell the memorabilia at ball games and military bases.[16] Still, he sees a declining interest in baseball among modern fans. "When I go to the bases, they give me a write-up in the paper, and ... several places [have] interviewed me [about] how it was growing up when I played baseball.

"But that's not enough," he added. "We'd like to tell the story. There's less than 200 of us living now, probably less than 150. Once we're gone, that's it."

JOHN MITCHELL

John Mitchell was born December 25, 1937, in Autauga, Alabama, the son of Willie James and Ola Bell Mitchell and the younger brother of Negro League star Jessie Mitchell. As Brent Kelley wrote, "There's no denying that Jessie was good, but he had an awfully good younger brother."[17]

The Mitchell family soon moved to Birmingham, where John attended Lewis Elementary and Parker High schools. "I was born in Autauga County, down below Selma, but I was raised in Birmingham," Mitchell said. "I came here when I was about five years old. Been living here ever since."[18]

John started playing the game at an early age on the streets of Birmingham. "I knew I wanted to play baseball when I was about nine or ten," he said. "We used to play stick ball in the street — hit that tennis ball from block to block."

John started playing organized ball with the Fairfield Tigers. He got his first chance at semi-pro baseball in 1956 at the age of 15 when he earned a position on the 24th Street Red Sox of Birmingham's industrial league. "Crip Chambers was our manager," Mitchell said. "We called him 'Crip' because one of his legs was shorter than the other."

His stay in the industrial league was a short one. In 1957, he joined the Detroit Stars for part of the season. His chance to join the Negro League came in April when Ed Steele, manager of the Stars, spotted Mitchell playing in an industrial league game. Mitchell was only 16 years old at the time. Steele approached Mitchell after the game and said, "I'm gonna take you with me. You ain't nothing but a baby, so I'm gonna have to ask your momma if you can go."

Steele went home with Mitchell to talk to his mother. "I'll take care of him," Steele told Mrs. Mitchell. "Don't worry about it."

She agreed, and John went on the road with the Stars for a two-month barnstorming tour before returning to Birmingham. "I'd gotten kind of homesick," he said. "I was in high school. I could only travel in the summer, when school was out. I couldn't travel when school was in, 'cause momma wouldn't let me go."

Still, he met some memorable players. "I played with Pedro Sierra, Art Hamilton, the catcher for the Detroit club, and a guy named Porter, who played first base. A tall boy, about 6-foot-6."

He found another local opportunity, joining the Birmingham Black Barons in 1958. "Most of the guys on the team were older than I was; they were four or five years older," Mitchell said. "But Jim Canada, the manager of the Birmingham Black Barons, said he wanted me to play with him, so I played in 1958 with the Birmingham Black Barons."

Mitchell had a great day in a double-header against the Memphis Red Sox in Martin Stadium. "I hit a home run in the first ball game," he said. "In the second ball game, we were tied up 5–5 going into the ninth inning. I hit a grand slam and won the nightcap."

Apparently he played well in a lot of other games, too — well enough to play in the 1959 East-West All-Star Game in Comiskey Park. The highlight of that game for him was a catch he made in the outfield. "The ball was hit over my head so I made an overhead catch like Willie Mays did," he said. "I had good hands. I didn't drop anything if I got my hands on it."

Another memorable game was a contest against the Indianapolis Clowns in Oklahoma. "We were playing against Sweetwater and Goose Tatum," he said. "Sweetwater was pitching, Goose was playing first base. Goose was a pretty good ballplayer. We had a good time playing them. It was great."

There wasn't much money. Mitchell was paid $200 a month plus two dollars a day for meals. "You could eat on two dollars," he said. "You could get a breakfast for about 30 cents. You could get a dinner for about 35, 40 cents."[19]

Mitchell quickly adapted to the discrimination he faced on the road with the Barons. "You play for the love of the game," he said. "It didn't bother me too much. We went through a lot of hard times with people calling you names and stuff like that.

Back in those days they used the 'n' word a lot, but that didn't bother me. It made me play harder."

The worst name-calling occurred when the Black Barons played a team of white players, games the black teams usually won. The Negro League teams seemed to play harder when facing a team of white players. Mitchell recalled one game in particular, played against a group of major leaguers, in Wichita, Kansas. "Willie Smith was pitching for us; he played for the Cubs," he said. "We beat that team 15–1 and all the ball players on the team were major league ball players."

His tenure with the Barons included the championship season of 1959 under manager Piper Davis. The Barons defeated the Memphis Red Sox, 6–5, to claim the title. "It was a good ball game," Mitchell said. "We had some good ball players in Memphis at that time. They had Isaac Barnes catching with Memphis; his brother [Frank Barnes] played in the St. Louis Cardinals organization. They had Rufus Gibson playing second base and Willie Harris was playing left field. They had a good ball team, but we beat them."

For the 1959 season, he put together a .295 batting average with 15 home runs. "I was hitting a home run practically every night," he once said. "I was hittin' the ball good."[20]

Mitchell again made the East-West All-Star Game in 1960, his final season with the Barons. Jim Canada returned as manager, and the Barons still had the makings of a good team. "We had some good ballplayers," Mitchell said. "We were killing everybody."

Along the way, Mitchell attracted the attention of major league scouts, but not enough attention to get a major league contract. Some scouts once came down to the field after a game, telling the team they were "the best ball players we have ever seen" and tossing around offers of $90,000 for a signing bonus. "A ninety thousand dollar bonus was a lot of money back there in the 50s," Mitchell said.

Mitchell had his share of scouts looking at him, including Joe Sewell of the Cleveland Indians. But he never made it to the show. "Joe Sewell wanted to sign me up. He followed me for about two months," Mitchell said. "The secretary said, 'He wants to sign you up.' I don't know what happened. I don't know if they wouldn't sell me or what happened."

Instead, he retired from the Negro Leagues after the 1960 season. "I had a lot of problems with my arm," he said. "I think the cold weather had a lot to do with it — playing in Des Moines, Iowa. It was cold and I hurt my arm and I had to give it up.

"I played a little sandlot ball for a while, but I was working hard in a steel plant," he added. "When I got off work, I was a little tired coming out of the steel plant but I played for a while."

But he has no regrets about playing in the Negro Leagues. "I enjoyed it, I really enjoyed it, traveling and meeting different people," he said. "I met a lot of movie stars — Sammy Davis, Lena Horne, Sam Cook. I met Wilt Chamberlain in New York City. I met a lot of musicians in New York City at the Apollo Theater."

He also had a chance to play against Satchel Paige at Rickwood Field. "He was up in age then, but he could pitch," Mitchell said. "I got two little scratch hits; they barely got through the infield. He struck out ten of us. He could bring it."

And he got to travel over much of the United States. "We went all over, to every state," he said. "We played ball in California, New York, Chicago, Cleveland, Philadelphia, Washington, West Virginia, St. Louis, Kansas City, Topeka, Kansas, Wichita, Kansas.

"When my career was over with, I had seen the world."

Chapter 6

Black Barons in the White Minor Leagues

As the decade of the 1950s entered the second half, the Black Barons were still playing, but to smaller crowds. By the late 1950s, many of the Negro League players were "playing for the scouts" as much as the fans in the stands. Many, in fact, were signed by the major league teams and assigned to the minor league organizations. Many of these players had solid minor league careers, but never made it to the show. Many of them became, as Larry Marthey argued, "buried in the minors."[1] Some didn't make it as players, but their knowledge of the game became valuable to the major leagues as scouts and coaches. They were relatively invisible, and yet they faced the same discrimination that the early major leaguers had to endure. In some ways, they had it worse since the relative anonymity in which they played would sometimes see a tolerance for more misconduct. Regardless, they played a major role in extending the fight against discrimination to smaller cities and towns across the nation.

Frank Evans

Frank Evans was born December 16, 1921, in Linden, Alabama, near Demopolis. It was a humble beginning for a man who would have a profound influence on baseball in general and the Negro Leagues in particular. He was a person, as Riley noted, who "was affiliated with ball clubs in organized baseball as an instructor, scout, and coach."[2] He played four different positions — outfielder, first base, pitcher, and catcher — but is best remembered for his managerial leadership. As Eugene Scruggs, his former roommate, said, "He was a man who could help young people choose the right way in life."

Evans started playing baseball in Linden when he was 15 years old. He then moved to Birmingham, where he faced better competition and honed his skills. During this time, he had the chance to play in his most memorable game — an exhibition contest between Negro League players and an all-star team of major leaguers that included such renowned players as Lou Boudreau, Preacher Roe, and a couple of other future Hall of Fame players.

"I watched Satchel walk the bases loaded for nine innings and no one got a hit off of him," Evans recalled. "Ted Williams fouled two off of him, and Joe DiMaggio fouled one and from then on, it was history. No one could touch it. This was 1941 in Wrigley Field."

Dizzy Dean was pitching for the All-Stars and also pitched well. "The score was one to nothing," Evans added. "Satchel beat him one-nothing."

Evans had his own great days as a player. He recalled one game in which he drove in all three runs in a 3–2 win. "I hit a triple and tied it up," he said. "The next inning, they walked the bases loaded and they made a mistake pitching to me. I doubled, and we beat them three-to-two."

Ironically, his first major break in professional sports came from another game — basketball. Evans was signed to a professional contract with the Harlem Globetrotters by owner Abe Saperstein. He stayed with the barnstorming basketball team for five years before returning to baseball. "Baseball was history for me from then on," he said.

He first broke into professional baseball in 1947 with the Raleigh Tigers, and moved to the Philadelphia Stars in 1948. In 1949, he joined the Cleveland Buckeyes as an outfielder and stayed with the team through the beginning of the 1950 season. He left midseason to play with the Winnipeg Buffalos in the Mandak League while also playing a little football.[3]

He stayed in Canada until mid-year of 1951, when he returned to the Cleveland Buckeyes for the remainder of the season. That was followed by three years in New Orleans, leading to early 1954, when he signed with the Cleveland Indians. He worked in the Texas League before making the major leagues as a coach and instructor. "I had an awesome experience with them, and they let me do a lot of things," Evans said. "I used to work with the pitchers, work with the hitters." His baseball resume also included stops in New Mexico, Alaska, Kansas, and one venture into Japan.

His association with the Birmingham Black Barons came in the twilight years of the team. He was the manager for the final seasons, in 1961 and 1962. "I started managing early," he said. "I started managing in 1948, and I managed two years. They picked me up again in 1959. I managed 1959 through 1962."

"As a manager, I tried to treat everybody right and teach my guys the basics," he added. "How to run the bases, how to bunt, how to play signals, how to shift to outfield. All the guys worked together. We didn't have a thing where we had one individual and he had his own. Everybody worked together and I never had any problems."

Evans also kept an eye out for other talent. Jake Sanders credits Evans with helping him find a place to play in the Negro Leagues. After trying out for the Barons, he was cut from the squad before the team broke from spring training. Sanders was sitting outside the stadium, crying after being cut, when Evans approached. "Now don't cry," Evans said. "I've just had a phone call from New Orleans. They're in the Negro League, and they want you to come play for them." Years later, looking back on his career, Sanders said of Evans, "Thank God for him."

Evans was a manager in the last two East-West All-Star Games, in 1961 and 1962. The '62 All-Star game epitomized the problems the Negro League was facing at the time. After five innings, the game had to be called because of heavy rain. Money from the ticket sales was refunded to the fans in attendance, but that action left the league in a serious financial situation. Evans had to go to downtown Chicago and borrow $10,000 to keep his team on the road. He also had to book some extra exhibition games to repay the funds.

Evans faced the same type of discrimination that was so common in the South during the 1950s and 1960s. The team bus developed mechanical problems in the Carolinas; the police would not allow the team to go to town while waiting on repairs. "We had to stay out there on the bus," Evans said. "A man came through with a truckload of watermelons, and we ate watermelons for a whole week until they got the bus fixed. Then we took off just like another day."

Evans' mother died while the team was headed to New Orleans. Evans learned of her death when the bus stopped in Phenix City. "I said, 'While we're here, I'll go and call home,'" he recalled. His brother answered. In the background, he could hear his uncle's voice and his father praying. His father came to the phone and told him they were getting ready for his mother's funeral. Instead of going to New Orleans, the team drove to Birmingham to the funeral. "All of them were with me on the bus," Evans said.

Evans made his mark in the Negro Leagues as a manager and hitting instructor. "All the guys that like to hit, they probably hit all day," he said. "That's all I work with them on. Teach them how to throw the bat shift, teach them how to follow the ball and drive the ball.

"Hitting is just like boxing; you're throwing a punch and you follow through," he added. "If you're on an outside pitch, you shift your body; inside, you're open up and you're swinging. It's easy when you know how, but trying to learn is hard if you don't catch on quickly. Baseball is just like mathematics; keep your mind on what you're doing, and you'll be all right."

His skills as a manger often showed up during the games. "If the score was tied, I used to get up, pick up a bat, and swing with the next hitter," he said. "Then the guys would bear down, be patient and get that hit."

Another technique was to pace the dugout as if he was in pain. The technique, he said, was his way of saying, "I want to win this one so bad." It usually worked. "They would always come through," he added. "We had very few times that we would lose a ball game. I had a good bunch of fellows here in Birmingham."

Evans would go to the mound for a conversation with his pitcher when the young man seemed to be in trouble. "I'd go out there to the pitcher, and I'd say, 'How do you feel?' 'Fine, fine,' they'd usually say." Evans would put his hand on the pitcher's chest and say, "Your heart is beating. Are you afraid?"

"Naw coach, I'm alright," the pitcher would say.

"Listen," Evans would say. "We need that one man. I want you to throw strikes. You're not following through. You're standing straight up. Bend your back. I don't want you to strike them out but let him hit the ball.

"If you hit the ball on the ground, we'll have a 100 percent chance of getting the ball. But if the ball gets loose in the air, it's no telling how far it goes," Evans explained.

Other times he would tell the pitcher, "You know you're making me look bad.

I've been bragging on you all this time and you can't throw any strikes. Do you want me to get somebody else?" After the pitcher protested, Evans said, "Then he'll go and give me all he has.

"You just have to work with them," he said. "I've never cursed a pitcher. I've never cursed a ball player. I always tell him things that I would do and add, 'I don't believe you can do it, but I can.'

"'Aw coach, now don't tell me that, I can do it,' the pitcher would reply. And they'd go out and do it."

Evans managed an all-white team in Wichita, Kansas. "We won the championship three years in a row," he said. "I never did burst that ball club up. Bobby Douglass, who played quarterback for the Bears, was one of my pitchers. Don Calhoun played with the New England Patriots; he was one of my catchers. So I have had a variety of athletes that I was able to help in football and baseball."

After the Black Barons shut down, Evans became an instructor and scout for some major league teams. These included the Cleveland Indians (1963), Chicago Cubs (1964–65), Montreal Expos (1967) and Kansas City Royals (1968–72).

He eventually retired from baseball full-time and moved back to Alabama. In his retirement years, he continued teaching the value of athletics to young people. One of his partners in the effort was University of Alabama football coach Paul "Bear" Bryant.

"Bear Bryant and I worked for fifteen years around through the South — places like Linden, Marengo County, Demopolis [in Alabama and] all the way into Meridian, Mississippi," he said. "We were motivating the kids, showing them that we love them and just giving them pointers that could try to change their lifestyle.

"We tried to build that kid up," he said. Once the youngster had a goal, they encouraged them to take a small step. "Aw, you can do it. Just put a little on it," Evans would tell a pitcher.

"You'll be surprised. That will motivate a lot of people," he said.

After a semi-retirement from baseball, he returned to the field by working with a semi-pro team — the Montgomery Wings — for three years. He always felt good when one of his players signed with a professional team. "As long as you're teaching the basics and the guys really want to play, you can help them," he said. "But if their mind is on nothing better, at doesn't help them it all. They have to love it. They have to be hungry for it."

He speaks from experience. Frank Evans was always hungry for it.

Donald "Donnie" Harris

Donnie Harris was born July 1, 1936, in Jefferson County, Alabama. He would become a key player for the Birmingham Black Barons, and was a charter member of the Alabama Negro League Association.[4] Harris also served as the first president of the organization.

Harris attended Washington Elementary School and started playing Little League at the age of nine. Four years later, he was in the industrial leagues as an outfielder for the 24th Street Red Sox. He continued playing for the team until he graduated from

Pullman High School. His rapid movement up the baseball ladder at such a young age drew comparisons that led to Harris being called "another Willie Mays."[5]

Harris saw the Black Barons play in 1945 and was impressed with the play of stars Alonzo Perry and Piper Davis. "I promised myself that day that I would someday play in that league," he recalled.[6]

Beginning in the fall of 1953, Harris enrolled in Alabama A&M. There he lettered in baseball, basketball, and track. By his senior year — 1956 — he was named the baseball team's MVP, named to the all-conference team, and was the school's Athlete of the Year as well as a star in Birmingham's industrial league. Those achievements marked him as a prospect for the Negro Leagues, particularly when an injury to Jessie Mitchell opened up an outfield slot.

"I was an all-star in the industrial league," he once recalled. "The Black Barons didn't have an opening for a center fielder. Jessie Mitchell hurt his arm, and the Barons knocked on my door. After years of watching a lot of their games, I had reached my goal."[7]

Harris got the job and spent one season in the Negro League, playing for the Birmingham Black Barons in 1957. "My first time on the [Rickwood] field was my mother's first time to watch a game," he added. "I made a catch and could pick out her voice from the crowd screaming from the stands."[8]

Life on the road wasn't always easy. "Mississippi Delta towns had the biggest mosquitoes I'd ever seen," he said. "They had to fog the field before we could play."[9]

Crowds were particularly enthusiastic in the Midwest. "In the Midwest, the bus would pull into a town with a sign reading 'Population, 5000,' and a crowd of what seemed like 5,000 would show up at the ball field," he said.[10]

Later in the year, he was named to the East-West All-Star Game, slamming a triple in the contest. That was good enough to earn him a contract with the Pittsburgh Pirates in 1958, playing for the minor league team in Jacksonville, Florida. In 1959, the outfielder was signed by the Kansas City A's and assigned to the Grand Island A's in Nebraska. After the season was over, Harris had a brief stint as a basketball player for the Harlem Satellites.

The military called in 1960, and that effectively ended his chance for a major league career. He served four years in the army as a medic, much of it stationed in Germany. He was in Germany when the Berlin Wall was constructed. "I saw people shot, people literally running toward freedom, as they tried to jump the wall from east to west," he recalled. "Some of the wounded we were able to pull across the line. Many others died as we watched."[11]

Harris continued playing baseball on military teams, winning the MVP Award for the 1962–63 season and earning "All-Europe" honors the following year.

Harris completed his military duty in 1965. By then, the Negro Leagues were gone. He settled for five more years of playing in the industrial league and then retired from the game. Still, he had made his mark.

"The Barons had a promotional placard proclaiming me 'the next Willie Mays,'" Harris recalled. "I preferred to think of myself as the first Donnie Harris, and I don't think I disappointed the fans."[12]

EARNEST HARRIS

Earnest Harris was born in Birmingham, Alabama, on December 2, 1936. His shot at a professional baseball career came and went quickly.

Harris started playing baseball as a kid in the streets in Ensley. "There wasn't too much to do but to get in the streets, get broomsticks, make you a little ball and rip and run and play baseball," he said. "That's how I actually started playing."[13]

His high school didn't have a baseball team, but he played football and basketball and ran track. While still in school, he started playing baseball in the industrial league for the TCI Plant in Ensley. "I played as a pitcher on the company team," he said. "I played when I was in high school from 1955 for about three years straight."

The industrial league teams had a large fan following. "In the Wyatt and Plant leagues we used to have in Ensley, there used to be buses that pass by and stop and stay there 15 or 20 minutes watching the ball game. If you didn't get in there at a certain time according to which team was playing, you didn't get in there.... They would be standing up all on the side of the road."

In 1957, he signed a contract with the Detroit Tigers as a pitcher. "One of the Detroit pitchers came and signed me up for a tryout," he said. "I went down and came back. I pitched fast curves. I threw it hard, trying to get the ball over the plate and throw strikes. I had to put a little curve to it.

"I don't know what they called it at that particular time, but when it got to the plate, it dipped a little bit," he added. "I was pretty good at that and plus, you didn't steal too many bases on me because I was a left-hander. I had a good move to first base."

He joined the Tigers for spring training in Florida in 1958, but didn't make the team. "The Detroit Tigers tryouts were around February in Florida," he said. "We had pretty good weather there at that particular time. It didn't last long for me in Detroit because when I got released, I was there around a month or so."

He returned to Birmingham to play with the Black Barons as an outfielder. "Our manager, Mr. 'Slick' Threatt, lived in Ensley and got me to go to the outfield and started playing center field.

"Our regular center fielder was a good ball player but didn't bat as good as me," he added, "so to keep him in the lineup, I chose to go to left field because he had good speed. He was a good outfielder. So, I went back to center field."

Switching positions was a good baseball move. "I switched to outfield because when I pitched, I had good speed and knew how to steal bases," he said. "I also batted left-handed and could get to the bases pretty good. I could lay the ball down or bunt the ball pretty good and was a good average hitter. I could get on base a lot.

"At the time I was pitching, I used to lead off in the batting order," he added. "If I didn't lead off, I was second or third because I was hitting the ball pretty good. I was one of the leading home run hitters on the team as a pitcher."

His stay in the industrial league was a short one. "My manager for the Barons ... was Lorenzo 'Piper' Davis. He came and scouted me and I started playing with the Birmingham Black Barons in 1959."

Harris remembered one game, soon after joining the Barons, when he was approached by an infielder for the Memphis Red Sox — a man named Gibson who had played against him in the industrial league. He told Earnest that Memphis would win the game because Ben Adams was pitching for the Red Sox. "The first time I faced Ben Adams, I hit him out the ballpark right there in Paris, Texas," Harris said. "Gibson just looked at me and shook his head."

In another game against Memphis at Rickwood, the Black Barons faced Memphis left-hander Ace Robinson. The crowded stands included a group of scouts who were watching Robinson. His first time at the plate, Harris kept trying to pull the ball while Robinson threw mostly curveballs. Harris struck out and went back to the bench, vowing to get a hit the next time.

He didn't. Instead, he struck out again. He returned to the bench shaking his head, vowing again, "I'm gonna git him."

He got one more chance late in the game with two men on base. When Robinson went into his stretch to check the runners, Harris stepped up in the batter's box. "That same pitch he was breaking off for me, I hit it right down the line for a double, and everybody in the stands started hollering and jumping up," he said.

Another highlight of the season was a road trip that included a stop at Brooklyn's Ebbets Field. The return trip included stops at St. Louis, Joplin, Missouri, and Memphis. Memphis was one of his favorite cities. "I enjoyed playing there because of the places to eat that had good soul food," he said. "Plus, they had an outdoor shower behind the grandstand."

Travel was still the hardest part of the job. "The bad part about it was some of the hotels we stayed in. The problem was not mice, but rats!"

Harris' roommate on the road was John Mitchell. Mitchell was older and had more experience in the Negro League. "He had been there a few years before I got there," Harris said. "He kept me up on what was going on."

Mitchell used a code word — "Red" — to designate the nights the two players would not go out on the town. When Earnest heard the term, he would "drop my head a little. That meant that I'm going to have to stay and fight the rats. You can't get the kind of sleep you want because you hear things crawling around.

"But when he says green, I know he is ready to go," Harris said. "When we hit the streets, we go down on Beale Street. We go down to get mullions.

"A lot of people don't know what mullions are," he said. "Mullions are women! I don't know how to spell mullions. If you give me a thousand dollars, I wouldn't know how to spell it. We would chase them all night long until two in the morning. It didn't bother me. I would rather be down there chasing them than to be in that room chasing rats."

Returning to play in Birmingham was always more relaxing. "I like that because I'm coming to see my people," Harris said. "I'm playing in front of the home crowd and another thing, I get that good soul food. I started not to go back on the road, but I love the game so much."

Other than in cities such as Memphis, eating on the road could be a problem. "Sometimes we didn't have anything for breakfast but bologna and crackers," he said. "For dinner we had souse meat, cheese, and crackers."

The game schedule was rugged. Double-headers were common, sometimes as frequent as three times a week. "On the bus, off the bus, on to the next town," he said. "You miss that good food. You pass by these places and smell that food, [but] you can't get it unless you go to the back door and they didn't want to serve you then.

"It wasn't the first time it's happened," he added. "If it happens right here, it will happen there. You had to put the bitter with the sweet. If I had to do it all over again, I would do it again.

"We had a pretty good season at Rickwood," he added. That they did; after all, the 1959 season was the year that the Black Barons won the Negro League championship.[14]

Harris was also the only rookie to make the East-West All-Star Game, played in Chicago's Comiskey Park before a crowd of 8,923. The West won, 8–7, in 11 innings. He had three hits in the game — two infield singles and a two-run inside-the-park home run — and made a sterling catch in the outfield. He also scored the winning run from third, driven in by a single to left field by Bill White. His speed put him on third; he reached first with an infield hit, then stole second base, and advanced to third on a passed ball.

For Earnest, the inside-the-park home run was the most memorable play. "I was fast," he said. "It was 415 feet up against that center field bullpen. I circled the bases on them."

His performance was good enough that he got another chance at the major leagues. "I can remember the place was real packed that particular day, and I didn't know who was in the stands," he said. "I couldn't pay it that much attention."

After the game, Piper Davis approached the team and said there were scouts in the stands and they were interested in one player. "I'm going to make a long story short," Davis said. "They're interested in Harris."

Harris received congratulations from the rest of the team. That afternoon, scouts from the Philadelphia Phillies visited Harris' house and signed him to a contract.

Again he traveled to Florida, this time to Leesburg. Leesburg was the

Earnest Harris was the only rookie to make the 1959 East-West All-Star Game in Chicago's Comiskey Park. He had three hits in the game: two singles and an inside-the-park home run.

organizational center for three of the Phillies' minor league teams — their rookie league team and those for the Class C and Class E minor leagues. Earnest moved up through the organization, rising to the Class C team before he was promoted again to Bakersfield, California. "When I was in the minor leagues, I didn't make it as a pitcher, but I made it for a few months as an outfielder," he said.

His teammates at Bakersfield included Pat Corrales, a catcher who is now a coach for the Washington Nationals. He also remembers two other players on an opposing team—first baseman Al Ferrara and pitcher Nick Wilhite. Both men played for Reno in the Dodgers' organization.[15]

Harris was particularly friendly with Ferrara. "I liked his style," Harris said. Ferrara often hit to center field, where Harris would inevitably catch the ball for an out.

"Hey Ernie, let one drop for me," he said. "I'll let one drop for you."

"OK, Al," Harris replied jokingly, not intending to keep his promise. Ferrara came up later in the game with two outs and the bases loaded. Again he hit one to the outfield. Again, Harris caught it.

Ferrara passed Harris between innings, and said, "Damn, Ernie. I thought you was going to let it drop."

"Man, you got to be out of your mind if you think I'm gonna let something like that drop," Harris replied. Ferrara shook his head and went out to first base.

Harris found that his speed was an asset in the minor leagues; he stole four bases in one game. "I stole home standing up on my own," he said. "I could have stolen more than that but [manager] Luke Horn wouldn't let me. 'Jim Crowe, manager,' that's what we called him.

"I was just running on my own," he added. "We didn't have anything such as a hit and run. Ninety percent of the time when I'm on base, I get the base stolen."

Once on base, he would use his speed to try and score. He usually started by stealing second base. That would set up a situation where the batter could bunt him to third. "But I didn't need to be bunted," he said. "When they hit the ball, I may lag around like a man's got a play on me at third base in order for him to get safe at first base. Now, you got two players on base with no outs."

From there he would try to score, sometimes surprising the defense by racing around third on a ground ball. "I scored from second base on a lot of infield outs," he said. "I have stolen second base and third base and then come home on fly balls or an infield out."

Sometimes he took chances. "I'm on first base and the ball is hit to the shortstop. I may challenge him, round second, and keep on to third," Harris said. "The ball has got to go to first base, and [the first baseman] has got to make a good throw back to third base to get me."

Sometimes, when going from first to third on a single, he would deliberately run slow to draw a throw from the outfield. "I may slow down to make the outfielder make a play on me so the batter can get a chance to get to second base," he said. "We won some pretty good games on plays like that."

When Harris was in center field, he was the captain of the outfield. "I'd tell them, if I call it, let me go. I can take it." If a runner was on third, Harris wanted the ball because his arm was stronger than the other outfielders. He would circle behind the fly ball and catch it moving forward. "I didn't just catch it and draw back and throw," he said. "I'd catch it coming toward the infield and make a good throw.

"You had to be smart," he added. "Who will outsmart one another? That goes a long way to winning the game."

He played with Bakersfield for two months before getting released. That was the beginning of the bad news. When he returned home, he discovered that his mother had died. "I didn't realize it until I got home and stepped on the front porch," he said. "I saw my sister and three other people sitting on the porch. It didn't dawn on me." He went inside the house, saw his uncle, and asked where his mother was.

"Son, you don't know?" his uncle asked. Earnest knew she had been sick when he left Birmingham, but he didn't realize the extent of her health problems. He didn't realize that she had died in May.

Earnest stayed in Birmingham for a while, playing baseball during the 1961 season. It would be his last year as a player. He moved to Detroit in 1962 to spend some time with his brother and sister before returning to Birmingham later in the year.

That's when a friend and his wife asked for help on a drive to California. Earnest took the challenge, and the trio arrived in Los Angeles on December 2, 1962, Earnest's 26th birthday, and he was back in the state where he had ended his minor league baseball career.

Back in California, Earnest started looking for employment. His first job was at Vick's Car Wash. It didn't pay much, but he started putting a little money aside. He soon moved from there to a pipe company. After that, he started looking for better pay, preferably with the U.S. Postal Service.

While in high school in Alabama, he had taken an exam required for all postal employees. He had passed the test easily, but was unable to get a postal job in Alabama. "At that time, very few blacks worked at the post office," he recalled. "I had my test transferred to Los Angeles. They kept it on file for a few months and then wrote me and told me the test had changed.

"I took the test again as a mail handler and passed it," he added. "The job I was working on paid about $4 an hour. That was pretty good money then. And it was regular." He got the job. "I started out making $2.37 an hour. I was a single man at the time and was taking a chance by working for the postal service. I passed my probation period and became a regular employee."

Good money, but there was one problem. "When I went to Los Angeles, I didn't go there to make it my home," he said. "I went there to make some money and try to come back and live with it."

He returned to Birmingham on February 15, 1988, working until he retired in 2002. His life in retirement is one of dominoes, television, and church. "What I do mostly now is play dominoes — I am a domino addict," he said. "I go down to McAlpine Park Recreation Center and play Monday through Friday. I meet other people who have retired and some still work. We play dominoes and chat with one another and check by home later and go to another place and play dominoes."

The routine is interrupted only on Sunday, when he attends True Love Missionary Baptist Church in Ensley. And on one Monday in each month, he attends the meetings of the Alabama Negro League Association. Baseball, after all, is still part of his life, even if he doesn't play it anymore.

"Baseball is my thing," he said. "I played it, coached it. I watched it, plus I officiated it. They want me to come back and officiate again. I said, 'No.' I have done it all now. I'm just going to sit back in the stands and watch while I drink me a cold beer!"

WILLIE J. LEE

Willie Lee was an outfielder who broke into the Negro Leagues with the Birmingham Black Barons. He went on to play with the Kansas City Monarchs before moving into the minor leagues. As Brent Kelley noted, Lee was a talented "slugging outfielder who might have made it to the major leagues, if a hose had been put away."[16] Stepping on that hose injured a ligament and ended his baseball career.

Willie Lee was born March 19, 1935, in Docena, Alabama, and grew up in Ensley. He attended Council Elementary School and Western-Olin, where Negro League scouts first noticed him. He started practicing his batting skills with a broomstick and developed into an all-around athlete. "I was really a sports-minded person," he said. "I'd get a broomstick and whip a tennis ball ... like Willie Mays used to do in New York."[17]

His favorite sport was boxing. He had a natural aptitude for the sport, and trained to become a boxer. But there were more opportunities in baseball.

Lee broke into the Negro Leagues in 1956 after trying out with the Birmingham Black Barons. He went to the tryout after seeing an ad in the newspaper announcing the team was looking for players. His first road trip was to Mobile, playing against a team headed by Tommie Aaron, Hank Aaron's brother. His manager for the trip was Satchel Paige.

His tenure with the Barons was brief—that one game. When the team returned to Birmingham, Lee spotted another ad in the paper. The Kansas City Monarchs were in town, and they were looking for players too. He went to his second tryout, made the Monarchs and stuck with them for the rest of the season.

Lee returned to the Monarchs in 1957, hitting .311 with 26 home runs. He also occasionally filled in as a pitcher; in a game played in Mound Bayou, Mississippi, Lee tossed a one-hitter against the Memphis Red Sox. "I think Rufus Gibson got the hit," Lee recalled. "The only reason he got that hit, the catcher called for a changeup curve."[18]

The highlight of the 1957 season for Lee was playing in the East-West All-Star Games. The 1957 contest was a doubleheader in Newark, New Jersey. The West lost the first game of the twin-bill, but Lee hit a grand slam home run in the second game to win it.

He stayed with the Monarchs in 1958, but that was his last season in the Negro Leagues. He moved to Grand Rapids, Michigan, and briefly joined the Grand Rapids Black Sox — another team owned by Monarchs owner Ted Rasberry.

While in Grand Rapids, Lee also played with a semi-pro team headed by Bob Sullivan, a major league scout. Sullivan signed Lee to a minor league contract with the Detroit Tigers organization, and the outfielder reported to the Tigers for spring training.

Willie Lee was known as a power hitter when playing in the minor leagues, thus his "big bat" award. While playing with Class-D Decatur in the Midwest League in 1959, the team's business manager pledged to pay one hundred dollars to the first player to hit a home run. The next day, Willie Lee won the prize. Indeed, Lee hit an opening day home run in each of his seasons in the minor leagues.

Hitting major league pitching was no problem, although Lee had some trouble adjusting to "Iron Mike." "I had never batted against Iron Mike — a pitching machine," he said. "Everything was new to me. I was used to live pitching."[19]

Despite that problem, Lee impressed the Tigers enough to make the team — at least that was the plan, until he stepped on a water hose and stretched a ligament in his left knee. The incident occurred in a game against a Cincinnati farm team. Lee chased a foul ball down the right field line and stepped on a water hose left there by the grounds crew manager.

Limping around after that, Lee was sent to Class D Decatur in the Midwest League in 1959. The team had a joint dinner the night before the season opened. At the meeting, Decatur's business manager pledged to pay one hundred dollars to the first player on the team to hit a home run.

The next day, Willie Lee won the prize. That wasn't particularly unusual. Indeed, Lee hit an Opening Day home run in each of his seasons in the minor leagues. He hit several more in 1959, finishing his rookie season in the minor leagues with a .241 average, 12 home runs and 64 RBIs.

That got him invited back to spring training in 1960. When the team broke from camp, he was assigned to Duluth in the Northern League. He hit two home runs and had 13 RBIs while batting .309 before an injury disrupted his season again. He jammed a shoulder while sliding into second base on a pickoff play, and he was sent back to Decatur to recover. "They said they thought I would do better in a warmer area," he recalled.

At Decatur, he hit .266 with three home runs and 16 RBIs. "I didn't do too well," Lee told Kelley. "They had to operate on my shoulder."[20]

He was invited back to spring training for the '61 season, but his injuries hampered his chances. "My arm didn't come around," he said. "I couldn't even bat right. That's when I got released by Detroit."[21]

Lee returned to Grand Rapids, playing for Sullivan's semi-pro team for a while. When his arm got stronger, Sullivan arranged a contract for Lee with the Minnesota Twins. The Twins sent him to Bismarck, North Dakota, in midseason. He was again playing in the

Willie Lee broke into the Negro Leagues in 1956 with the Black Barons. His first road trip was to Mobile, playing against a team headed by Tommie Aaron — Hank Aaron's brother.

Willie Lee was a power-hitting outfielder who seemed slated to play for the Detroit Tigers until a spring training injury tore ligaments in his knee. This photo shows him catching a deep fly ball in centerfield while with the Kansas City Monarchs.

Northern League and finished the season with a .270 average, 14 home runs and 74 RBIs.

Lee noted that he ran into racial prejudice while playing with the Twins organization in Bismarck. Most of it was directed toward teammate George Scott, who later made the major leagues with Boston. And the guys behind the prejudice were other teammates.

"I'm sitting on the bench next to 'em, and when he'd make a good play they'd call him bad names," Lee recalled. "They'd look over at me and say, 'I'm sorry, Willie.' But I was used to it, being born in the South."[22]

Lee started the 1962 season at Wilson, in the Carolina League. He managed only one home run, 14 RBIs, and a .174 average before being sent to Erie in the New York–Penn League. His average there was only .253, but he had his best season as a slugger—24 home runs and 87 RBIs. It marked the third time in his four minor league years that Lee hit double figures in home runs.

He was released by the Twins in 1963. Again he returned to Grand Rapids and played with local teams. He still had an occasional chance to play against top competition, traveling with the Al Kaline All-Stars and playing in the National Baseball Congress tournament in Wichita.

He eventually retired from baseball and got a job working for American Seating, a factory in Grand Rapids that specialized in making automotive and stadium seats. After retiring from that, he moved back to Birmingham in 1985.

In retirement, he still supports the game of baseball. "I try to tell the kids to get into sports, to get into baseball," Lee told Kelley. "I know it's only a game, but it teaches you different things."[23]

CARL LONG

Carl Long broke into the Negro Leagues with the Birmingham Black Barons at the end of the 1951 season. The outfielder played two seasons with the Barons before moving to the minor leagues. Kelley described Long as "a five-tool guy" who could "hit, hit for power, run, throw, and field."[24]

Once, while playing right field, he threw out Larry Doby when the Hall-of-Famer tried to go from first to third on a single. "He just put his hands on his hips and shook his head," Long recalled.[25]

Born May 9, 1935, in Rock Hill, South Carolina, Long joined the Black Barons as a 16-year-old in 1952 and stayed through the 1953 season. "I had a good year; I don't know what I hit—they didn't keep the records—but I know I did real good," he told Kelley.[26] After the last game of the season, a teammate told him there was a scout in the stands "who wants you to join the Pittsburgh Pirates."[27]

Long was signed by the Pirates organization after the 1953 season and worked his way through the team's minor league system. He spent the 1954 season with St. Johns, hitting 20 home runs. He moved to Billings in the Pioneer League in 1955—with a brief, mid-season visit to Waco in the Big State League. He returned to Billings and finished the season there with 18 home runs.

Long was with Kinston in the Carolina League in 1956, becoming the first African

American to play for Kinston. He made the all-star team, was leading the league in hitting for part of the season (but was eventually beat out by Curt Flood), and set a league record with 111 RBIs. In one of his most memorable games, he hit two home runs and had six RBIs in an 18–3 win over Greensboro.

His most memorable game, though, was an exhibition game he played as part of the Roy Campanella All-Star team. His teammates included Campanella and Jackie Robinson. What made the game memorable, though, is that it was the only game in which his father saw him play. "I asked him if he was coming to see Jackie Robinson," Long recalled. "He said, 'No, I'm coming to see you.'"[28]

Long started 1957 with Mexico City in the Mexican League, where he batted .407. Branch Rickey spotted him there and said, "You can't stay here." Long moved to Beaumont in the Texas League later that year in what would be his final season in professional baseball.

He got one more shot at the majors, going to spring training with the Pirates again in 1958. A shoulder injury ended his career at the age of 22. "I tore a muscle in my shoulder and that was the end of my career," Long said. Pirates general manager Branch Rickey suggested surgery, but Long refused. "I wanted to play baseball, and I got a chance to play baseball," Long said later. "I'm satisfied."[29]

Instead, he retired to his native state of North Carolina. In his post-baseball career, Long became the first black deputy sheriff in the state.[30] In 2003, he was inducted into the Carolina League Hall of Fame.

Long now lives in Kinston, North Carolina, spending his spare time speaking to youth groups. His son is a minister who oversees 40 churches in the area. Long visits each of those churches with two messages: play sports and get an education.

JESSIE MITCHELL

Jessie Mitchell was born in Autauga County, Alabama, on April 25, 1936, the son of Willie James and Ola Bell Williams. He grew up in a family of four — two sisters and two brothers — that moved to Birmingham when he was five years old. By the time he was nine or ten, Mitchell was playing basketball and running track for his public school, first at Lewis Elementary School in Birmingham and then Parker High School but graduating from Ramsey High. His brother John would also develop as a local athlete who played in the Negro Leagues.

When some Little League teams were put together, Jessie became a baseball player. "We had a pretty good team," he said. "We used to play at Memorial Park, Ensley, different teams around here."[31]

By the age of 14, he had attracted the attention of the Birmingham Black Eagles, a semi-pro team in the area. "The manager asked my mother if I could go play with them," he recalled. His mother agreed, and Jessie joined the team for a summer as a teenage traveling pro. His early career included games against such teams as the New York Cubans, the Zulu Clowns, and the Pittsburgh Stars.

Jessie recalled a number of games against the Stars during an extended road trip in Texas. "The Pittsburgh Stars dropped out of the Negro League in about 1950, so we got a chance to play them out there in Texas," he said. "We played about a month out there, in Dallas, San Angelo, Houston, Corpus Christi—us and the Stars moving from town to town."

When the summer was over, Jessie returned to school. "I was still in high school," he said. "That was about 1948 or '49."

He soon returned to baseball, playing with a local industrial team. From there, he was recruited to play for a competing team—ACIPCO (the Alabama Cast Iron Pipe Company), the most powerful industrial team in the Birmingham area.

Bob Bolin was the team's manager, and he sought out Mitchell during the 1951 season. "Jessie, don't you want to come play with us?" he asked.

When Mitchell responded positively, Bolin said, "I tell you what we're going to do. We're going to give you a game, your league team against our team."

Mitchell agreed. His team started off well behind the hurling of pitcher Joe Elliot. "We actually had them beat in the eighth inning. But we had a guy who called himself a manager. He wanted to get in there and pitched himself.

"Joe had them shutout, 6–0," Mitchell added, "but the manager started pitching and they started hitting him. They beat us, 7–6."

Mitchell may have lost the game but he found a job. The next year, 1952, he and several of his teammates joined ACIPCO. "The principal was good friends with the manager of ACIPCO," he said. "He used to let me take all my subjects in the morning, then let me out at two o'clock to go play ball."[32]

Although it lacked the renown of the Negro Leagues, Acipco was a local baseball powerhouse. "ACIPCO was one of the best teams I played with," Mitchell said.

Jessie soon discovered he was playing the wrong position. "I was trying to play shortstop," Mitchell said. "I could always catch the ball, but I'd always over-throw first base."

The solution came in the addition of another player named Cooper, who took over the shortstop position. "Mitch, we've got another shortstop here now," Bolin told Mitchell. But, he added, "I can't sit you down, because you're a good hitter. I'm going to put you in the outfield.

"Have you ever played outfield before?" he asked.

"Yeah, I can play it," Mitchell said.

Jessie moved to right field for a game against Hightower. "Somebody hit a ball to right field, and I threw the ball to home," Mitchell said. "The first baseman threw up his hands to cut it off and the ball nearly hit him in the face."

Bolin was impressed. "Wait a minute," the manager said. "Your arm's too good. I'm gonna put you in center field."

It was Jessie's first chance to play the position that would become his home on the baseball diamond. "If I had done that when I was much younger, I probably would have made the majors," he said. "I was good enough to be one of the best outfielders around there."

The following year, 1953, the Birmingham Black Barons asked the young outfielder to join their touring professional team. Mitchell turned them down, choosing instead to stay with ACIPCO during a championship season. "I think we lost one game that whole season," Mitchell said. "We beat everybody in the city league."

As a reward for their performance, the company treated the entire team with travel and tickets to a World Series game in New York to see the Yankees face the Brooklyn Dodgers. "It was the first time I had really been to a big city like New York," he said.

The following season, Mitchell joined the Negro Leagues — not with the Black Barons, but with the Louisville Clippers. "Several of us who played with ACIPCO, myself, Buddy Ivory, Robert Baldwin, we started playing with the Clippers," he said.

Instead of playing for the Black Barons, he was playing against them. The early tours of the team included visits to Birmingham and to Texas.

His tenure with the Clippers was short-lived. The beginning of the end was a game of pool in Nashville, Tennessee, following a game on the diamond in which Mitchell had pounded out several hits against Barons left-hander Kelly Searcy.

"We went to Nashville, and the Birmingham Black Barons owner (S. Bridgeport) lived in Nashville and had a pool hall up there," Mitchell said. Mitchell and some other players were shooting pool when Bridgeport came out of his office, walked up to the center fielder, and tapped him on the back.

"What's your name?" Bridgeport asked.

"Mitchell."

"Mitchell, I've heard a lot of talk about you," Bridgeport said. "How would you like to play with Birmingham?"

"Why, I live in Birmingham," Mitchell replied.

"You want to play with us? I'm going to buy you."

Bridgeport knew the Clippers' touring bus had recently broken down during a trip to Mississippi. Noting that, he said, "I'm going to buy you to help Louisville get themselves a bus."

"That'll be fine with me," the 19-year-old Mitchell said.

"You need any money?"

"I can always use some money."

"Take this four hundred dollars," Bridgeport said, handing the youngster four one hundred dollar bills, "and I'm going to buy you."

The Clippers accepted the swap and added another player to the deal, future country-western singer Charley Pride. "They sold me and Charley that night," Jessie recalled. "Charley stayed about a month and they sent him to Memphis to play with the Memphis Red Sox, but I stayed with Birmingham."

Mitchell had to compete with another center fielder, Sidney Bunch, for the starting job. "(Willie) 'Chico' Wells was the manager. When I first got to Birmingham, (Wells) told me to sit with him on the bus."

Sidney Bunch was sitting nearby. "Ain't no need for him to come over here," Bunch said loudly. "He ain't gonna play no center field here."

Wells turned to Mitchell and called him by his nickname — "Little Chief" — and said, "Little Chief, don't you worry. You just do your job. We'll see who's going to play." The next month, Mitchell had taken over the starting position. Bunch was sent back to Nashville.

Mitchell faced the typical discrimination faced by black athletes in the South. "Traveling was rough at times," he said. "We couldn't stop and eat like we needed to.

But it was all right. I think it just made me a better man. Red Harris was light skinned, they thought Red was white, so he'd go into a place and order food for all of us, and bring it back to the bus.. We'd sit on the bus and eat it."

Another memorable teammate was one-armed pitcher Willie Young. "Willie was a really good pitcher," Jessie said. "He only had one arm, but he had good speed. And he could run. He could really run."

The Black Barons had a good team in 1954, but Mitchell's personal best came in 1957 when he hit 17 home runs and won the Negro League batting title with a .338 average.

Defensively, he played the outfield with both skill and knowledge. "I knew how to play center field at Rickwood," he said. "I knew exactly where the dips were out there, how far I was from the scoreboard, how the ball bounced off the wall. If you didn't know that outfield, you could miss some balls out there.

"I could always go after the ball," he added. "When you hit it, I went to get it. I could always do that. Even when I was playing against Willie Mays and the Major League All-Stars, they'd say, 'Don't hit it to him. He'll catch it.'

"You can watch the pitcher and you can tell by the way the batter's swinging which way the ball is headed," he explained. "I'd look up at the ball, and I'd just take off. You don't have to keep you eye on the ball all the time; you go to a spot.

"I was playing left field once, and a boy hit a foul ball down the line away from me," he added. "I started running and I just kept running and before you know it, I caught the ball.

"Somebody said, 'I thought you were going to give up on that ball.' I didn't give up."

In 1957, he moved from center to left field. "Anything to help the team," he said. "But I could play any position anyway. I played outfield, first base and third base."

One highlight of his career was playing in the East-West All-Star Game in Chicago. He made the all-star team three consecutive times, from 1955 to 1957. "We got to meet a lot of movie stars. Eartha Kitt used to be our grand marshal. Sometimes they'd have somebody to throw out the first ball."

He didn't play as well in those games as he would have liked. "I never did get a home run in the all-star game, because they always had good pitching. It was just like the all-star game in the major leagues."

During the off-season, he made extra money by barnstorming with the Willie Mays All-Stars from 1955 to 1958. He particularly remembers a game in Dallas, Texas, when Willie Mays hit a line drive to left field.

"I saw where it was going, and took off running." he said. "Just as I got to the spot, I looked up, reached up, and caught the ball by reaching back."

When he was running in from the outfield after the inning, Mays met him going out and said, "Lucky catch."

Ernie Banks was nearby, overheard Mays' remark, and said, "He must be lucky all the time. He's always making catches like that."

"Actually, I didn't play in 1958," he said. "I signed a contract to play a couple of games in Hawaii, but [the promoter] didn't really want me to continue playing. So I stopped [playing] for a while."

He rejoined the barnstorming troupe when they made an appearance in Birmingham. "I went out to Rickwood, and Gene Alvin, the man who ran the minor league all-stars, wanted me to play."

Some of the minor league all-stars objected, though, because Mitchell wasn't a member of their league that season. Mitchell went and talked with major leaguers Willie Mays and Larry Doby.

"They don't want me to play," Mitchell told the major leaguers. "They voted me out."

"You've been playing all the time," Mays replied. "I don't understand that."

After a pause, Mays added, "I tell you what. You're going to make some of this money some way. Have you got a blue suit?"

"Yeah," Mitchell answered.

"Go get that blue suit and come back. You're going to umpire," Mays said.

And that he did. Jessie Mitchell served as third base umpire for the game.

"The minor league all-stars beat the major league all-stars that day," he recalled. "Stanley Jones was pitching and he beat them something like 3–2 or 4–2. Stanley got signed that night. He blinded the major league all-stars that night.

"They were swinging at the ball before it got there," he added. "Stanley had a real good motion, but he didn't throw that hard. But he got the ball up there, and he beat 'em."

Major leaguer Hal Smith approached Mitchell after the game and said, "I don't know why we can't get this guy."

"It's because y'all are swinging at the ball before it gets there," Mitchell replied.

"They were used to swinging quick," he said. "Those guys in the majors throw it hard, and Stanley was just walking the ball up there. He beat 'em that particular night."

Mitchell recalled another exhibition game in which the minor league all-stars came out the winners. Charley Pride defeated the major leaguers at a game in Austin, Texas. "Charley had a knuckleball, and he beat them, 4–2."

Mitchell's most memorable game in the Negro League came in a 1959 contest in Canada when he hit a game-winning home run. "I wasn't one of these powerful home run hitters, but if I got it right, I could hit one," he said.

Jessie Mitchell won the Negro League batting title in 1957 with a .338 average while also hitting 17 home runs.

He got it right for this game. The Black Barons were behind, 5–2, coming out of the eighth inning. First, Paul Gilbert hit a home run to make the score 5–3. Then Willie Watkins hit another solo home run, and the Barons only trailed by one run.

The next batter worked around and got a walk. Mitchell came to the plate, representing the potential winning run.

"I got an inside fastball," he said, "and I hit it over the wall. When I rounded first base, people came out of the stands to celebrate. The umpires had to hold up the ball game.

"I don't know why they were so happy, unless they had some money on the game. But finally I was able to get around to home. But that was one of the most moving moments in my life."

Another memorable game was facing legendary pitcher Satchel Paige. The Barons went to the other team and said, "If y'all won't hit our pitchers that hard, we won't hit Satchel that hard."

In the first inning, one of Satchel's teammates hit a home run. The Barons abandoned their vow and went after Satchel's pitches with vengeance. "We were hitting him all over the place."

After the game, the Barons were taking their showers and celebrating, when Satchel came in. "Y'all got me tonight," he said, "but the next time we play, y'all ain't gonna hit nothing."

"I thought he was joking," Mitchell said, "but if that man didn't bring that ball next Sunday — low, hard and fast. When he changed up on you, he would almost break your bat.

"When he wanted to pitch, he was one of the best I ever faced in my life, and we had some good ones," Mitchell added. "Even when Satchel was getting up in age, he was still something out of sight. He could put a quarter or a dime out there and throw the ball over it.

"I saw Satchel when I was a boy, and here I was playing against him. And he was still throwing hard."

Mitchell's one shot at the major leagues came a year earlier, in 1958. "I was having a good day of running the ball down in the outfield," he remembered. "All of a sudden, they held the game up. Two scouts came out of the stands, said they wanted to see me throw some.

"We were in the middle of a ball game," he added. "But I made about six throws. After the ball game, they came around and offered me a contract."

Three teams were actually competing for his signature: the Baltimore Orioles, the St. Louis Cardinals and the Cleveland Indians. Mitchell first eliminated Cleveland.

"The Cleveland scout wanted to change my batting style. He wanted me to get up on my toes. But the ball would get up on me too quick. I didn't figure there was anything wrong with the way I stood as long as I was hitting the ball."

Instead, he signed with the Baltimore Orioles and joined their Double-A team, the San Antonio Missions, in training camp in 1955. "I was hitting the ball well. The first week I was down there, this guy with the Yankees, Fred Hoffman, he was hitting me fungos in the outfield. He hit me about ten balls, and I was catching them. Finally, he said, 'Come on with me.' We went to the manager Joe Schultz. Fred said, 'Joe, This is your outfielder here. This man can go get 'em.' Joe said, 'OK.'"

Later, in a spring training game against Charleston, the Triple-A ball club, none of the African American players were playing in the game. "There were 11 of us black guys down there," Jesse recalled, "and ninety-something white kids. We were facing a left-handed pitcher, Herb Score, and, brother, he was bringing it. In the eighth inning, he hadn't given up a base hit."

The manager came down the bench, approached Jesse, and said, "You want to pinch-hit?"

"Yeah, I'll pinch-hit," Jesse replied.

He got up, grabbed a bat, went to home plate and slammed a double. It was the only base hit his team got that day.

In a team meeting after the game, the manager offered an explanation. "I didn't put no black ballplayers in the game today, but I had my reason," he said. "The reason I didn't is that I wanted to show y'all that these black kids are excellent ballplayers. All of y'all are down here saying you're gonna stay and all this. If I had my way, I'd send all of y'all home tonight. But it's up to the front office, and I've got a quota of guys that I've got to keep. I can't keep no more than what the front office says I've got."

Mitchell described the manager as "a mean ol' man, had a big chew of tobacco in his mouth," and he continued talking. "I just can't keep but a certain amount of guys," he said.

"So that's what they done," Jesse said. "After that, they cut me, Billy Springfield, Denny Green, who used to play with the Washington Senators, and one more.

"When I came out of the office, this player, Mark Regan — he used to play second base with the Dodgers — he thought I was going to Vancouver. 'You going to Vancouver, Mitch?' 'No man, they're fixin' to cut me.' 'Cut you! You're out-hitting everybody in the camp!' 'I don't know.' I was young and naive, and I didn't know.

"I flew to Mobile a couple of days later and met Satchel and Hank Aaron to play in an all-star game down there in Prichard. I got in about 2:30 that morning, and Satchel was still awake. I walked into his room, and he said, 'What happened?' I said, 'They cut me.' Satchel said, 'I'll tell you what happened. They had a quota of how many black players they would keep. I know you can play.'"

So he stayed and played in the Negro Leagues and an occasional appearance against the Willie Mays All-Stars. "The first time I played against them after my tryout, they didn't expect me to be there," Mitchell said.

"I thought Baltimore signed you," Mays told him. "They couldn't believe I'd been cut," Mitchell recalled.

Jessie said it was often hard for players to know how much money they had earned. "They'd count the money, and you didn't know what you were getting," he said. "You could look at the ballpark and tell how many people were there, because you played there all the time. You'd have a ballpark that was jam-packed, and they'd say there was only four or five thousand there.

"Rickwood always drew a crowd," he added. "We had 12 to 13 thousand out there practically every time we would play. Standing room only, with areas in the outfield roped off. Ground-rule double if you hit it into the roped area. One player hit a grand slam home run, and the crowd just erupted. We drew more than the white teams. Sometimes we'd play three ball games a day — a double-header with Memphis on Sunday and another game with another team that night."

Mitchell still stays in touch with former teammate Charley Pride. "That's a man that I talk a good bit with in the phone. He's not a snooty person to be a celebrity. Some people when they make it, don't look back at the other guys."

"My manager at ACIPCO, Bob Bolin, was one of the best managers you'll ever see. He taught the fundamentals of baseball from the ground up. He knew the game."

Bolin once noticed that Mitchell was having trouble hitting. "There's got to be something wrong with you," Bolin told the young outfielder.

He was right. Mitchell was sick and had a mild temperature. "Being young, I didn't really talk to him about it. But he sent me to the doctor."

Mitchell was playing center field during a game in Asheville, North Carolina, against the Willie Mays All-Stars, with his team leading, 3–2, in the bottom of the ninth. The All-Stars got one runner on base, with one out, when Mays came to bat. Mays hit a long blast. Mitchell, standing in center field, said to himself, "There's no need to run after that one." He stood still, but turned and watch the blast go over the fence and hit a nearby football field.

He recalled one time when he made a rookie mistake by running with his head down on a stolen base. He took off from first, planning to steal second. As he neared the base, he heard someone say, "Slide." He did. When he looked up, he realized that the batter had gotten a hit and that he should have continued running to third base.

He stayed with the Birmingham Barons from 1954 through 1957, and joined the Kansas City Monarchs in 1959. "I wasn't a long ball hitter. I was mostly a line drive hitter. I was a smart hitter. I played for Kansas City. Sometimes I'd get a hold of one. One time we were playing a game and the pitcher threw me a knuckleball. Pow. Over the left field fence. He glared at me as I rounded the bases. The next time I came up, he threw me a fastball. I hit a shot, a straight foul ball. The manager jumped up off the bench and said, 'Put him on.'"

Mitchell retired from professional baseball after his 1959 season with the Monarchs and moved to Birmingham's industrial league. He joined Stockham, a team that reunited him with former Black Barons Henry Elmore, James Ivory, and manager Piper Davis. During an August 21, 1965, game, Mitchell went 3-for-4, with two singles and a home run, in leading Stockham to a 9–6 win that gave them the "Y" championship that year.[33] He finished that season with a .396 batting average.[34]

He eventually retired from baseball to take a steady job in the health care industry. That wasn't anything new to the athlete. During the 1950s, most professional baseball players (including major leaguers) had to find an off-season job to pay the bills during the winter months. Mitchell was no exception. His most common job out of baseball was working as a hospital orderly at Highland Avenue Baptist Hospital (now Montclair) in Birmingham. He was joined there by two other professional athletes, John Williams and Willie Ivory.[35] After baseball, he worked for 25 years at Princeton

Hospital, before retiring on September 23, 1999, from Birmingham's Health South Medical Center.

But baseball remains close to his heart. "If I had it to do all over again, I'd do it again," he told Karen Lingo.[36] "Because I enjoyed it, and I met so many good people. If they started a league tomorrow and I could play, I'd go right out and sign a contract and play with them."

He also remains one of the most respected Negro Leaguers to never make it to the major leagues. Larry LeGrande, a six-year veteran of the Negro Leagues, identified Jessie Mitchell as the second-best player he ever played against,[37] while Kelley notes that "several former ballplayers say that Jessie Mitchell was one of the best ballplayers they ever saw."[38]

"It was fun. Most of the time, we were winning, but it was fun still, whether we won or not," Mitchell said. "The only thing I hate is that I didn't start off playing outfield. Starting at shortstop hurt my career.

"I was a pretty good ballplayer," he told Karen Lingo. "I should have made it. But I have no anger in my heart about what happened in baseball. It was a sign of the time and the people."[39]

Alonzo Perry, pictured here with his two children, Diane [Favors] and Alonzo, Jr. Perry's hitting accomplishments earned him the nickname "His Majesty" in the Mexican League.

ALONZO THOMAS PERRY

Alonzo Perry was a pitcher-first baseman for the Birmingham Black Barons, starting in 1946. Perry caught the attention of major league scouts, who came to watch him play at Rickwood Field. While there, they spotted a teenager on the team named Willie Mays, and signed both to contracts with the New York Giants organization. Perry never made it to the major leagues, but he did rise to the Triple-A level of the minor leagues.[40]

Born April 14, 1923, in Birmingham, Perry broke into professional baseball in 1945 as a pitcher for the Atlanta Black Crackers. He started the '46 season as a curveball pitcher with the Homestead Grays,[41] posting a 4–0 record before getting in trouble with the team over a gambling issue. He returned to Birmingham and joined the Black Barons. Because of Perry's strong hitting skills, the Black Barons started splitting his time, using him at first base or as a pinch-hitter on those days when he wasn't on the mound.

Sam Williams recalled joining the Black Barons with Perry. "Alonzo Perry and I went to the Barons the same year," he said. "In fact, we was the two youngest fellas on the team when we went there in '47."[42]

He was still primarily a pitcher in 1948 when he put together a 10–4 record on the mound and a .325 batting average. Those numbers got the attention of major league scouts. He reinforced their interest with a 12–4 record and 3.45 ERA in 1949. Manager Piper Davis also used Perry as an assistant coach, due primarily to Perry's adeptness at stealing the signs of opposing teams.[43]

Later in 1949 season, the Black Barons sold his contract to the Oakland Oaks in the Triple-A Pacific Coast League.[44] He posted a .200 batting average in his brief stay there. In 1950, he was back with the Black Barons, playing primarily at first base. He stroked a .313 batting average and was named to the East-West All-Star Game. He finished the all-star contest with two hits.[45]

Such numbers interested New York Giants scout Ed Montague. He attended a Black Barons game to watch the power-hitting first baseman. The Giants wanted to sign Perry to their Sioux City farm team,[46] but they also spotted an outfielder named Willie Mays. "I had no inkling of Willie Mays [before that]," Montague later said.[47]

Montague signed both players, and Perry got another shot at Triple-A baseball in 1951. This time it was a nine-game stint with Syracuse in the International League, where he hit .278 before finishing the season with Brandon in the Mandak League.

Beginning in 1951, Perry started playing in the Caribbean leagues, winning batting titles in 1954 and 1957. He also earned the nickname "His Majesty" for his prowess at the plate. He might have acquired the moniker after hitting a ball over the left field wall in San Diego in the Dominican Republic. Perry was one of only two players to accomplish the feat.[48]

In 1955, Perry left the states and started playing in the Mexican League with Mexico City. During five seasons with the team, Perry posted batting averages that ranged from .333 (1959) to .392 (1956). His best season came in 1956 when he reached his peak in batting average and led the league in hits (177), doubles (33), triples (13), home runs (28), runs scored (103) and RBIs (118).

Carl Long described Perry as "a heck of a good hitter," recalling that he played

Alonzo Perry (front; the other ballplayer is unidentified) started his career as a curveball pitcher for the Homestead Grays until he joined the Black Barons. The Birmingham club took advantage of his power hitting. Scouts for the New York Giants traveled to Birmingham to see Perry.

against him in Mexico. "He bent down in a crouch — way down in a crouch — and he come forward," Long recalled. "I just played deep and deeper."[49]

Perry retired from professional baseball after two years with Monterrey in the Mexican League in 1962 and 1963, where he batted. .318 and .353. His son, Alonzo Perry, Jr., continued the family baseball tradition by playing briefly with the barnstorming Birmingham Black Barons in the 1960s. Such blasts caused Negro Leaguer Melvin Duncan to say, "This guy Alonzo Perry — whew, he could mash that ball."[50]

Alonzo Perry, Sr., died September 14, 1982.

WILLIAM "BILL" POWELL

Bill Powell had an impressive baseball career, playing in the Negro Leagues, Latin America and the minor leagues, winning more than 250 games in all venues combined. He made multiple appearances in the East-West All-Star Game, giving up only one run in six innings and emerging as the winning pitcher for the 1948 contest.[51]

Powell was born May 8, 1919, in Comer, Georgia, but his family moved to Birmingham when he was nine years old. He started playing baseball at the YMCA at the age of 15 and soon moved up to the semi-pro team, the 26th Street Red Sox. When he was 17, the pitcher started playing in Birmingham's industrial league with ACIPCO. Powell played in the league for six years until his career was interrupted by World War II.[52]

In 1942 he was called into military service with the army, eventually being assigned to the 234th Army Aircraft Unit. The war took precedence, but Powell was able to play some more baseball before he was discharged.

After leaving the army, Powell joined the Birmingham Black Barons in 1945. "They came to me when I got out of the army," he told Brent Kelley.[53] It would be the beginning of a six-year career with the team. He had a mediocre 4–5 record his rookie season, but jumped to 5–0 in 1946.

One of Powell's most memorable games was not a pitching matchup, but a comeback against the Indianapolis Clowns that featured offensive firepower. Trailing the Clowns, 10–1, the Barons fought back to win the game, 11–10.

Powell was a key player in the Barons' 1948 pennant-winning season, keeping hitters off-stride with a curve, slider and — his best pitch — a fastball. He posted an 11–3 record and a 3.81 ERA, and started two games in the Negro League World Series against the Homestead Grays.[54] He was crucial, though, in the Barons playoff wins over the Kansas City Monarchs for the NAL pennant. Powell recalled the game to Brent Kelley:

> All they had to do was win one game and we beat 'em two in Birmingham. [Manager] Piper [Davis] told me that night, "I'm gonna let you pitch in Memphis under them dark lights.... That night I pitched and I won that game. I beat Kansas City, 3–2. Boy, you talk about some big games. They come to us with just one game to win, and I beat 'em 3–2, and there went the championship.[55]

He was also the starting pitcher for the 1948 East-West All-Star Game, surrendering only one hit and picking up the 3–0 win for the West with three shutout innings. Powell tailed off in 1949, posting a mediocre 11–11 record. He rebounded in 1950 with a 15–4 record, a 3.00 ERA, and his second trip to the all-star game, when he pitched the last three innings of a 5–3 victory for the West.[56]

Another memorable game was an exhibition contest in Atlanta against a team of major league all-stars. The all-stars included Larry Doby, Roy Campanella, and Junior Gilliam. Powell won the game, 3–0. "I didn't give 'em but three hits," Powell recalled. "Doby didn't get nothing."[57]

At various times, Powell also played in Cuba and Puerto Rico. He had a combined record of 4–6 in the Cuban League in the late 1940s. He played one season (1949–50) with Ponce in the Puerto Rican League, posting a 7–6 record and 2.83 ERA. He appeared in two games for Puerto Rico in the inaugural Caribbean World Series, winning one and losing one. The combination of his wins abroad and his performance in the Negro League gave him three consecutive years—1948 to 1950—when he won at least 20 games.

His 1950 season attracted the attention of major league scouts. He also had a falling out with the Barons owner during the 1950 season. "That's the year Cincinnati and Chicago and all of 'em was after me, but ... they just looked me over. [Roy] Campanella was trying to get the Dodgers to sign me," he told Kelley.[58]

Powell believed he was almost signed by the Milwaukee Brewers of the American Association. The Brewers apparently tried to sign him and Bob Boyd in a package deal. "Tom Hayes, my owner, wanted a $30,000 package deal for the two of us, but they only wanted to give $15,000, so Tom Hayes wouldn't sell us. We got messed around. I could've been in the majors."[59]

Consequently, he left the Barons and signed a minor league contract in 1951. He joined the Sacramento Saints in the Pacific Coast League, posting a 0–1 record in his only decision.

"That was better than the majors," he once said. "You'd meet good players."[60] He spent most of the season at Colorado Springs in the Western League. The team was nicknamed the Millionaires when it was founded in 1901.[61] Powell didn't become a true millionaire, but he did compile a 14–8 record and a 4.69 ERA.[62]

In 1952 and 1953, he moved to the American Association. The 1952 season was an off-year for the right-hander; he posted a losing record (5–15) and a high ERA (5.05). But he bounced back in '53, posting a 14–9 mark and a 3.06 ERA. That was the high point of his minor league career.

Cincinnati signed Powell in the offseason and he went to spring training with the team in 1954. He broke camp with the Reds, but then was optioned to the minor leagues. "They had a boy lost 15 games and won five," he said. "I had won 15 and they took him up. That hurt me, you know."[63]

Instead, Powell entered the International League, splitting his time between Toronto and Havana, and posted a 10–8 record with a 4.23 ERA. But his career went downhill after that.

Powell finished his career by pitching seven more years, most coming in the low-level South Atlantic League. His best season during that period came with Savannah in 1956 when he put together a 6–12 record and a 3.12 ERA.

In 1957, Powell opened the season with Savannah and won his first two decisions.

He then signed with Nuevo Laredo in the Mexican League and put together a 3–7 mark and a 3.96 ERA while batting .286. He returned to the Sally League in 1958 with Knoxville as a player-coach. His main job was that of pitching coach, but he appeared in 70 games as a reliever and spot starter. He finished his career with Charlotte in 1961 with a 15–8 record. "I was the winningest pitcher just about everywhere I went," he said.[64]

After retiring from baseball, Powell developed a career in sales for Birmingham Beverage. He retired as a sales supervisor in 1987. Powell died August 21, 2004, in Birmingham.[65]

James E. "Jake" Sanders

James E. "Jake" Sanders was born August 31, 1934, one of twelve children born to Mary and Dobie Sanders in Fairfield, Alabama. He grew up in a poor section of the city, one that he still describes as the "slums." But baseball brought a welcomed relief from the surrounding poverty.[66]

"The only thing we had to do was play baseball," he said. "Actually, it was a tennis ball and a broomstick. We weren't allowed on the parks to play with the white kids, so we just played ball every day. To get up there and hit that tennis ball a block and a half away, it was a big thrill at the time."

He started playing while attending Englewood Elementary School. By the age of twelve, street ball became a daily afternoon activity. "Every day, we would all gather in the street around three or four o'clock in the afternoon. We'd go to church on Sunday and it would be the same way."

By the age of 15, Sanders was attending Fairfield Industrial High School and playing for the Fairfield Graystones, a team in the local YMCA/industrial league teams. It was his first opportunity to play with an organized team.

"The only thing I hated about that is that I had to catch," he said. "We didn't have any equipment. Even during the sandlot days, I made my own mask. I didn't have a face mask. I just made one out of some wire, because I didn't want the ball to hit me. The mask was a pretty good mask, just made out of some wire. Just enough to keep me from getting hit in the eye.

"And no breast protector," he added. "I made the breast protector out of a croaker sack. That would keep some of the sting off of me when the ball was fouled back."

One adjustment that had to be made was playing with a real baseball bat. The real equipment was heavier than the broomstick used for street ball.

"I think that's what made me a better ball player, batting with that broomstick against that tennis ball," he said, "because I had no problem once I started using a 33-ounce bat. That's all I ever used, all through my life, a 33-ounce bat. I would choke up on it, kinda like Pete Rose."

Baseball's role in his life became more important, eventually leading to Sanders dropping out of high school. He returned after a couple of years to get his degree. By then, he had established a local reputation as a player who could hit, run, and throw. He started playing for a variety of semi-pro teams until Birmingham Black Barons executive James Bolin suggested that Sanders consider playing in the Negro League. "Toward the end of the season, the Kansas City Monarchs were looking for players," Sanders said. "I started playing with them PC — a percentage of the gate.

"My first payday in Birmingham was $380," he said. "I thought I was rich. Three hundred and eighty dollars. Man, I was smiling from ear to ear. That was a lot of money." Few paychecks, though, matched that first game in Birmingham.

"Birmingham was the best city," he said. "All the ball clubs loved to come to Birmingham, especially when they were on PC, because they knew they were going to make a good payday.

"If you didn't get out there early, you'd probably have to stand up," he added. "They'd rope off areas to get all the people in. The Black Barons out-drew the white Barons. The community supported the Birmingham Black Barons."

Other times, the players' pay was sporadic. "When I did sign with the Monarchs, my contract was $225 a month," he said. "Sixty dollars of that money had to be paid back at the end of the month. That's what they gave you for your food, so you had to pay that back."

Sanders played with the Monarchs for three years, but even though he was initially contacted by Black Barons executive James Bolin, he never played for the Birmingham team.

"I played exhibition games against Birmingham with other teams. But when it came down to cutting day, I was cut from Birmingham," he said.

"I couldn't understand it. The way I'm hitting this ball? Why'd they cut me? But they cut me for Donnie Harris."

Sanders was sitting out by the stadium, crying after being cut, when Frank Evans approached. "Thank God for him," Sanders said.

"Now don't cry," Evans said. "I've just had a phone call from New Orleans. They're in the Negro League, and they want you to come play for them."

The New Orleans Bears were loaded with talent, including such names as Evans, Pat Patterson, Elijah Gilliam, and Sam Thompson. "I left Birmingham and went on to New Orleans," Sanders recalled, "and I'm thankful that I did. I stood out. I bet I batted .600. I could hit and I could throw. For a little fellow, I had all the qualifications."

Sanders was particularly proud of his speed on the base paths. "If you bobble a ball, you might as well throw to second, 'cause that's where I was gonna end up at," he said. "That was my speed. I remember once when I was in the Dodger organization. That was '57. They said they clocked me at 3.2 going to first base. I could fly."

Sanders' most memorable game in the Negro League came on the road. "We were in Illinois and I hit three triples in one game," he said. "I was tickled pink. I could always hit, but when you hit three triples in a ball game, man that was something. I can't remember the team we played, but I know it was in Illinois. That game stands out."

He also fondly remembers the road trips. "I liked traveling, because I could see a lot that I never would have been able to see if I had never gone out with New Orleans," he said. "I was just thrilled and excited."

Others agreed that Sanders was a talented player, and he was selected to represent New Orleans in the 1956 East West All-Star Game.[67] "In that game, I hit a triple,"

Sanders recalled. "I stood at the plate, and the ball hit the 420-foot wall, and bounced back, and I had to run. As I rounded the bases, fifty thousand people stood up and hollered."

After the game, six scouts came down to the dugout to talk with him. "Baltimore was the one really trying to sign me," he said. "If I'd had sense, that's where I would have gone."

Soon after the all-star game, Sanders experienced one of his most troubling moments with the team. The New Orleans team was driving through South Carolina when its bus broke down near the city of Aberdeen. There had been some racial problems in the town earlier in the week, including a report of the lynching of a black man. A white man selling watermelons by the side of the road warned them of the problems and suggested they avoid going to town.

"About ten minutes after we had broke down, the police came up," Sanders recalled. "They never said one word to us, but they took turns watching us day and night."

The watermelon vender helped the team get a mechanic, but a part had to be shipped in for the repair. That took a week, during which time the team stayed beside the road with the bus.

"For one week, sitting out there on the side of the road, we ate watermelon. No bathroom. We just ate watermelons for one week."

The bus was repaired on Friday, and the team left town without playing its scheduled game. Before they left, though, Sanders and Evans made one trip to town.

"We were so hungry, we wanted food," Sanders said. "Frank Evans and I were nominated to go into town and get some food. While we were there, I was scared. God knows I was scared. Frank was scared, too."

Soon afterwards, Sanders' contract was sold to the Brooklyn Dodgers. "I did sign that contract," he said. "Actually, I wasn't old enough, so my dad had to sign the contract. That was in 1957.

"I don't know how much money was involved," he added. "Some said $7,500. Some said $75,000. I just don't know. But back then, they wouldn't give no black kid no $75,000. They would give it to the team, then the team would compensate you.

"Baltimore had offered $8,000 for me, and I had begged the owner to take the $8,000 so I could get out of there."

The Dodgers signed Sanders to a contract for $300 per month and assigned him to their Class B team in Cedar Rapids. He joined the team for spring training the following year. "During spring training in 1957, I hit .462," he said.

"This was the same year that big Frank Howard came from Ohio State," he added. "He (Howard) got $118,000. I don't know how much money they got for me. I do know that on that team, I was the only black. I was the only one who wasn't a big bonus boy. And I could out-hit and out-throw all of 'em."

Sanders didn't make the team, but he earned a promotion to Triple-A. "They weren't gonna send me to no Class B with the speed and arm I had, and the way I could hit."

He was partly correct. They didn't send him back to Class B, but he didn't get the promotion either. "They called me to the office, and I'm thinking, 'I'm going to Triple-A now.' But they called me in and cut me.

"I was hurt. I didn't understand it. Why? The manager couldn't understand it either. I was the best on the team."

What happened to Sanders happened to a number of blackball players of that time. While the major leagues were eager to get talented blacks on their teams, they didn't want too many.

"It was the quota system," Sanders said. "They were only going to allow so many blacks to go in and play on those teams."

The teams, though, had to give a non-racial justification for the cut. "The Dodgers said I couldn't hit a fastball, and I know that wasn't true. Some other people said they cut me because I hurt my arm, but I know that's not true. I never hurt my arm. My arm's just like rubber."

Once Sanders heard about the quota system, he actually felt better about getting cut. "It made a lot of sense," he said. "I was a different person. I walked around for years with my stomach in knots because I couldn't understand why.

"This black and white thing—I couldn't understand it," he said. "Being a kid, I couldn't believe it. I finally had to get an operation for a bleeding ulcer."

Still, the Dodgers weren't his last shot at the major leagues. He returned to Birmingham after being cut from the Dodgers and was approached by the Baltimore Orioles' Luman Harris, who offered him a Triple-A contract. Sanders turned it down.

"No, I'm not going no place," Sanders told Harris. "I'm gonna stay home. The Dodgers almost killed me. What if you do me the same way? I'll just go on and die."

Harris promised that the Orioles would honor the contract, but Sanders was adamant. "No, I'm not going."

Instead, he returned to the Negro Leagues with the Kansas City Monarchs, and stayed in the league until his retirement in 1961. He played with and against some of the best in the Negro Leagues, including Dodger shortstop Earl Robinson (the first black to sign for a $100,000 bonus), Sollie Great, John Kennedy, Bobby Robinson, Stanky White, Jessie Mitchell, Tony Taylor, Sam Thompson, Elijah Gilliam, and Ben Adams.

He had some memorable games, including one in which he hit three triples. He scored three runs off those hits because, as he noted, "If I got on base, I scored."

His only regret was never winning a championship during that time. "We never made it to the championship. Seemed like every team I played on was on the bottom."

He also wonders if he ever had a real shot at the major leagues. "I felt that I had the tools to go to the major leagues," he said. "I know I had the speed, because when anybody compared you to Cool Papa Bell, folks said Papa Bell didn't have nothing on me. And I could always hit, bunt, and steal home.

"It was nothing to steal home for me. It wasn't just speed. I could read a pitcher. I just look at the pitcher and see what he's looking at. I'm gonna get me a good lead. Whenever he goes into his motion, I'm off running.

"You just take off. I always let the batter know I'm taking off. They were always aware that I'd take a base, so they were always aware. I love that.

"It was fun to steal home. Left-hander or right-hander, it didn't make no difference. It's easy to steal on a right-hander, but, as far as I was concerned, I could steal on a left- or right-hander. I didn't pick em, but it was hard for the left-hander to keep an eye on you at third.

"I was never a big home run hitter," he added. "The Dodgers thought I would be a home run hitter. I hit some home runs, but I always liked to just meet the ball so I could get on base and run. People loved to see me run."

Sanders most memorable moment as a player was a home run over the center field wall at Birmingham's Rickwood Field. "That was back over the concrete wall. They've done brought it in now," he said. "That was my best game at Rickwood.

"I just loved to come home. When you were going to Rickwood, you'd just smile because you know people were going to jam the ballpark.

"But they did that at every place we played," he added. "We were starting to out-draw the major leagues. You go to Comiskey Park, and the major leagues would draw 19,000. When we played there, we got 40,000 people."

The popularity of black baseball prompted some talk about expansion. "In 1942," he added, "there was some discussion about putting two black teams in the major leagues, but the law wouldn't allow them to do it."

Expansion probably would not have directly benefited Sanders. An eye injury led to his retirement from the game. "I was pitching, and we were fighting for a championship game. The batter hit a ball through the box, I went to field it."

A few weeks earlier, Sanders had been in a car accident. One result of the accident is that he occasionally lost his balance. As he moved to field the ball, he stumbled slightly to his right.

"When I did, the ball hit me in the left eye," he said. "They said they could hear it all over the stadium."

Oddly enough, Sanders wasn't even supposed to pitch. "I just pitched that night because we were short of players," he said, noting that he normally played in the outfield. "Since I had a strong arm, I thought I could get these guys."

Sanders was taken to the UAB eye clinic. A few days later, a surgeon used 68 stitches to repair his damaged eye socket.

Sanders retired as a player after the injury, but he remained in the game as a YMCA coach in Fairfield. Many of his students later earned college scholarships. "I would teach kids," he said. "Black or white, scouts would always tell kids to go to Fairfield and Jake Sanders. He's gonna teach you the fundamentals.

"For black kids, often their arm was gone by the time they turned 14 years old, because they weren't taught how to properly throw a baseball. This was my thing, to teach them the fundamentals so they could protect themselves. Even today, a mother or father will call me to come look at their kid and tell them what's wrong. I love to do it."

Sanders also gets frequent requests to speak to schools and churches about the Negro League. "I have at least 15 engagements this month," he said. "When they find out that Jackie Robinson wasn't the first black to play in the majors, that is something new to them. Moses Fleetwood Walker was the first black to play major league baseball.

"The second guy was his brother, Welday. After that, in 1884, they banned all blacks because of racial problems. Jackie came along 60 years later, so that made Jackie the first modern day (black) ball player.

"I tell them about Josh Gibson hitting 89 home runs in one season in 1942," he added. "They're surprised, because they've never heard that.

"And you see players sliding into bases," he said. "Do you know who started that? Rube Foster, a black man. White major league managers would come and watch him play and take it back to teach to their players on their major league ball club.

"Josh Gibson hit 962 home runs in 17 years in the Negro League," he added. "They were tape measures. He is the only guy to ever hit a ball out of Yankee Stadium over the roof. He's the only one. There's so much we could tell them, but we just don't have the time to tell them."

One reason many of today's youngsters do not know much about baseball history is because many have shifted their interest to other sports. "Since Michael Jordan came on the scene, all they want to do is play basketball," Sanders said. "I tell the kids to stick with baseball. In basketball, there's only a spot for four or five (players in an organization). In baseball there's a spot for 150 out there. But it's basketball now, football tomorrow. Baseball's forgotten and dying out."

While baseball has taken a backseat to other sports among black youths, Sanders noted that the integration of the major leagues led to the demise of the Negro League. "The major leagues actually killed the Negro League," he said. "The Negro League was the third-largest money-making business in the United States at one time."

That changed when the major leagues starting combing the Negro Leagues for the top players. "The last four teams were Memphis, Birmingham, Kansas City, and the Detroit Stars," he said. "After the 1962 season, that was it."

Sanders still has much of his old memorabilia. "I always kept stuff," he said. "I don't throw it away."

Nor does he forget the memories of that former time.

Sam Williams

Sam Williams had a four-year career as a pitcher for the Birmingham Black Barons, from 1947 until 1950. His tenure included a 6–3 record and a 3.21 ERA during the 1948 championship season. As the Negro Leagues started to diminish, he sought other baseball opportunities in 1951 by playing in Mexico before signing a minor league contract.

Williams was born October 12, 1922, in Birmingham. He grew up playing on neighborhood teams until he was old enough to join the military, where he played some more baseball. He was discharged from the army and returned to Birmingham in 1946.

He was soon playing in the industrial league, pitching for Clow Pipe Company. Williams said the industrial league was loaded with talented players. "At one time, you could go to Birmingham and pick up any kind of good ballplayer that you'd want," he said, "but ... the fellas didn't want to leave. They was working for those plants and they didn't wanna leave."[68]

The Clow Pipe team was talented enough to win the city championship in 1946. After the season was over, the league formed an all-star team to play an exhibition game against the Black Barons. Williams was selected as the starting pitcher for the all-stars, scheduled to pitch three innings before passing the ball to someone else.

When he arrived at the park that day, the manager told him the other two pitchers had refused to play. When Williams asked why, he was told, "I think they're afraid [to pitch against the Black Barons]."[69]

Williams had to pitch the entire game. That didn't bother him. "I just loved to play," he said.

He didn't win the game, but he pitched well. Williams went the entire nine innings, losing to the Barons, 2–1. The next day, he received a visit from Barons manager Tommy Samson and shortstop Artie Wilson. The two men, impressed by his performance against them, tried to get him to join the Black Barons.

At first, Williams was hesitant. "I'd never been out of Birmingham, except for my time in the army," Williams said. "I wasn't sure that I wanted to go." The Barons got him, though, when Wilson promised to look after the youngster. "I'll take care of you," Wilson said.

Williams joined the Barons for the 1947 season. That first season, he didn't see much action. "The Barons had a set pitching staff when I got there," he said. "They had four or five good starters.

"They didn't let rookies pitch league games; they had a starting rotation for that," he added. "I would pitch all through the week when we'd play other teams. You didn't get to start in league games until you had learned the other hitters in the league.

"I was a good pitcher, but I just didn't have much experience in pro ball," he said. "I could throw hard, so hard that very few fellows in the industrial league wanted to catch me."

His arm was so strong that he could throw the ball past most hitters in the industrial league. That was good enough to compete in the Negro Leagues. He finally learned that fact from former player Chet Brewer. Brewer, who was sometimes compared to Satchel Paige for his pitching ability,[70] taught Williams the importance of pitch placement.

"The strike zone was different," Williams said. "Chet told me that I was wild in the strike zone. I'd never heard that before."

To handle the problem, Brewer taught Williams to warm up by playing catch with another player while throwing to spots on the player's body. His routine was to start with tosses to the player's belt buckle, and follow that with throws to each kneecap. By doing that, he learned to hit the corners with his fastball. "After I got it down, I figured I was on my way," Williams said.

He received a chance to demonstrate his skill in a midweek game against a city team in Connecticut, the New Haven Sailors. The team included some ex-major leaguers. "The manager came to me, gave me the ball, and said, 'This is your game,'" Williams recalled. He took the ball and made the most of his opportunity.

He won the game, shutting out the Sailors in a 2–0 win. He later learned that his shutout was the first the team had suffered that season. "That game really gave the Barons an idea of what they had," Williams said.

It also gave the New Haven team an appreciation of their opponent. The Barons visited the Sailors again the following year. The owner offered Williams a new suit if he could toss another shutout. He won the game but lost the new suit, beating the New Haven team, 2–1.

Williams improved each season, notching a 6–3 record in the Barons' pennant-winning campaign in 1948. He improved to 8–6 in '49. After the season, he was one of the Barons chosen to face the Jackie Robinson All-Stars in an October exhibition game.[71]

In 1950, Williams improved to 13–7. He also started helping the bus driver on long hauls between games. "When I was in the service, I drove heavy equipment and the driver [would] get tired and I'd relieve him and give him some rest," he said.[72]

As he became a starter for the Barons, Williams particularly enjoyed pitching against the Memphis Red Sox and the Kansas City Monarchs. He liked pitching against the Red Sox because he usually won. "I could beat them," Williams recalled. "They had a big hitter named Casey Jones, and I used to strike him out. The others would come to me and ask, 'How can you strike him out and he beats us to death?' I don't know, but I could get him out."

But the financial situation of the Negro League teams was deteriorating. Williams left the Barons and went to Jalsico, Mexico, for 1951. "The owners in the Negro League didn't have the funds," he said. "We wasn't makin' no money. This is why I chose to go to Mexico, because we could make more money down there."[73]

He soon found that the pay was better and the fans loved baseball. "Down there, a baseball player was a god at that time," he told Brent Kelley. "You were a big-time celebrity in Mexico. You were treated well."[74]

Williams, though, had an off-year. His 5–10 record was the worst he would experience as a pro. He returned briefly to the Barons in 1952 before signing with the Wisconsin Rapids, a member of the Wisconsin State League, late in the year.

Williams moved to the West Texas–New Mexico League in 1953. He would have his best year as a pro, winning 25 games and losing only 12. That performance earned him a brief promotion to Oklahoma City for the start of the '54 season, but he lost his first three decisions and was returned to Pampa. He finished '54 with a 15–10 record for his old team.

Williams split the 1955 season between Superior (Northern League) and the Eugene Emeralds (Northwest League), putting together a combined record of 9–8 and a 3.42 ERA. The Eugene team won the league championship.

One game from that season was particularly memorable since it featured an appearance by baseball comic Max Patkin. Part of Patkin's show was hanging upside-down on the netting behind home plate and hitting a pitched ball from that position. The feat required a good batting eye on Patkin's part, and good control on the part of the pitcher.

Emerald manager Cliff Dapper selected Williams as the pitcher for the stunt. He and Patkin practiced before the game and then pulled it off without a hitch before the crowd. "I should hire you," Patkin told Williams. "You make me look good."[75]

Williams moved up to San Jose in 1956, finishing with a 15–9 record. It was back to Mexico in 1957, this time with Veracruz. He posted an 8–8 record before signing with Dubuque (Midwest League) late in the season. He had only three decisions in this trip to the minors, winning two and losing one.

"I had a winning season everywhere I went," he said. "It didn't matter who I pitched against, I was going to pitch my game. If you hit me, you hit me, but I figured I was going to get you out. I figured you had one chance to get a hit, and I had nine chances to get you out. That's the way I approached pitching."

He finished his career in 1958 with Poza Rica in the Mexican League, compiling a 9–11 record. By then he was married with two children. His wife encouraged him to quit and come home. "That was the hardest thing I ever done in my life," he said.

His work as a part-time bus driver for the Barons paid off in his post-baseball career. He got a job driving a bus in San Jose, California. He retired from the company in 1983.

His years with the Barons remain memorable. "We look back on it and we say that was real tough, but, you know, we got to where we was enjoyin' it," he said. "We all loved the game. We weren't playin' for the money, because we wasn't makin' no money."[76]

He is particularly proud of the 1948 Black Barons. "It was the best team I ever played on," he said, "the all-around best. We were like brothers. We were the most close-knit ball team I was ever on. It was just like a family."

Williams' final assessment of baseball? "That's the best job I ever had in my life," he said. "I wouldn't take nothing for the experience."

JIM ZAPP

Jim Zapp was born April 18, 1924, in Nashville, Tennessee. He found an unusual way to break into the Negro Leagues — by enlisting in the U.S. Navy to serve in World War II. And he had the distinction of serving two tenures on the Birmingham Black Barons. The first came in 1948 when he was part of the team that went to the Negro Leagues World Series. The second came in 1954.

Zapp did not play baseball as a teenager. "As a boy, I played just a little softball around town.... We didn't have a baseball team, especially where I went to school, a private Catholic school in Nashville."[77] His first stab at the game came when he enlisted in the navy in 1943 and was stationed at Pearl Harbor. After arriving in Hawaii, he soon became the third baseman for the navy's black baseball team on the island.

The navy also had an all-white team on the base. The coach for the white team was Edgar "Special Delivery" Jones, a former All-American football player from the University of Pittsburgh. On August 8, 1941, three months before the bombing of Pearl Harbor, Jones had made national news on the football field when he led the Pittsburgh Panthers to a 13–0 upset over previously unbeaten Fordham. Pitt historian Sam Sciullo called it "the greatest upset victory in the history of Pitt football."[78] Jones would later have a five-year career as a running back for the NFL Cleveland Browns,[79] becoming part of a team described as "pro football's greatest dynasty."[80]

At Pearl Harbor, though, Jones was coaching baseball. When he spotted Zapp playing third base for the black team, he saw a chance to improve his own diamond nine. At Jones' request, Zapp was transferred and Jones' team became the first segregated military baseball team on the island. "He took me and the first baseman [Andy Ashford]," Zapp recalled. "The first baseman didn't stay long, but I stayed with them until we moved away."[81] Zapp finished the season with Jones' team. The team finished the season by winning the military championship in 1943.

Zapp's unit was transferred to another location — Manana Barracks — after the '43 season, effectively removing him from Jones' segregated team. Zapp returned to the all-black team, which won the 1944 championship. He was then transferred to Staten Island, New York, at the end of World War II.

He continued to play baseball, this time under manager Larry Napp. Napp was a former player who eventually became a professional umpire. "It didn't seem like he was going to make the majors, so he turned to umpiring," Zapp said.[82]

Zapp's play got the attention of the Negro Leagues. After he was discharged, Zapp was one of two players on the military team signed by "Fat Puppy" Green to join the Baltimore Elite Giants in the Negro National League on a part-time basis by playing in weekend games. His new teammates included future major league Hall-of-Fame catcher Roy Campanella.[83]

Zapp joined the Giants' farm system and finished the 1946 season with the Nashville Cubs. In 1947, he returned to the Negro Leagues, playing with the Atlanta Black Crackers. The Black Crackers played their home games at Ponce DeLeon Park, in Atlanta's East Point area.[84] Zapp was described as "a great long-ball hitter" for the team.[85]

The problem, however, was the Crackers were having financial problems; sometimes, the players didn't get paid. About halfway through the season, while on a road trip in New York, a disgruntled Zapp left the team to stay with family there. "I quit the team right there because the owner of the Atlanta Black Crackers, you had to almost fight him to get your money," he said.[86]

His absence from baseball was a short one. He had hit 11 home runs during his brief stay with the Crackers; that was enough to get the attention of the Birmingham Black Barons.[87] He was soon offered a job on the team. It would be the first of his two tenures with the Black Barons. He joined the team in Montgomery, where they were playing a game on the campus of Alabama State University.

Zapp entered the lineup as the left fielder for manager Piper Davis; he was joined in the outfield by Ed Steele in right and Willie Mays in center. The team finished the season by beating the Kansas City Monarchs in seven games for the conference championship before losing to the Homestead Grays in the Negro Leagues World Series.

Zapp played a major role in the championship series against the Monarchs. In the third game, played in Memphis, he came to the plate in the ninth inning with the Barons trailing, 2–1. He hit a two-run homer to give the Barons a 3–2 win.

In the fifth game of the series, he hit a home run in the bottom of the ninth to tie the game at 3–3. The Barons scored another run later in the inning to win the game, 4–3, and take a 3–2 lead in the seven-game series.

Zapp dropped off the Barons' roster after the 1948 season when he was assigned to a barnstorming tour with the Indianapolis Clowns. Zapp wanted to be assigned to the higher profile team playing against the Jackie Robinson All-Stars. "So who would you think was going to make the most money?" he asked.[88]

Rather than join the Clowns, Zapp asked for his release. His request was granted. "That's probably one of the biggest mistakes I ever made in my life," Zapp said. "Piper Davis always said I was the only man he ever saw in his life to leave a championship team."[89]

"One time Piper mentioned ... that I was the best prospect on the team at that time," he added. "I don't know why I didn't stay with the Black Barons."[90] He played semi-pro ball in the Nashville area for a year. These include stops with the Morocco Stars in 1949 and the Nashville Stars in 1950.

In 1950, he returned to the Baltimore Elite Giants, now a member of the realigned Negro American League, under new owner Sue Bridgeforth. He remained with them in 1951 when he had one of his better seasons — at least until mid-season. When the selections for the East-West All-Star Game were released, Zapp had been omitted.[91] Outraged at the oversight, Zapp quit the team.

Again, his absence from baseball was brief. Zapp was signed by owner John Gibbons to play for an integrated minor league team in Paris, Illinois, in the Mississippi–Ohio Valley League (now the Midwest League). It was his first chance to play integrated baseball as a professional. "I said I'd never play in the Negro Leagues again, and I didn't," he said.[92]

Zapp ended that 1952 season batting .330, leading the league in home runs (20), and setting a team record for RBIs with 136. Zapp credited teammate and friend Butch McCord with helping him obtain that record. Zapp batted clean-up or fifth in the batting order, while McCord hit in the third spot. McCord hit about .390 that season and was often on base for Zapp to drive home.

Still, once the season was over, he was released. "Something happened during the season that they didn't like about my personal life, so they gave me an unconditional release during the winter," he told Kelley.[93]

The following year, Zapp went to Danville in the Mississippi–Ohio Valley League. That was the beginning of an odyssey around the minor leagues that would include stops at Lincoln and Corpus Christi in the Western League [94] and Odessa in the Texas League. Tired of the trades, Zapp tentatively retired again and returned home to Nashville.

No explanation for the trades of such a talented player were provided, but Zapp's temper may have been a factor. His reactions to missing the 1951 East-West All-Star Game may have been one example, but another story is also on the record. It occurred during an unspecified spring training game in southern Illinois. Zapp was apparently the target of name-calling and obscenities during one of his plate appearances. He responded by swinging hard, but popping the ball up for an easy out. That outcome triggered even more jeering from the crowd as Zapp returned to the dugout. Zapp then responded by running toward the offending fans. His teammates intervened to keep him from going into the stands.

Zapp later admitted he had a problem with his temper. As he told Brent Kelley:

> My biggest problem was I was very temperamental. I think that's one thing that held me back. That's why I didn't advance any further.... If I didn't think the owners was treating me right, I'd quit, ask for my release, or whatever, as long as they didn't give me enough money. Sometimes they did not.[95]

After a short stay in Nashville, he decided to make a comeback with Odessa. Odessa had no openings, but Zapp was referred to the team in Big Springs in the Longhorn League. Owner Bob "Pepper" Martin purchased Zapp's contract and was rewarded when his new third baseman hit a home run in his first at-bat for the team.

"The team was in San Angelo," Zapp recalled. "I was out of shape and fat.... It was hot in San Angelo and it was a day ballgame and ... the first time up I hit a ball over the center field fence."[96]

That happened on June 6, already late in the season, but he finished the campaign with a .290 average and a league-leading, record-setting 32 home runs in 90 games. The last blast — and the one that gave him the home run title — came despite playing with one swollen eye that came from being hit in the face by a thrown ball. "I was warming up on the sideline and one of my own ballplayers, a pitcher warming up with somebody else, hit me in the eye. Closed my eye," he said.[97]

After the minor league season was over, Zapp returned to the Negro American League, playing about a month with Baltimore and Birmingham. Zapp returned to Big Springs for the 1955 season, but was shifted to first base, a position he didn't like. He was batting .311 with 29 home runs in 89 games before he dropped off the team again. While away from the team, he was traded to Fort Arthur where he hit another eight homers. After the season was completed, Zapp retired from the game again.

This time, he was really out of organized baseball. He had completed a professional career that included years with two Negro League teams, several minor league teams, and a few semi-pro organizations. Along the way, he set a minor league record and helped the Black Barons capture a conference championship.

That's quite an achievement for a player who didn't start until he was playing for a military team.

CHAPTER 7

Black Barons in the Major Leagues

Once Jackie Robinson broke the major league color barrier in 1947, Rickwood Field became a favorite spot for visiting major league scouts. After all, the Black Barons were considered one of the best teams in the Negro League. The team was stocked with talented players.

The most famous Black Baron player to make the major leagues was Willie Mays, but the first was Dan Bankhead. He followed Robinson to the Brooklyn Dodgers, joining the team later in the 1947 season.

Artie Wilson made it to the majors with the New York Giants in 1951, while Sam Hairston had a brief appearance with the Chicago White Sox. Then Willie Mays, a rookie on the 1948 Black Barons, replaced Wilson in the Giants lineup.

There were other major achievements. John Irvin Kennedy, a member of the 1955 Black Barons, became the first African American to play for the Philadelphia Phillies. Jehosie "Jay" Heard broke the same barrier for the Baltimore Orioles. Bill Greason was mentioned as a possibility to break that barrier for the Boston Red Sox before making it to the majors with the St. Louis Cardinals.

Still, the person who may best represent how much progress had been made was Bob Veale. Veale started out as a ball boy for the Black Barons, but he put together an award-winning career as a pitcher for the Pittsburgh Pirates.

Below are profiles of some of the Black Barons who reached the majors.

DAN BANKHEAD

Robert Daniel "Dan" Bankhead was one of five Bankhead brothers who played in the Negro Leagues.[1] Dan Bankhead was one of four brothers who played for the Birmingham Black Barons and the only one of the five to make the major leagues. Dan made his Negro League debut in 1940 with the Black Barons. He would go on to be a three-time all-star, become the second black player in the National League [2] and the first black pitcher to play in the major leagues.[3]

Dan Bankhead was born May 30, 1920, in Empire, Alabama. He received a tryout with the Memphis Red Sox in 1939 as a third baseman[4] and broke into the Negro Leagues in 1940 as a shortstop with the Barons. He switched to the mound in 1941, compiled a 6–1 record, was third in the Negro American League with 15 strikeouts in a shortened (24 games) season, and was named to the East-West All-Star Game.

He had a 3–0 record in 1942 before getting drafted into the U.S. Marines for World War II. He returned to baseball with Memphis in 1946 when he tallied a 6–2 record and made his second all-star appearance. The Negro Leagues had two all-star games in '46, and Bankhead was the winning pitcher in both games. He had a 4–4 record in 1947, made his third all-star appearance, and was again the winning pitcher for the game. He also became the highest-paid player on the Memphis team.[5]

In between the 1946 and '47 seasons, Bankhead played winter ball in Puerto Rico. He ran up an impressive tally of 179 strikeouts with the Caguas team. One of his wins was a victory in an exhibition game over the New York Yankees.

The Negro League stats and his performance in Puerto Rico was enough to get the attention of the Brooklyn Dodgers. Advance scouts George Sisler and Clyde Sukeforth were so impressed that they described Bankhead as "the next Satchel Paige" and "the colored Bob Feller." He was on Branch Rickey's list of potential recruits as early as 1946.[6]

In early August 1947, Bankhead increased his stock by being the winning pitcher in the annual East-West All-Star Game.[7] On August 23, 1947, Branch Rickey flew to Memphis to see Bankhead pitch.[8] He saw Bankhead toss a win over his former team, the Black Barons, while striking out 11 of the Birmingham players.[9] Rickey paid the Red Sox $15,000 for Bankhead's contract—a record at the time—and signed him to a major league contract.

Bankhead made his Dodger debut four days later, on August 27, 1947, the same year that Jackie Robinson broke the color barrier, and became one of Robinson's teammates.[10] When he took the mound, Bankhead became the first African American pitcher to appear in the major leagues.

At the plate, he had a spectacular

Dan Bankhead. One often overlooked fact is that Jackie Robinson did not spend his entire rookie season as the only African American on the Brooklyn Dodgers team. Former Black Baron Dan Bankhead joined the Dodgers before the end of the 1947 season and became Robinson's roommate. Bankhead was one of five Bankhead brothers who played in the Negro Leagues, one of four who played for the Birmingham Black Barons and the only one of the five to make the major leagues. Bankhead was the winning pitcher in the 1947 East-West All-Star Game.

debut. He hit a home run in his first at-bat. On the mound, he was less than spectacular. He lasted less than four innings, giving up ten hits and eight runs. Bankhead admitted that he was intimidated by his first major league experience. "I was scared as hell," he later said. "When I stepped on the mound, I was perspiring all over and tight as a drum. I wound up to throw to the first batter and I thought I'd never get unwound."[11]

Robert Paige, son of Negro League legend Satchel Paige, recalled that Bankhead "was a superb athlete," adding that Branch Rickey had high expectations for Bankhead. After his disastrous debut, Rickey met with the press and told the reporters that the former Black Baron would be a great pitcher in the major leagues. But, as Paige noted, "He never did. It takes assurance and poise to be a great pitcher. Dan Bankhead never found his balance."[12]

Buck O'Neil believed he knew why Bankhead never "found his balance" in the major leagues.

> Dan was scared to death that he was going to hit a white boy with a pitch. He thought there might be some sort of riot if he did it.... Dan was always from Alabama.... He heard all those people calling him names, making those threats, and he was scared. He'd seen black men get lynched.[13]

Dan Bankhead, Jr., believes that such problems made it harder for pitchers to succeed in the major leagues. "Nothing against Jackie Robinson, ... but it was harder to be a black pitcher in those days," Bankhead said. "People would say, 'Okay, maybe black guys can hit or run, but they can't pitch.'"[14]

Bankhead finished the season with only ten innings in four games with a 7.20 ERA, but that included four scoreless innings on Jackie Robinson Day at Ebbets Field. Writers speculated that the performance might be good enough for him to return to the Dodgers in 1948.[15]

Instead, Bankhead was returned to the Dodger minor leagues in 1948, playing with Class B Nashua. He put together a 20–6 record, becoming the first player in the league to win 20 games. He also struck out 240 batters in 204 innings. His wins included a no-hitter before being promoted to St. Paul. He finished the season with a 4–0 record at Class AAA St. Paul.

Bankhead found himself in Montreal, in the International League, in 1949. He again won 20 games, compiling a 20–6 record and leading the league in strikeouts while batting .328 for the team. He also led the league in walks, earning him the label of "the wild man of the International League" by local sportswriters.[16] That stat was overlooked, though, after he won ten games in Puerto Rico, including a five-hit shutout to clinch the pennant. He earned another promotion to the Dodgers in 1950.

The season started roughly, with a racial incident during a spring training game in the South spoiling the appearance of black athletes. The players, including Bankhead, ended the issue by leaving the field.[17] When the team returned north the 1950 season ended up as his best in the majors. His ERA was a bit high (5.50), but he compiled an impressive 9–4 record and three saves while appearing in 41 games as a relief pitcher and spot starter.

The first sign that his major league career would soon be over came in June 1950 when he was hampered by a stiff shoulder. The problem turned out to be an old dislocation injury that had caused the bone to become calcified.[18] Bankhead got off to a poor start in 1951 losing his only decision in seven games, while getting pounded for a 15.43 ERA. He was demoted to the minor leagues, finishing the season with a 2–6 record at Montreal. He never made it back to the majors, concluding his career with a record of nine wins, five defeats, and a 6.52 ERA.

He had another bad year in Montreal, losing his only decision. He was sold to the Escogido Lions of the Dominican Republic League in 1952. In August, he got into a physical confrontation with catcher Luis Rosario of the Estrellas Elephants. After a hard slide from Bankhead, Rosario threw a baseball at him and Bankhead responded by hitting Rosario in the head with a catcher's mask. Bankhead was knocked unconscious in the resulting melee, jailed for his role, and fired from the team.[19]

With his pitching stats declining, Bankhead tried to make the transition to first base—first by playing in Canada and then in the Mexican League.[20] He finished his career playing for another 12 years in the Mexican League, with some of the final years spent as a manager.[21] He retired from the game in 1965 and died in Houston, Texas, on May 2, 1976.[22]

In many ways, Bankhead never received much recognition. "I just don't understand why my father has never gotten his due," Dan Jr. has said. "My father was not the best pitcher, obviously. But he was the first. And that story, I think it's an important story. I think it's as important in its own way, you know, as Jackie Robinson."[23]

Lorenzo "Piper" Davis

Piper Davis. "Mr. Birmingham Black Barons." Satchel Paige and Willie Mays may be more famous, but no player was more identified with the Birmingham Black Barons than Davis. When the Birmingham Barons, the Southern League affiliate for the Chicago White Sox, established the Barons Hall of Fame, the first inductee from the Black Barons was Piper Davis.

He was a legendary player and manager in the Negro Leagues,[24] but a person who came up just short on the fame meter.[25] Bill Greason, who made the major leagues, described Davis as "one of the greatest ballplayers" that he ever knew. "Piper was better than Mays when Mays started. Mays was just a rookie in 1948, but after that he developed," Greason added. "I would put Piper Davis up with any second baseman."[26]

Greason also lauded Davis' skill as a manager, saying he "could've managed in the major leagues. He had everything," Greason added. "He was a student. He was smart, stern, and yet he could be nice to you. He knew how to approach you. He was the greatest manager I ever played for."[27]

Some folks expected Davis to be the first black to break the color barrier, a role that instead went to Jackie Robinson. Then many expected him to be the person who would integrate the Boston Red Sox, the last major league holdout to hiring a black player. That role went to Pumpsie Green instead.

Lorenzo Davis was born in the coal-mining community of Piper, Alabama, the small community south of Birmingham that no longer exists. The only trace of its previous existence is the nickname that it provided to a Negro League legend. His father was a miner in the local mine for the Piper Coal Company.[28]

Davis worked in the mines and attended high school in Fairfield, where he played baseball and basketball. The multi-talented athlete attended Alabama State University on a basketball scholarship, but dropped out of school after a year to get a job in a Birmingham steel mill. That job provided a chance for Davis to play in Birmingham's industrial league.

Davis briefly moved into professional baseball at the age of 19 in 1936 by signing with the Omaha Tigers, an all-black team that barnstormed around the Midwest. He returned to the Birmingham industrial teams at the end of the season when the Tigers ran into financial problems. He played in the industrial league for another five years, playing for ACIPCO from 1939 until 1942. His tenure there ended when Winfield Welch signed Davis to play two different sports. Welch was the manager of the Birmingham Black Barons baseball team and also the head coach of the Harlem Globetrotters basketball team.

Welch met Davis at Bob's Savoy Café, the biggest black café in Birmingham, and signed him to contracts with both teams — playing second base for the Black Barons during the spring and summer, and basketball during the off-season.[29]

Davis earned $350 a month to play baseball, $300 a month plus two dollars a day for basketball. It was a dual role that Davis would continue during the years of World War II, decades before Michael Jordan would try to duplicate the feat.[30]

Davis told Fullerton how the double signing happened.

> Now that particular day, I went down to sign my contract [with the Black Barons] because they were going to play here that Sunday, and the Lord was just in the plan. I got the pen in my hand to sign for a certain figure, three hundred fifty dollars, or something like that, and Bob Williams, the owner of the Savoy Café, came by. He said, "Welch, that boy can play basketball too."
> Welch said, "You can play basketball too?"
> I said, "Yeah, I played one year in college."
> He went back to the phone and called up Abe Saperstein and he said, "Abe, this boy can play basketball too. Yeah, Bob says he's his best player. And Abe said, "Give him another fifty dollars and let him play for the Globetrotters."[31]

Davis became a member of some of the most successful teams in the history of the Black Barons. The Birmingham team won the Negro American League pennant in 1943 and 1944, but lost the Negro World Series to the Homestead Grays both years. Davis hit an anemic .142 in 1944, but improved to .313 in 1945.

Davis was the team leader and was named to the East-West All-Star Game four times, from 1946 to 1949. He hit safely in all four contests, had a .385 all-star average, and scored four runs in the games.

"Wasn't nothing the white Barons did, we couldn't do," Davis told Dave Kindred. "We outdrew 'em playing in the same ballpark. We'd have a few whites come to see us, couple hundred a night. They appreciated good ball."[32]

Unfortunately, Davis reportedly had a short temper. One example of his anger occurred in 1945 during a game between the Black Barons and the Cleveland Buckeyes. During an argument with umpire Jimmie Thompson, Davis hit the official. In an unusual move for the Negro Leagues, NAL president J. B. Martin fined Davis fifty dollars and suspended him indefinitely.[33]

Regardless, Davis' play during the 1945 season impressed Branch Rickey, who was searching for a player to break baseball's color barrier. Rickey considered Davis to be a prime candidate, but eventually eliminated him from consideration because of his age — 29.[34]

In 1947, after Robinson broke in with the Brooklyn Dodgers, other major league teams started scouting the Negro League players. The St. Louis Browns signed Davis to an option, but the team and Davis never reached an agreement. The Browns wanted to assign him to their Elmira, New York, farm team; Davis wanted to go directly to the majors. The Browns let the option expire, and Davis remained with the Black Barons.

In 1948 Davis became the Black Barons' player-manager. In his first year at the helm, Davis led the Barons to the league championship. As a player, he hit .378, led the league in RBIs, and was again named to the East-West All-Star Game. He also signed a 16-year-old youngster named Willie Mays to his first professional contract.[35]

Several Black Barons echoed Greason's opinion that Davis was the best manager and coach they ever played under at any level in baseball. "I learned more baseball from him than I did in four years of college," Tony Lloyd said.

"When I got with the Barons, I was playing and I was in the wrong position," Lloyd added. "Simple things about where I should be and how to pivot on second base to keep from getting spiked. Piper Davis showed me all that."

Davis had his own way with dealing with the racism the Black Barons faced on the road. When the Barons bus pulled up at a gas station to refill the tank, Davis would ask if the team could use the bathrooms. If the attendant refused, Davis would say, "If we can't use the rest room, then we can't buy no gas." "Pretty soon, people started letting us use it," Greason recalled.[36]

Davis also had a reputation for punctuality. "He was a good manager," James "Sapp" Ivory said. "But you had to be on time. Whenever he said the bus was going to leave at a certain time, you had to be there, 'cause he wasn't gonna wait on you."

The Rev. Bill Greason agreed. "I've seen the bus pull out with somebody running behind it, trying to get him to stop," Greason said. "He'd tell the driver to keep going."

In 1950, Davis became the first African American signed by the Boston Red Sox.[37] The Red Sox paid $15,000 for his contract, a figure that tied the Dodgers' signing of Dan Bankhead for the highest contract fee for a Negro League player.[38] He was assigned to their Class A affiliate in Scranton, Pennsylvania — a move that looked like the first step in Davis breaking the color barrier in the major leagues for the Red Sox.

There was talk that Davis might go directly to the show, but there didn't seem to be room on the Red Sox roster. Riley attributed the minor league assignment as a necessary one since rookie first baseman Walt Dropo was off to a great start and couldn't be sent back down.[39] Boston manager Joe Cronin confirmed that the Red Sox intended for Davis to join the team quickly. "If he makes good, I'm going to waste no time moving him to Boston," Cronin said.[40]

The move looked even more likely when Davis got off to a hot start and was leading the team in hitting, home runs, RBIs, and stolen bases when, on May 30, 1950, he was suddenly released by the Red Sox. Davis was shocked at the decision. He thought he had a deal to get promoted if he was still in Double-A by mid–May. When called to the manager's office, he was expecting a promotion, at least to Triple-A.[41]

Davis recalled the moment for Fullerton.

> I'm leading [the farm team] in hitting, RBIs, and home runs. I went out and practiced that May 15th morning and I went back to where I lived and [my wife] asked me where I'd been. "They'd been calling all morning for you." So I called them up and they said, "We've got to give you your release."
> I said, "For what, man?"
> "Economical conditions."
> When Boston released me, that took all the joy out of it for me.[42]

Tony Lloyd thinks he knows why. "Piper was a better ball player than Jackie Robinson, but he was something of a hot head," Lloyd said. "He couldn't take the racial slurs and the catcalling."

Instead of playing in the majors, from 1951 to 1955 Davis played for the Oakland Oaks in the Pacific Coast League. That tenure included one incident in which Davis and Ray Noble, the other black player on the team, were threatened following an in-game brawl.[43] Later in the season, as a promotional stunt, manager Mel Ott had Davis demonstrate his versatility by playing all nine positions on the field.[44] "Piper Davis is the best all-around player I ever saw," Ott explained.[45]

Davis then spent a few years with the Los Angeles Angels in the same league.[46] During this time, his batting average ranged from a low of .288 to a high of .316 — all respectable numbers.

Davis ended his playing career in 1958 as the player-manager for the Double-A Fort Worth Cats in the Texas League. His average for the year was a solid .282, but still low by his standards. As a final season tribute, the Cats played one game in which Davis played all nine positions, replicating the feat he previously performed for the Oakland Oaks during his days in the Pacific Coast League.[47]

Davis never actually made the major leagues as player, but he spent another 25 years as a scout for a number of major league teams, including the Detroit Tigers, Montreal Expos, and St. Louis Cardinals. His scouting achievements included signing future major leaguer Lee May to a contract. He and Buck O'Neil also made an infamous visit to a ballpark in Jackson, Mississippi, lured there to watch a ball game, only to discover the Ku Klux Klan holding a rally.[48]

Davis finally retired in 1986. In retirement, he seemed to hold little resentment toward the racism that kept him out of the major leagues. Instead, he considered his years in the Negro League to be "time worth remembering."[49]

"Wasn't the game's fault," he told the *Sporting News* columnist Dave Kindred. From his view, the game of baseball was a path to a better life. As he also told Kindred, "Praise the Lord, baseball got me out of the mines and into the sunlight."[50]

In 1993, Davis was inducted into the Alabama Sports Hall of Fame. He joined Willie Mays and Satchel Paige as the only Black Barons honored by the Alabama shrine. Davis died May 21, 1997.[51]

William "Bill" Greason

Count the Rev. Bill Greason as one of the lucky ones. He had an enviable baseball career as a pitcher, got a shot at playing in the major leagues, and retired from baseball for a career in the ministry. He has been a success in both fields.

William Greason was born in Atlanta, Georgia, on September 3, 1924, one of five children of Lizi and James Greason. He learned to pitch while playing stickball. He eventually developed a fastball, a change-up and three different curveballs — an overhand drop, a three-quarters throw, and a sweeping sidearm curve. He polished his early athletic abilities playing football and baseball at David T. Howard High School and Booker T. Washington High School. He preferred football and played two years at quarterback and halfback with the semi-pro football team, the Atlanta All-Stars.

But baseball was his ticket to a better life. "We lived in the alleys," he told Rob Trucks. "And I was determined, not only to get out of the alley, but to get the alley out of me."[52] After graduating from high school in 1943, he was called into the U.S. Marines to serve in World War II, becoming one of several baseball players in the war.[53] He wasn't playing baseball. Instead, he took part in the invasion of Iwo Jima, serving in the 66th Supply Platoon, a group of black Marines providing a support role in the battle.[54] Greason and his platoon went ashore on the island on the fourth day of the invasions, digging mass graves for some of the 6,800 who died there.

"They would take off the dog tags and put the bodies wrapped in ponchos on top of each other. They kept records of who was on that stack," Greason recalled. "Then they would cover it up and put a cross on top. For the enemies, they'd just dig a trench and push bodies in."[55]

Greason finished his military service in occupational duty in Japan, at Nagasaki and Sasebo, serving in Nagasaki after the atomic bomb was dropped. "People haven't seen war as it really is," he once said. "If they would really see what takes place, the body parts, see somebody step on a land mine, they wouldn't want to go to war so quick. They'd want to reach some kind of solution to keep people from being destroyed for nothing."[56]

After the war, he started playing semi-pro baseball in the Atlanta area. That got the attention of the Atlanta Crackers, who signed him for a couple of games. From there, he went to Nashville to play with the Nashville Black Vols. The next year, the Vols sold him to the Asheville Blues in North Carolina.

He joined the Birmingham Black Barons in 1948 after pitching against them in an exhibition game. The Black Barons were in spring training, playing an exhibition game in North Carolina, and Greason was the starter for Asheville. He tossed eight solid innings against the Birmingham team, enough for the Barons to decide they wanted to add him to their squad.

"The deals they made, I don't know," Greason said. "We were not knowledgeable of what the transactions were, nor did we receive anything, but they did bring me here in 1948. I pitched on Saturday night, and on Monday I was in Birmingham."[57]

He joined a team with three other rookies: Jim Zapp, Joe Scott, and Willie Mays.[58] Rookies, he found, had to fend for themselves. "They didn't try to teach you too much,"

Greason recalled. "If you didn't have the gift, they didn't want to teach you because you could move them out. So if you didn't have it, you didn't stay."

All three stayed and helped the Barons win the Negro American League pennant that year. He finished the season with a 6–4 record and a 3.30 ERA. The Barons tied the Kansas City Monarchs for the regular season lead and won the title in a playoff series. Greason was the winning pitcher. Greason called the game his most memorable outing.

"We had a rainout or two, and most of the pitchers were tired," Greason said. "I was a rookie that year. Piper came in and didn't know who to pitch that night because the other guys were tired. I asked him to let me pitch and I beat Kansas City six to one. They got one run and we got in the World Series because of that game.

"I had an unusual night," he added. "I pitched a five-hitter. They had some power back then. Gene Baker, Curt Roberts, Buck O'Neil, and Herb Sewell. I pitched against Jim Lamarque, a left-hander who was a great pitcher. But that night I just had my stuff and that was one of the greatest memories I have as far as baseball is concerned."

The victory put the Barons into the Negro League World Series against the Homestead Grays. They lost the series to the Grays, but Greason pitched in three of the games and was the winning pitcher in the Barons' lone win in that series, picking up the victory in relief. "We [the Barons] really had something. But, they [Homestead] had something too," he said. "It was a good series. We were blessed to get in."

He considers those 1948 Black Barons to be one of the best teams he ever played with. "I enjoyed playing on that team," he said. "As far as camaraderie, we looked out for each other and that's how we were able to win.

"Our catchers were Herman Bell and Lloyd Pepper Bassett," Greason recalled. "We used to call him [Bassett] rocking chair. Some games they would bring a rocking chair and he would just sit and catch.

"We had Joe Scott from California, who played first base; Piper Davis, second base; Artie Wilson, shortstop; Johnny Britton, third base; Bobby Robinson, left field; Willie Mays, center field; and Ed Steele, right field. Our pitchers were Nat Pollard, Sam Williams, Alonzo Perry, Jimmy Newberry, Jehosie Heard, and Bill Powell. We had a real good team."

Good enough for five of the players from that team to make it to the major leagues — Greason, Mays, Artie Wilson, Piper Davis, and Jehosie Heard.[59]

Greason was particularly impressed with Piper Davis, whom he called "the greatest manager I ever played for." "He was knowledgeable about baseball and could play any position," Greason said. "He knew how to use his pitchers and he knew the game."

Greason recalled that the Black Barons were a team with a sense of pride.

> When the Black Barons would leave Birmingham to go on the road, we were always clean and dressed right. We looked out for each other. We didn't come into another town lookin' like tramps. If one of our players didn't have the proper clothes to wear, we'd chip in and buy him a suit. People respected us everywhere we went.[60]

After the season, Greason received his first opportunity to play winter baseball in Puerto Rico. "Artie Wilson, who played with us then, got me the chance to go to Puerto

Rico, but I didn't stay that year," he recalled. Still, his interest in the place was piqued, and he would later return to the island to play.

He stayed with the Barons from 1948 to 1951. In 1949, his record dropped to 7–12, but still made the all-star team.[61] He tossed three shutout innings for the West.

In 1950, his last year with Birmingham, he bounced back, winning nine games against only six losses while compiling a 2.41 ERA. By then, he had also started playing winter baseball in the Mexican League. He signed with Jalapa and finished with a 10–1 mark and a 3.88 for his south-of-the-border team.

During this time, one Negro League opponent—Sherwood Brewer, who played with the Indianapolis Clowns and Kansas City Monarchs—identified Greason as one of two pitchers that were the hardest to hit in the league (the other was another Black Baron, Bill Beverly). But he considered Greason the tougher of the two. "I just couldn't hit him," Brewer said. "He'd laugh at me sometimes. He told me one time, 'Sherwood, I'm gonna lay one right down the middle.' Right down the middle. Medium speed. And I popped it about a hundred feet right over the catcher. And I knew it was coming."[62]

Mel Duncan, a veteran with the Monarchs and Detroit Stars, had a similar opinion. "Everything he [Greason] threw started out not much over your knees—fastball, the curveball, and all," Duncan said. "You'd swing at that ball and it would hit in front of the plate—it wouldn't even get there. That last one, he'd drop it over or either he'd blow it by you. He just kept you thinking, kept you thinking."[63]

Many of those games were played on the road, with the Black Barons moving from town to town to entertain more fans. "We didn't mind traveling," he said. "We had a lot of fun on the bus.... We had one of the best drivers in the world. He really took care of us. He could drive all night and seem to not get tired."

On the road, though, discrimination was rampant. "There were places where we couldn't stop and eat or hotels where we couldn't sleep, so we traveled and slept on the bus," he said.

When they couldn't eat in a restaurant, the players would pool their money. "One guy would buy a loaf of bread, the other one would buy cold cuts, another would buy mayonnaise and mustard and we'd make sandwiches and buy sodas," he said. "That would hold us until we got to a town where we could sit down and have a meal."

"You don't allow it to get you down," he later told *Birmingham News* writer Greg Garrison. "You know it exists. You can't change it by yourself. One thing you can do: You can maintain your integrity."[64]

Two of the Black Barons—Red Harris and Jim Zapp—were light-skinned. The team sometimes took advantage of that by sending one of them into a restaurant to get meals for the team.

Abuse from white fans in the stands was common. "Of course, you got a lot of abuse. Even when we were playing with the Black Barons in different parks and all, folks would give you a hard time," he told Rob Trucks. "They'd call you everything but nobody paid that much attention. We even called each other nigger. We'd been called that before, but when other people said it, it was in a derogatory manner. But we didn't pay any attention."[65]

Sometimes the Barons would leave Birmingham in the afternoon and go to Mississippi to play at night. They only had one uniform, and sometimes they would have to wear the same uniforms to play in another town. "Sometimes our uniforms would be wet, and we would change sweatshirts," he recalled. "But we did it because we loved the game."

The team took their problems in stride. "It didn't bother us because we would sing, play cards, and tell jokes," he said. "We just had a lot of fun and didn't think too much about the traveling."

The U.S. Marines called again in 1951 during the Korean War. Initially stationed at Camp Lejeune, North Carolina, he expected and wanted to go to Korea. Instead, he found himself playing baseball.

"I asked to go to Korea out of frustration because I was having a good year with Birmingham," Greason said. "The company commander said I couldn't go because he was having a base team, Camp Lejeune baseball team"

Greason went to the commanding officer, and said, "Sir, I want to go to Korea."

"You're angry, aren't you?" the commander replied.

"Yes sir, I'm angry."

"You're about to have a good year," the commander said. "I'm not going to send you to Korea. Now get outta my office."

The next week, Greason returned to the office and again made his request. "I still want to go to Korea," he said.

"You're not gonna go," the commander said. "There's a ball team here, and I want you to play on it. Don't come back to my office no more."

Greason's reply: "Thank you, sir," and he spent the rest of his year playing baseball.

Greason had seen plenty of discrimination while playing baseball in the South. He found even more in the military. When his unit went to Florida for spring training, he was refused admittance to one restaurant. Earlier, at an exhibition game in Orlando, he was ordered to leave the stands because of his color. He was supported by his fellow soldiers, but was still bothered by the incident. "I looked at my manager, and he got up and all of us left," Greason said. "I thought that was one of the worst things that could be done. Men in uniform couldn't sit and watch the game, not bothering anybody. That really hurt me."[66]

While playing for the Marine Corp, Greason met Bob Motley. Motley was an umpire in the Negro Leagues, but he started out officiating games for the military. Later he ran into Greason on a barnstorming tour. Motley recalled the moment in his book, *Ruling over Monarchs, Giants, & Stars*:

> I spotted Bill immediately as I boarded a bus with the Black Barons on one of my many barnstorming trips. He later became one of the many Negro League players to be drafted by a major league club, and appeared in a few games for the St. Louis Cardinals. Although he never became a household name, he was one of those gifted players that the Negro League was blessed to call its own.[67]

Greason drew that attention of some major league baseball scouts when he defeated future Dodger Don Newcombe, 1–0.[68] One scout, representing the St. Louis Browns, recommended him to their minor league team in Oklahoma City. The Oklahoma City Indians were the Double-A farm team for the Cleveland Indians in the Texas League.

Greason had to try out for the Oklahoma team by pitching against a prison team. The prisoners provided surprisingly strong competition, but Greason did well enough to get the contract.

"They offered me a contract for $2,000 to sign," Greason recalled. "I'm just out of the Marines, and I'm happy and broke."

He was happy to get the money, but there were some stipulations. "When I talked with them, they said, 'I tell you what I'm gonna do. I'm going to give you a thousand now. If you stay six months, I'm gonna give you five hundred more. If you stay for the whole season, I'll give you the other five hundred.'"

He joined the team in July under manager Jim Tatum, a former teammate of Jackie Robinson's at Montreal.[69] On July 31, 1952, he won the first game he pitched before 5,751 fans — the largest home crowd of the season.[70] Greason finished the season with nine wins and only one loss. He helped the Oklahoma City Indians make their league playoffs, one they eventually loss to the Dallas Eagles. "We were leading Dallas three games to one and they beat us out," he recalled.

He faced more discrimination from the fans of the Texas League teams, but he felt comfortable with the Oklahoma team. The owner, a man named Humphries, helped smooth the transition by taking Greason into the clubhouse and introducing him to the other players, saying, "Even though this fellow is black, I don't want you to look at him as being the first black ballplayer. He's a ballplayer. I bought him because I feel he could help our team."

"And those fellows I played with in Oklahoma City were some of the best fellows I ever played with, and they were a white team," Greason added.[71]

At that time, the Texas League had only one other black ballplayer — pitcher Dave Hoskins with the Dallas Eagles. On August 3, 1952, four days after Greason's Texas League debut, he and Hoskins made history by becoming the first two black pitchers to face each other in a minor league game. The a match-up was repeated other times during the season.[72] "We filled the parks wherever we went, because Dave was a good pitcher, too," Greason said.[73] Adelson noted that the two "showed southern whites they could play baseball."[74]

Hoskins, already considered the "savior of the league,"[75] entered the game with a 16–8 record. Greason pitched a complete game and won the historic contest, 3–2. He gave more details of what the two men faced to Rob Trucks:

> In that Texas League, there was just two of us so it was tough, but I'd just smile and go on and pitch and did a good job. I didn't let it upset me. I'd look right at the person and smile, nod my head, and keep going. Why should I pay attention to that? I know who I am. I don't have to pay attention to what folks say. So that's the way it was with us, but we had already learned that, growing up in the South.... The South has always been, to me, more real than people up north. We used to go into restaurants and the waitresses would walk by you, not paying you any attention. And we'd ask them, Can we get some service? And they'd say, Do you see that sign up there? Because they'd have these signs that said, "We reserve the right to refuse service."[76]

His 9–1 record and 2.14 ERA at Oklahoma City got the attention of other teams. There were immediate offers from the Boston Red Sox and the New York Yankees, with the offers reportedly reaching $100,000 in cash plus some players.[77] The Oklahoma City owner, though, refused to sell, thinking he could get a better deal.[78] "He said, 'No, I'm going to wait until next year. I can get twice as much,'" Greason recalled. "Here I am still waiting on part of my two thousand dollars. And he wants to wait until next year."

Interestingly, if the Red Sox had been successful in their efforts to buy his contract, he would have been positioned to be the first black player to join Boston's major league roster.[79] When they missed on signing Greason, the Red Sox waited until 1959 before adding Pumpsie Green to the roster and becoming the last major league team to integrate.

With both the Yankees and the Red Sox out of the picture, Greason's marketability dropped despite a 16–13 record, 193 strikeouts, and a 3.62 ERA. Oklahoma eventually traded him and Texas League batting champion Joe Frazier to the St. Louis Cardinals in the off-season. The Cardinals made the purchase after beer magnate August Busch purchased the team from Fred Saigh, who had strongly opposed integrating the team.[80] *Jet* magazine noted that "it was reported that [Greason] would be given 'every chance' to make the Cardinals next spring."[81]

Greason's part of the deal was an outright purchase, but the Indians received only $25,000 for the pitcher.[82] Greason didn't see any of the money. "I was supposed to get that bonus for signing when I left the Marines, $2,000," he said. "I never did get it all."

The Cardinals sent Greason to their farm team in Houston in 1953. He finished the season with a 17–4 record and a 3.48 ERA.

For the 1954 season, he moved up to Columbus, Ohio, playing for the Columbus Red Birds under manager Johnny Keane. "Johnny Keane was a great manager," he said.

"I was having a great year there," he recalled. So great, in fact, that he caught the attention of the major leagues. *Sport* magazine named him one of the ten top prospects in the minor leagues.[83]

After pitching against Herb Score, and beating him, 2–1, Greason got called for his "cup of coffee" in the major leagues.[84] "Eddie Stankey, who was from Mobile, was the manager of the Cardinals, but they were not having a good year," Greason said. "I didn't want to go, not in the middle of the season while the team was losing."

Greason said he later talked with Monte Irvin, who also disliked his mid-season call-up to the major leagues. "He didn't want to do it," Greason said. "The reason was, it was too much of a strain on you. I didn't feel comfortable going up at that time of the year."

And there was the pay cut involved. Greason was making $1,200 a month in Triple-A. The Cardinals offered him $900 a month for the major leagues.[85]

Still, joining the Cardinals meant making the major leagues. "I wanted to see what it was like even though I wasn't happy about going up there," he said.[86]

Further, Columbus manager Johnny Keane insisted that Greason accept the call-up. "So I went and I was happy I was able to make it," Greason said.

He was not happy with his new manager, Eddie Stanky. "I knew the manager and the kind of person he was. He was one of the guys who gave Jackie Robinson a hard time when he went up and he didn't care much for blacks."

Greason first got the silent treatment from Stanky. "When I went up, he didn't even speak to me except once when I was pitching batting practice in Philadelphia," he said.

That mirrored the action from most of the team. "The reception I got was cool," he later recalled. "There was no overt hostility. But the worst feeling you can sometimes get is being ignored. People don't speak to you, don't look at you. Things were cool enough in Columbus, but St. Louis was like goin' from the refrigerator to the freezer."[87]

He also saw little action, and soon found that his pitching skills were getting rusty. "I did not touch the ball for two or three weeks," he said. "When I went up, I didn't do any throwing or anything but go out and run.

"They wouldn't let me [throw]," he said. "You couldn't go to the bullpen unless they told you. I don't know if race had anything to do with it. That was just they way things were."[88]

When he finally got a chance to pitch, his release point was off. Stanky, upset with his lack of control, finally came out to the mound and yelled, "Get the damn ball over the plate!"

"What the hell do you think I'm trying to do?" Greason replied. "Do you think I have a string on it?"

Stanky stared at Greason, then turned and walked back to the dugout. "That was the only time he spoke to me," Greason said.

Greason was 29 years old when he joined the Cardinals. He was happy to reach his goal of making the major leagues, but disappointed at how long it took. "To make it at that age is tough," he told Rob Trucks. "I figure if I had got a shot earlier, then I wouldn't have had any trouble."[89]

Greason became the second black on the Cardinals. First baseman Tom Alston was the first, and the two men became roommates for Greason's brief stay. Alston, Greason noted:

> was really hurting because he had so much pressure on him. They wanted him to be the big guy on the team, him and Stan Musial.... Tom wasn't doing anything.... We became roommates, but Tom was really under a lot of stress and it didn't change much after I arrived because they were still looking for him to be productive and he just didn't do it that year.[90]

Greason's major league experience was limited to three games. "I started a game in Chicago, I started one in St. Louis against Philadelphia, and I pitched in relief in the Polo Grounds," he recalled. "But other than that, I didn't do any pitching. I didn't do too well at that time because I hadn't thrown much."

He saw action in only four innings, giving up eight hits (including four home runs). Most of the action came in that first game against the Cubs on May 31, 1954. He went three innings, giving up six hits, five runs, and a walk while striking out three. He finished his major league stint with an ERA of 13.50. After nine weeks in the show, he was sent back to Columbus.

"It didn't bother me," he later said. "I was happy to get out of there. They wouldn't let me go to spring training because I started playing winter ball. They said, 'If you give up winter ball, you can go.' But I said, 'Who's going to take care of me during the winter?'"[91]

"I made more in the minor leagues than I did with the Cardinals," he added. "They gave me a $900 contract when I went up there. I said, 'What is this?' They said, 'You got to prove yourself.' I said, 'You brought me up here. That ought to prove something.' So I went ahead and signed it, but I was glad to leave."[92]

Brooks Lawrence, Greason's roommate in Oklahoma City, recalled Greason's call-up for Peter Golenbock:

> They called him up to St. Louis before they called me. St. Louis was taking any good pitchers they could find. He went up there and stayed a week at the most, maybe ten days. They hit him like he stole something, they beat on the ball so bad. So they sent him back and took me and a (white) pitcher from Cincinnati named Ralph Beard. He didn't last either. They didn't play fair with him.[93]

In 1951, Greason started playing winter baseball in Mexico. In 1953, he finally played in Latin America, signing with the Puerto Rican team of Santurce. It was the beginning of a six-year relationship with the team and its owner, Pedro Zorilla.

After the 1954 season, he headed south again to play with Santurce. "We had a major league team when I pitched down there," he said. Indeed he did. The Santurce team included a number of major league players on its winter squad, including Willie Mays, Don Zimmer, Ruben Gomez, Sam Jones, George Crowe, Ron Sanford, Buzz Clarkson, Roberto Clemente, and Bob Thurmond. Mays had joined the team after helping the New York Giants win the 1954 World Series. Santurce eventually went to Caracas, Venezuela, where they swept the Caribbean World Series.

For 1955, he returned to the states and back to the minor leagues. This time he was sent to Houston, where he compiled a 17–11 record. As the season approached an end, Houston had a chance to play in the Dixie Series. One potential opponent was the Birmingham team from the Southern League. Greason told a teammate, "I'm from Birmingham. If we win, we may have to go in there and fight the Ku Klux Klan."[94]

The following year he put together a 10–6 record before he was promoted to the Rochester Red Wings in the International League. He finish out his professional baseball career there, compiling a 16–18 mark from 1956 to 1959.

He was still pitching for Rochester in 1959 when he was traded to a team in Charleston, West Virginia. He and the Charleston team never reached an agreement on his contract and he decided to retire. He left Rochester and returned to Birmingham—the site of his memorable years with the Black Barons and his wife's hometown.

He left professional baseball, working at a local department store [Pizitz] for 14 years. Greason, however, did not drop out of baseball entirely. He joined the local industrial league, playing for Fairfield. His team won a city championship during that time.

He also got a chance to play against Jackie Robinson when the Hall-of-Fame player brought an all-star team to Birmingham. Bill Greason pitched for the local team, limiting Robinson's team to one hit. After the game, Robinson came to Greason and complained, saying, "They didn't come to see you. They came to see me."[95]

His success against Robinson's All-Stars didn't surprise Greason. He had always thought the competition in the Negro Leagues was of a high caliber — at least equal to the Double-A or Triple-A minor leagues. The problem was that the Negro League players never had a chance to demonstrate their skills against white players.

"Here in Birmingham, you couldn't even play sandlot ball against the whites in the city," he said. "We couldn't even play out in the streets with whites. Police would come and break it up. When I came in 1948, they didn't allow that."[96]

The industrial league also gave Greason a chance to meet Capp Brown, a coach at Parker High who also played for Fairfield. Greason started working with the kids on Brown's baseball teams.

He also went back to school, graduating from Birmingham Baptist Bible College after three years of study with a degree in religion. After that, he did post-graduate work at both Birmingham's Samford University and Birmingham Baptist Bible College. By then, Greason felt his calling was in the Christian ministry. "I began going to the Sixteenth Baptist Church, and went there about eight years before I became a member," he told Karen Lingo.[97] "Being around the church, something happened. I announced my call on Sunday morning, and by that afternoon I was in the pulpit."

He was preaching once a month at the church when it was bombed in 1963. "I just happened to be in Tuscaloosa that Sunday the church was bombed," he recalled.[98] Greason had gone to Tuscaloosa with another former Black Baron, Jake Sanders, as part of a program to get young people into organized baseball programs. Meanwhile, the other Negro League players look up to him as a religious leader and fun-loving spokesman for their organization. As Willie Curry said, "I like to sit down and talk to him. He keeps you laughing all the time."

Looking back, he has no regrets about his baseball career. "Baseball gave me a chance to see a lot of the world," he said. "I had a great career in baseball and I was blessed to have been called here to Birmingham."

SAM HAIRSTON

Sam Hairston's time on the Birmingham Black Barons was one season in 1944 — before the post–Robinson era — but he was still in the Negro Leagues until 1950.[99] He became one of several former Black Barons to make the major leagues, although his time at the top was a brief one, featuring five at bats in four games.

Hairston was born January 20, 1920, in Crawford, Mississippi. He grew up in Birmingham, getting his semi-pro start as a catcher in the industrial league for ACIPCO. His teammates included two other future Black Barons — Piper Davis and Artie Wilson.

Hairston joined the Black Barons in 1944 as "a remarkably talented young catcher-third baseman."[100] He made the team as a backup catcher after Double Duty Radcliffe broke a finger and the Barons needed another backstop. Hairston told the Barons he could play the position, knowing he might not make the highly competitive team as a third baseman.

Still, he was released by the Barons after his first season.[101] He moved north, joining the Cincinnati Clowns for the 1945 season, one of Syd Pollock's barnstorming teams in black baseball.[102] The Clowns moved to Indianapolis in 1946, and Hairston moved with them.

The new environment seemed to help him, as he became a star for the team. He was hitting .465 for the Clowns in 1950 when the Chicago White Sox signed him in the middle of the season. He became the White Sox's first American-born black player, preceded only by Minnie Minoso. Hairston was assigned to the Triple-A Pacific Coast League, becoming one of nine African American players in the league.[103]

Hairston made the major leagues in 1951, appearing in four games and getting five at-bats. He had two hits, giving him an impressive .400 career average. His stats also included a double, one run scored, and one RBI.

"Sam was one of those players who shined in that time just before baseball integrated in 1947, ... he was thirty years old when he signed with the Chicago White Sox," Joe Posnanski recalled. "His best days were gone."[104]

After the 1951 season, the White Sox obtained Sherm Lollar as their new catcher. He would hold down the position for the next 12 seasons. Hairston was sent back to the minor leagues, spending most of his remaining career at Colorado Springs in the Western League.

He became a local legend in Colorado Springs. He hit .316 for the team in 1952, falling only four percentage points shy of the batting title. He won the league's MVP award in '53, finishing the season with a .445 mark in his final 121 at-bats. Hairston spent the 1954 season in Charleston, but returned to Colorado Springs again in 1955. Again he won the batting title, this time with a .350 average.

The highlight of his minor league career came during that 1955 season when the team set aside a night in his honor. The recognition was partly for his baseball accomplishments, but was also spurred by his civic work in the community to fight juvenile crime. This was no typical "honor" night in which he was merely recognized and presented with a plaque. Instead, the community poured out a series of gifts for the beloved Hairston, including a new Pontiac, a television set, a radio, luggage and a cash award. Appropriately, after the ceremony, Hairston went 3-for-4 in the game.[105]

When Hairston retired as a player, he stayed in the White Sox organization as a scout and coach.[106] As a scout, he signed his two sons to major league contracts. John Hairston had only a brief stay in the major leagues, but Jerry Hairston played 14 years in the show.[107]

In his later years, Hairston became a coach in the White Sox minor league organization. Those years included a popular stint as a coach for the Birmingham Barons, the White Sox's Double-A affiliate in the Southern League. Hairston finished his professional career where it began — in Birmingham. He died October 31, 1997.[108]

BILLY HARRELL

Billy Harrell reached the major leagues in 1955 at the age of 27 as a reserve infielder with the Cleveland Indians. Harrell made his major league debut on September 2 of that year and played in 13 games. He returned to the majors again for 22 games in 1957.

His best season came the following year when he appeared in 101 games, compiling a .271 batting average and seven home runs. Harrell finished his major league career in 1961 with the Boston Red Sox, appearing in 37 games.

For his career, Harrell played in 173 games over his four seasons in the show, compiling a .213 batting average with eight home runs and 26 RBIs. His career numbers also included 54 runs, seven doubles, one triple and 17 stolen bases.

Harrell was born in July 18, 1928, in Norristown, New Jersey. He was a two-sport star at Sienna College from 1949 until 1952, playing baseball and basketball.

Basketball may have been his best sport. Harrell was named honorable mention on the United Press All-American team in 1952. He played basketball for the Saratoga Harlem Yankees during the 1951–52 season, and turned down offers from the Minneapolis Lakers of the NBA and the barnstorming Harlem Globetrotters to pursue a baseball career.

Harrell's only year with the Birmingham Black Barons came during the summer of 1951 when he was a shortstop for the team.[109] After returning to Sienna for the 1951–52 basketball season, Harrell was signed by the Cleveland Indians to a baseball contract. He worked his way through the minor leagues before joining the team in September 1955.

JEHOSIE "JAY" HEARD

Jehosie "Jay" Heard was one of five players from the 1948 Birmingham Black Barons who made it to the major leagues. Heard's stay, though, was short — two games and three innings in 1954 for the Baltimore Orioles.

Heard was born January 17, 1920, in Atlanta, Georgia, and grew up in Birmingham. Unlike most kids of the day, Heard never played baseball as a child. He was introduced to the game while serving in the military during World War II. The 5'7" athlete first tried the outfield, got hit in the head by a fly ball, and took his strong arm to the pitchers mound.

After completing his military service, Heard returned to Birmingham and joined the Birmingham Black Barons. He was a key player in the Barons claiming the Negro American League pennant in 1948, finishing the season with a 6–1 league record and making a relief appearance in the World Series.[110]

Heard played for the Memphis Red Sox in 1949, and shifted to the Houston Eagles in 1950. In Houston, he was spotted by Rogers Hornsby and Bill Veeck, eventually signing a minor league contract with the Baltimore Orioles.[111]

Heard cut five years off his official age to make himself more attractive to major league scouts and made his debut in the Orioles organization in 1952 with Victoria, a Class A team in the Western International League.[112] Heard got the attention of the league when he pitched a no-hitter. He also raised some eyebrows by pitching both games of one double-header; he lost both games, but only by a 1–0 margin in each. Victoria won the league championship while Heard compiled a 20–12 record with 216 strikeouts and a 2.94 ERA.[113] His performance at Victoria earned him a promotion in 1953 to Portland of the Pacific Coast League. He finished that season with 16 wins and a 3.19 ERA.

That was good enough to move to the Orioles for spring training in 1954. He opened the season with Baltimore, becoming the first African American to play for the team. The stay was brief; in June he was optioned back to the Pacific Coast League. The Orioles recalled him to the majors in September, but he was optioned back to the minors in October. He spent the next year, 1955, in Tulsa and posted a 10–15 record. That was followed by a stint with Havana in the International League, registering a 3–5 record, but that completed his baseball career.

His two short tenures with the Orioles left him with a limited statistical record. Heard made it into only two games, getting no decision in either, and appeared in only 3⅓ innings. During that brief appearance, he gave up six hits, three walks, and two strikeouts, while posting a 13.50 ERA.

But those appearances were historic, particularly the first one. Heard was one of three relief pitchers to appear in a 14–4 loss to the Chicago White Sox on April 24, 1954. That appearance made him the first black player to play in a game for the Baltimore Orioles.[114] Mfune and Stodghill argued that Heard was brought to the major leagues only "as a token on a team of twenty-three whites."[115]

Maybe so. But another barrier had been broken.

Jehosie Heard died November 18, 1999, in Birmingham.[116]

JOHN IRVIN KENNEDY

John Irvin Kennedy was a shortstop in the Negro Leagues with the Birmingham Black Barons and the Kansas City Monarchs in the 1950s. He was born November 23, 1934, in Sumter, South Carolina. Kennedy was a talented player who had a solid career in the Negro Leagues, but he is best remembered as the player who broke the color barrier for the Philadelphia Phillies — the last team in the National League to integrate — and as the last player to make the jump from the Negro Leagues to the major leagues.[117]

Kennedy was initially signed out of the Negro League by the New York Giants in 1953. Assigned to St. Cloud in the Northern League, he batted .262 with 30 doubles and 33 stolen bases, but was released by the Giants after the season. He joined the Birmingham Black Barons for the 1954 and 1955 seasons. He played for the Kansas City Monarchs for the 1956 season and had an all-star year, hitting .385 with 17 home runs.

The Philadelphia Phillies invited him to a tryout at Connie Mack Stadium late in the season. He was signed as a free agent and invited to spring training for the 1957 season.

He made the team, but Kennedy's future with the Phillies became somewhat tenuous when they signed another shortstop. That came the day before the first games of the 1957 season; the Phillies picked up another African American, Chico Fernandez, from the Brooklyn Dodgers. Fernandez eventually ended up as the Phillies' starter at the position.

Kennedy made the team out of spring training anyway, but had to shift to third base. Both he and Fernandez made the trip to Philadelphia and were met by a large crowd of happy Phillies fans.

Kennedy made his major league debut on April 22, 1957, becoming the first African American player to appear in a game for the Phillies. Other than that, nothing much happened. Kennedy entered the game against the Brooklyn Dodgers in the eighth inning as a pinch-runner for Solly Hemus. Hemus had doubled, and Kennedy replaced him at second base but did not score. The Dodgers won the game, 5–1.

Two days after his debut, Kennedy was again used as a pinch-runner, this time against the Pittsburgh Pirates. He replaced Harry Anderson at first base and scored the only run of his career when Ed Bouchee hit a bases-loaded triple. The Phillies won the game, 8–5.

Kennedy played in only three more games, capping his career with an appearance on May 3, 1957. He finished his five-game major-league career going 0-for-2 at the plate. In the field, he had only two chances — one assist and one error. The assist came on his participation in a double play. A shoulder injury ended his major league career and led to a demotion to Thomasville, North Carolina, the Phillies' Class B team.

After being released by the Phillies, Kennedy played several more years in the minor leagues with Des Moines, Jacksonville, Miami and Tulsa before retiring from baseball.[118] He died April 27, 1998, in Jacksonville, Florida, at the age of 71.

WILLIE MAYS

The most famous of the post–Robinson era Black Barons is Willie Mays. The "Say Hey Kid" is no longer a kid, but he is still a baseball legend — arguably the greatest player in the history of the game. He played in 24 all-star games (a record), was a Gold Glove winner for 12 consecutive seasons, and won two MVP awards in two different decades, 1954 and 1965.[119] His career numbers include a .302 batting average, a mark that is 46 points higher than the league average of his time.[120] His 660 home runs rank fourth on the all-time list; only a year of military service prevented him from having a shot at topping Babe Ruth's career total of 714. And it all started with the Birmingham Black Barons.

Mays was born May 6, 1931, in Westfield, Alabama, near Birmingham. He played three sports — baseball, football and basketball — at Fairfield High School, but baseball was his passion. By the age of 16, he was seeking a professional career. He found it later that year in 1947, the same year Robinson broke into the major leagues.

Former Black Barons manager Tommy Sampson took credit for first spotting Mays on a local sandlot team and signing him to a barnstorming team that Sampson was putting together.[121] Former Baron Jim Canada made a similar claim,[122] and did play a significant role. But Sampson got Mays on a barnstorming team. He asked Mays to join the team, but knew he would need permission to sign him to a contract. Mays lived with his aunt, and Sampson said he had to beg Mays' aunt to get her consent, promising that he would take care of the youngster. Sampson purchased a new set of spikes for Mays and took him to Macon, Georgia, for a game against the Newark Eagles.

Sampson's makeshift team lost, 2–1, but the Eagles were impressed. They tried to sign Mays to a contract, but Sampson refused. "I said, 'I couldn't let you have that kid. I just picked him up.'"[123]

But he did sign to play another game the following Sunday, this time traveling to Tennessee to face the Chattanooga Choo Choos. After that game Sampson realized he wasn't going to be able to keep his team together. The teams he was playing paid their players a salary; Sampson was having to pay them based on a percentage of the gate.

Sampson broke up the team, sending most of the players back to Birmingham. Mays, though, signed a brief contract with the local Chattanooga team. At age 16, he was in the Negro Leagues, playing for the Chattanooga Choo Choos.

He also made his first headline. On May 14, 1948, Mays hit a home run and two singles to lead Chattanooga to a 3–0 win over the Atlanta Crackers, a story that was reported the next day with the headline, "Mays homer big blow in Choo Choo triumph" in the *Chattanooga Times*.[124]

Piper Davis and the Birmingham Black Barons ran into Mays soon thereafter. Davis already knew the young outfielder; Piper had once played with his father, William Howard Mays. Davis already knew Mays was a talented young athlete. What he didn't know was that he was already playing professionally.

Davis sought Mays out and talked to him. "You know, if they catch you playing out here, you won't be able to play high school sports." Mays replied that he was making good money and didn't care.

"If you want to play ball for money, have your daddy call me."[125]

Mays first day with the Barons was a Sunday double-header at Rickwood Field. Davis sat Mays' on the bench for the first game, but started him in left field — batting seventh — for the second.

The move caused some grumbling by some of the veterans on the team. That caused Davis to turn to the team and say, "Anybody doesn't like that lineup ... , you can go in and take off the uniform if you want."[126]

Mays responded with two hits in the game, but as Riley noted, "he was still the fourth-best center fielder on the team."[127] Davis signed him to a contract, but only to play home games. The manager refused to allow him on road trips while school was in session.

During the summer, Mays got his first taste of the road. Davis and the other Barons quickly took the youngster under their wings. "I came from Fairfield very cocky, knowing I could make it. But I had no know-how," he later recalled. "But those guys wouldn't let me go out at night and they wouldn't let me have any girls."[128]

Davis assigned Jimmy Newberry to be Mays' bus pal. Once in a city, most of the other players took turn as the youngster's chaperone.

> Every night he would have a different player babysit for me, but there were two he would not leave me with — Newberry, who was good enough for bus rides but not to be trusted in the evenings, and Alonzo Perry, our first baseman.... They liked the ladies and they liked their beer. But I couldn't go anywhere unless I was chaperoned. Piper made good and sure of that.[129]

Mays also learned the importance of promptness, particularly when playing for a manager who expected his players to be on time. Once he was late arriving for the bus that was departing on a road trip to play the Monarchs. Davis ordered the bus to leave without Mays.

The youngster caught a cab and caught up with the bus outside of Birmingham. Davis allowed him on the bus, but only after a tongue-lashing. "You don't want to be left, get your little chicken butt on your seat and sit down so we can get going to Kansas City," he yelled.[130]

Negro American League of Professional Baseball Clubs

Uniform Player's Contract

Parties   The _Birmingham Black Barons_ herein called the Club, and _Willie Howard Mays Jr_ of _Birmingham Ala._, herein called the Player.

Recital   The Club is a member of the Negro American League of Professional Baseball Clubs. As such, and jointly with the other members of the League, it is a party to the Negro American League Constitution and to agreements and rules with the Negro National League of Professional Baseball Clubs and its constituent clubs. The purpose of these agreements and rules is to insure to the public wholesome and high-class professional baseball by defining the relations between Club and Player, between club and club, and between league and league.

Agreement   In view of the facts above recited the parties agree as follows:

Employment   1. The Club hereby employs the Player to render skilled service as a baseball player in connection with all games of the Club during the year _1948_ including the Club's training season, the Club's exhibition games, the Club's playing season, any all-star games and the Negro World Series, (or any other official series in which the Club may participate and in any receipts of which the player may be entitled to share); and the Player covenants that he will perform with diligence and fidelity and service stated and such duties as may be required of him in such employment.

Salary   2. For the service aforesaid the Club will pay the Player a salary of $ _250.00_ per month from _July 4, 1948_ to _Sept 6, 1948_, as follows:

In semi-monthly installments after the commencement of the playing season on the _1st_ and _15th_ day of each month covered by this contract, unless the Player is "abroad" with the Club for the purpose of playing games, in which event the amount then due shall be paid on the first weekday after the return "home" of the Club, the terms "home" and "abroad" meaning respectively at and away from the city in which the Club has its baseball field.

If the player is in the service of the Club for part of the month only, he shall receive such proportion of the salary above mentioned, as the number of days of his actual employment bears to the number of days in said month.

Loyalty   3. The Player will faithfully serve the Club or any other Club to which, in conformity with the agreements above recited, this contract may be assigned, and pledges himself to the American public to conform to high standards of personal conduct, of fair play and good sportsmanship.

Service   4. (a) The player agrees that, while under contract or reservation, he will not play baseball (except post-season games as hereinafter stated) otherwise than for the Club or a Club assignee hereof; that he will not engage in professional boxing or wrestling; and that, except with the written consent of the Club or its assignee, he will not engage in any game or exhibition of football, basketball, hockey or other athletic sport.

Post-season Games   (b) The Player agrees that, while under contract or reservation, he will not play in any post-season baseball games except in conformity with the Negro Major League Rules, or with or against an ineligible player or team.

Assignment   5. (a) In case of assignment of this contract to another Club, the Player shall promptly report to the assignee club; accrued salary shall be payable when he so reports; and each successive assignee shall become liable to the Player for his salary during his term of service with such assignee, and the Club shall not be liable therefor. If the player fails to report as above specified, he shall not be entitled to salary after the date he receives notice of assignment.

Termination   (b) This contract may be terminated at any time by the Club or by any assignee upon five days' written notice to the Player.

Regulations   6. The Player accepts as part of this contract the Regulations printed on the third page hereof, and also such reasonable modifications of them and such other reasonable regulations as the Club may announce from time to time.

Above and opposite: The most famous of the ex–Black Barons is Willie Mays, the Hall of Fame outfielder for the Giants. The New York Giants purchased Mays' contract from the Black Barons after he graduated from Fairfield Industrial High School in 1950.

Agreements and Rules	7. The Negro American League Constitution, and the Negro Major League Agreements and Rules and all amendments thereto hereafter adopted, are hereby made a part of this contract, and the Club and Player agree to accept, abide by and comply with the same and all decisions of the League President or Board of Owners, pursuant thereto.
Renewal	8. (a) On or before April 1st (or if Sunday, then the succeeding business day) of the year next following the last playing season covered by this contract, by written notice to the Player at his address following his signature hereto (or if none be given, then at his last address of record with the club), the Club or any assignee hereof may renew this contract for the term of that year except that the salary shall be such as the parties may then agree upon, or in default of agreement the Player will accept such salary rate as the Club may fix, or else will not play baseball otherwise than for the Club or for an assignee hereof.
	(b) The Club's right of reservation of the Player, and of renewal of this contract as aforesaid, and the promise of the Player not to play otherwise than with the Club or an assignee hereof, have been taken into consideration in determining the salary specified herein and the undertaking by the Club to pay said salary is the consideration for both said reservation, renewal option and promise, and the Player's service.
Disputes	9. In case of dispute between the Player and the Club or any assignee hereof, the same shall be referred to the League President as an umpire, and his decision shall be accepted by all parties as final; and the Club and the Player agree that any such dispute, or any claim or complaint by either party against the other, shall be presented to the League President within sixty days from the date it arose.
	10. This contract is subject to Federal or State legislation, regulations, executive or other official orders, or other governmental action, now or hereafter in effect, respecting Military, Naval, Air or other governmental service, which may, directly or indirectly, affect the Player, the Club or the League; and subject also to all rules, regulations, decisions or other action by the Negro American League or the League President, including the right of the League President to suspend the operation of this contract during any National emergency.
Supplemental Agreements	11. The player expressly covenants and agrees that in the event of his breach of contract the Club shall have the right to apply to any court of competent jurisdiction, domestic or foreign, for an injunction, or for relief, in such manner as shall be deemed necessary.
	12. The Club and Player covenant that this contract fully sets forth all understandings and agreements between them, and agree that no other understandings or agreements, whether heretofore or hereafter made, shall be valid, recognizable, or of any effect whatsoever, unless expressly set forth in a new or supplemental contract executed by the Player and the Club (acting through its duly authorized agent) and complying with all agreements and rules to which this contract is subject.

Signed in duplicate this *July 4th 1948* day of _____, A. D. 194___.
[SEAL]

Witness: _____

Birm. Black Barons (Club)

By *Tom Hayes Jr.* (President)

X *W. H. Mays* (Player)

X *216-57 St. Fairfield, Ala* (Home Address of Player)

#82590

Tom Hayes Jr.
680 No. Lauderdale St.
Memphis, Tenn

> **WESTERN UNION**
>
> NGA065 PD= 7UX NEWYORK NY 21 1011A= 1950 JUN 21 AM 9 52
>
> TOM HAYES PRESIDENT AND OWNER BIRMINGHAM BARONS=
>
> 680 LAUDERALE ST MFS=
>
> THIS WILL CONFIRM TELEPHONE CONVERSATION TODAY WITH OUR MR SCHWARZ IN WHICH WE OFFERED TEN THOUSAND DOLLARS FOR THE ASSIGNMENT OF CONTRACT OF PLAYER WILLIE H MAYES JR AND YOU AGREED TO ASSIGN HIS CONTRACT TO THE MINNEAPOLIS BASEBALL CLUB FOR THAT AMOUNT= 100 W 42 ST,
>
> =HORACE C STONEHAM PRESIDENT MINNEAPOLIS BASEBALL CLUB
>
> *Accept your offer of 10000 for Willie Mays...*

In June 1950, Black Barons owner Tom Hayes received this telegram from Horace Stoneham, president of the New York Giants triple-A affiliate, who was offering the substantial sum of $10,000 for one of the Birmingham players. Appearing at the bottom (and partially shown above) is Hayes's handwritten response: "Accept your offer of 10000 for Willie Howard Mays Jr."

"I was not late again," Mays said. "I knew that if I was, why, I'd simply be stranded again, and the next time it might not be in my home town."[131]

Mays also endured some of the problems of road trips in the Negro Leagues. The bus broke down in Montgomery, and Davis commandeered an ice truck to get to their next game. On another trip to the Polo Grounds in New York, the bus broke down in the Holland Tunnel.

Mays retrieved his suitcase as the team abandoned the bus, which caught fire and exploded, ruining the team's equipment.

Davis also taught the youngster some of the psychological aspects of the game. After Mays hit a home run off Chet Brewer, Brewer pegged Mays on the arm with a fastball his next time up. Mays was twisting on the ground in pain when Davis walked up.

Without bending over or offering to help him up, Davis said:

"Don't let this guy show you up. You see first base over there? I want you to get up, and I want you to run to first base. And the first chance you get, I want you to steal second and then third."[132]

Mays' talent was quickly apparent. "When he got there, he just took over," former Baron Bill Powell recalled. "That was a ball player. You couldn't hit nothing up the middle."[133]

Umpire Bill Motley, who worked the Black Barons games that year, had a similar memory.

> Willie Mays was Hank Aaron, Ernie Banks, and every other great player — black or white — rolled into one.... Greatness has a way of calling attention to itself, and that was the case with Willie. He had the quick hands, the extra zip in his swing, the serious look on his face as the stepped up to the plate, the smooth glide in his stride as he sped across the base paths. There was also a hunger evident in how this youngster played the game.[134]

The opposing teams started noticing too. In a game against the Kansas City Monarchs, Mays threw out two runners at home. When a third opportunity arose, Monarchs manager Buck O'Neil — coaching third — stopped the runner at the corner base. "Whoa, whoa," O'Neil told the runner. "That man's got a shotgun."[135]

That same season, Mays got his first chance to bat against Satchel Paige. "I got a double off Paige, my very first time up," he later recalled. "I stood on second base, dusting myself off, feeling pretty good."[136]

> Paige left the mound, walked over to Mays on second, and said. "That's it, kid."
> Mays faced Paige three more times in that game, striking out all three times.

Mays became the Black Barons center fielder on June 1, 1948 — a few days after finishing high school. His opportunity came after the regular centerfielder, Norman Robinson, broke a leg.

When Robinson returned later in the season, Mays stayed in center and Robinson took over left field. Piper Davis told Mays he kept him in center because he had the stronger arm of the two. "Willie can go get it, and Willie can bring it back," Piper told others.[137]

Indeed he could. Archie "Dropo" Young remembered a game where he hit two long blasts in a park with no outfield fence. Young thought both hits were deep enough into center field for home runs. The problem, though, was that Mays was playing center field. "The first one I hit, they threw me out coming home," Young said. "When I hit the next one and got to third base, I stopped. Willie Mays had that type of arm on him so I just stopped. I didn't try to come home.

"We knew he was a natural from the time he joined us," Powell added. "Only thing he couldn't do was swing the bat, but after he stayed with us ... he started swinging the bat."[138]

Former teammate Bill Greason agreed. "Mays was a talented young fellow," Greason said. "He could catch the ball, run, and throw. [But] he was not a good hitter."

That's right. One of the greatest hitters of all time was a defensive specialist and not much of a hitter when he broke into the Negro Leagues. As Mays' father told Piper Davis before Mays was signed to the Barons, "Piper, he thinks he's Joe DiMaggio, but he can't hit a curveball none."[139]

"Well, he's got to learn by next season if he's gonna play with us."[140]

Eventually, he did learn. Mays had a .262 average his first year as a utility hitter, but only one home run and one stolen base. "What surprised us was that he developed all that power," Monte Irvin recalled. "He was not that big, but he was tremendously strong and coordinated."[141]

He played well in the league playoffs, when the Black Barons swept the Kansas City Monarchs in four games.[142] His bases-loaded single in the 11th inning gave the Barons a 5–4 win in the first game. He had three hits in the Barons' 6–5 win in Game Two.

In retrospect, that's not really all that surprising, considering the level of competition he had faced in high school and on the sandlots. He'd never seen pitching like the curveball and heat that a Negro League pitcher could bring. It took some time to adjust.

"Piper Davis helped him," Greason said. "A lot of fellows couldn't hit the curveball. If they pitch you right with the fastball, you didn't hit that either."

Under the tutelage of Piper Davis, Mays changed his stance to more directly face the pitcher. That gave him a better view of the curveball.

The youngster's average moved up to .311 in 1949. He played on the Barons team that faced the Jackie Robinson All-Stars in a barnstorming game in October 1949.[143] Mays was hitting .330 in 1950 before leaving the team.

Mays was spotted in 1950 by Giants scout Ed Montague. Montague had attended a Black Barons game to scout power-hitting first baseman Alonzo Perry.

Mays was impressed by Perry. When the Barons played a double-header in the Polo Grounds with the New York Cubans, Mays hit a home run, but Perry had three dingers for the day. "He was big and strong, and I was just a little guy compared to him," he recalled.[144]

"I had no inkling of Willie Mays," Montague later said.[145] Mays knew Montague was in the stands, because manager Piper Davis had alerted Mays to the visit. Mays, however, didn't expect to be signed because "he was not there to look at me."[146]

Mays left the Barons when owner Tom Hayes sold his contract to the New York Giants for $10,000. Hayes gave Mays $6,000 of the money,[147] and the young players joined the Giants' minor league team in Trenton.[148] The next year, he was promoted to the Minneapolis Millers of the Triple-A American Association. He stayed with Minneapolis for only 35 games, hitting .477 before the Giants called him to the major leagues.

Giants manager Leo Durocher made the decision to call up the 20-year-old after talking with Mays on the phone. There are, however, two different versions of the conversation that occurred. Mays had one version of the call that he recounted for *Birmingham News* reporter Doug Segrest. According to that version, Durocher asked Mays, "Can you hit .274 (in the majors)?"

Mays' response: "I can walk that."[149]

The second version of the call was based on Durocher's memory of the conversation. In this version, Mays was reluctant to join the Giants, so Durocher called the outfielder to encourage him.

"Why don't you want to come?" Durocher asked.

"I can't play that kind of ball," Mays replied. "I'm not ready for the big leagues."

"You're hitting .477 right now where you are," Durocher answered. "Hit half that for me, and I'll be satisfied."[150]

He made his major league debut on May 25, 1951, against the Philadelphia Phillies at Shibe Park. Davis described him as "young, scared and bewildered."[151] Maybe that's why he got off to an unimpressive start, going hitless in his first 12 at-bats.

He broke out of the slump with a home run off future Hall-of-Famer Warren Spahn. "I still say he let me hit the ball because I was 0-for-12 at the time," Mays told *Birmingham News* writer Doug Segrest.[152]

Mays went on to hit 20 home runs and win the Rookie of the Year award. His roommate, future Hall-of-Famer Monte Irvin, recalled that he helped the youngster adjust to the major leagues, at least briefly. "I became a sort of mentor to him," Irvin recalled. "Then after a while he taught me a few things. He had a special way about him of picking things up quickly."[153]

The Giants went on to win the National League pennant that year, coming from 13½ games back to catch the Dodgers. As Davis noted, "No small part of the inspiration of that onrushing Giant club came from the day-to-day heroics of the rookie centerfielder."[154]

The comeback was capped by Bobby Thomson's ninth-inning home run that defeated the Brooklyn Dodgers. Mays watched the blast from the on-deck circle, where he was waiting to bat next.

Mays missed the 1952 and 1953 seasons while serving in the military. He returned to the Giants in 1954, led the National League with a .345 batting average, and was named the league's Most Valuable Player.

Great achievements, but that's not what most people remember about that season. Instead, it was a play that occurred in the first game of the World Series, where the Giants were facing the Cleveland Indians. With the score tied late in the game, Cleveland's Vic Wertz hit a long drive to the deepest part of the Polo Grounds' center field. Mays raced toward the wall, made miraculous catch over his shoulder, then spun around and threw the ball back to the infield. The Giants went on to win the game and the Series, sweeping the Indians in four games.

The play became a part of baseball lore. Mays, though, typically dismisses the hoopla. "I made better catches than that," he told Segrest, "but that one happened to be in the World Series."[155]

Buck O'Neil wasn't surprised that Mays caught up with the ball on that play. "There were men faster than Willie Mays," O'Neil once said. "But I never saw one faster with a fly ball in the air."[156]

Regardless, after that play, Mays was a baseball legend. He spent parts of the next three decades adding to that legend with achievements that are too numerous to mention. He capped his career with election to the Baseball Hall of Fame in 1979 — his first year of eligibility.

He was baseball's first great five-tool star, a player who could run, field, throw, hit and hit with power. Further, "he not only did it all, he did it with a flair and a style seldom matched."[157]

But Mays and the Black Barons both know that it all started in Birmingham. Mays is open in his appreciation of the start he got from the Black Barons, crediting his Birmingham teammates with helping him make it to the major leagues.

In January 2007, he invited the four surviving teammates from the 1948 team — the Rev. William Greason, Jimmy Zapp, Sammy Williams, and Artie Wilson — to Los Angeles, where he commemorated their role in this career. "What they did for me, I'll never forget," Mays said. "Those four guys knew I could play baseball, and even though they were older than I was, they would say to me, 'You have a better chance of getting to the big leagues than we do, and we want to make sure you get there.' I want to give them as much credit as I possibly can."[158]

According to Mays, the Birmingham Black Barons "were good. Very good. How good I didn't appreciate until years later, when going into organized ball was almost easy for me, because I actually had been playing at a higher level with the Barons."[159]

Mays particularly gives credit to Davis, whom he has described as being "like a second father to me."[160]

"My education as a baseball player took on a new dimension under Piper," he also said.[162]

Despite his success, some folks say that Mays is still trying to come to grips with the discrimination that he faced as a youngster in baseball. Buck O'Neil once cautioned a photographer about getting too many personal shots of Mays.

"Careful around Willie, now," O'Neil told the photographer. "He has a lot of sadness and pain in him." When the photographer asked why, O'Neil answered, "Hard being everybody's hero, I suppose."[163]

"Wonderful Willie" Smith

Willie Smith broke into the major leagues as a pitcher with the Detroit Tigers on June 18, 1963. "Wonderful Willie" had a nine-year career in the major leagues, playing both in the outfield and on the mound for the Tigers, the Los Angeles Angels (1964–66), Cleveland Indians (1967–68), the Chicago Cubs (1968–1970) and the Cincinnati Reds (1971). His brief tenure with the Black Barons came as a pitcher in 1958.[164]

Smith was born February 11, 1939, in Anniston, Alabama. After signing with the Tigers, Smith was assigned to the minor leagues, where he picked up his nickname because of his dual role as both a hitter and a pitcher. He became "Wonderful Willie" during his 1963 season with Syracuse, where he hit for a .380 average and compiled a 14–2 record on the mound.

Those numbers earned him a promotion to the major leagues, where he appeared in 17 games for the Tigers in '63, 11 as a pitcher. He compiled a 1–0 record, a 4.57 ERA, and two saves on the mound. He had eight at-bats that season, with only one hit.

The Tigers traded Smith to the Angels for Julio Navarro at the beginning of the 1964 season. Smith was primarily an outfielder during his three seasons with the Angels, hitting .301 with 11 home runs and 51 RBIs in 1964. His most memorable game came against Cleveland on June 4, when he entered the contest as a pinch-hitter, played the outfield following his plate appearance, and then came on as a reliever in the eighth inning.

In 1965, Smith put together a .261 average, with 14 homers and 57 RBIs. His only stint as a pitcher for the Angels came in '64, appearing in 15 games while compiling a 1–4 record and a 2.84 ERA.

Smith was primarily a reserve outfielder for the Indians in 1967 and '68. He also made two appearances (for five innings) on the mound in '68 before being traded to the Chicago Cubs. He finished his pitching career with one stint on the mound for the Cubs that year, but continued to play in the outfield. He finished his career with 37 games as a reserve for Cincinnati in 1971.

Smith ended his major league career with a .248 lifetime average, 46 home runs, 211 RBIs, and 20 stolen bases. On the mound, he was 2–4 in 39 games, with a 3.10 ERA. He still holds the distinction of being the only African American major leaguer to appear in at least 20 games as both a pitcher and a fielder.

Smith died January 18, 2006, in Anniston.[165] He is buried in Anniston's Maple Grove Cemetery.

Smith was highly respected by his teammates. That opinion was summarized by former Cubs teammate Don Kessinger, who said, "I really thought the world of Willie Smith. Willie was an exceptional hitter, but he was also an exceptional person."[166]

In June 2006, Smith was posthumously inducted into the Calhoun County (Alabama) Hall of Fame.[167]

BOB VEALE

Bob Veale is best known for his years as a hard-throwing left-hander for the Pittsburgh Pirates.[168] He had a 13-year career in the major leagues, led the National League in strikeouts in 1964, and was a two-time all-star (1965–66). He finished his major league career with a lifetime strikeout ratio of 7.96 per nine innings — a number that still ranks fifth among all-time hurlers. In 2006, Bob Veale was inducted into the Alabama Sports Hall of Fame.

In a way, he got his start in baseball with the Birmingham Barons as a bat boy. And while it doesn't show up on any official records, Veale pitched one game in the Negro League.

Born October 28, 1935, in Birmingham, Veale built up his arm as a youngster by throwing bricks at turtles sunning on rocks around a nearby creek. His strong arm eventually developed as a hard-throwing pitcher. As he got a little older, he found he could make some extra money by chasing baseballs at Rickwood Field.

He would hunt down errant throws, foul balls, and home runs. When the Black Barons or visiting teams sought the balls, Veale would return them — for a price. "I remember many times at Rickwood when I was running balls, the Barons had to buy their balls back," he said. "We'd have them in a bag behind the ball park the next day. But we'd give 'em back to 'em — fifty cents a piece."[169]

The experience also gave him a chance to see some Negro League legends play. He particularly remembers the power in the bat of home run hitter Josh Gibson. "He was a behemoth," Veale said. "God gave Josh his strength like he gave it to Samson. I've seen pitchers throw at Josh's head, and he'd just lean back and knock it over the right field fence."[170]

He broke into organized baseball after working out for the St. Louis Cardinals.[171]

The Cardinals didn't sign him, but the Pittsburgh Pirates witnessed the tryout and signed him to a free agent contract on January 1, 1958.

Veale made a name for himself while still in the minor leagues.[172] On August 10, 1962, the 6'6", 210-pound left-hander struck out 22 batters while playing for Columbus in the International League. He went twelve innings and defeated the Buffalo Bisons, 6–5.

During this time, the switch-hitting pitcher also played in a game for the Black Barons. He did so, though, under an assumed name.

He made the Pirates and the major leagues in 1963, reporting early to spring training to enhance his chances.[173] He finished the season with 78 innings and only nine earned runs. Bill James noted that the numbers were identical to those that future Hall-of-Famer Rollie Fingers had that season.[174]

In 1964, he led the National League in strikeouts. In a September 30 game against the Cincinnati Reds, he struck out 16 batters in a 12-inning game.

In 1965, Veale was named to the All-Star Game and finished second in the league in strikeouts and tossed seven shutouts. One of those came in a June 1 game against the Phillies. He set a Pirates team record by striking out 16 players for the second time in a game — this time a regular nine-inning affair — as Pittsburgh beat Philadelphia, 4–0.

As Maraniss noted, Veale was quickly "emerging as [the Pirates] best pitcher."[175] He put together two more winning seasons in 1966 and 1967. In 1966, he was again named to the All-Star Game. He was also the winning pitcher in the Pirates' 7–5 win over the Chicago Cubs on September 2, 1966. The victory put the Pirates in first place for the season. By then, Veale was arguably the best left-hander in the National League.[176]

Veale was doing it almost entirely by throwing heat. His two best pitchers were simply identified as "his fastball and low fastball."[177] He also wore thick glasses while pitching, which was intimidating. Tim McCarver once noted that Veale "would open my eyes wide before he even threw his fastball — by wiping off his glasses with his bandana."[178] No wonder Koppett said that the Pirates pitchers were "led by the intimidating Bob Veale."[179]

Early in the 1967 season, he won a key game against the St. Louis Cardinals.[180] But danger signs were apparent in 1967, particularly when he gave up seven quick runs in a June game.[181] The problem was a simple injury — an injured back — that hampered his effectiveness.[182]

Three losing seasons followed from 1968 to 1970. By then, his injured back was increasing his control problems; he led the league in walks four times and had 90 or more walks in seven consecutive seasons (1964–1970). Initially, he discounted the wild spells, saying they were not important as long as he was winning.[183]

But it started catching up with him in '68. Critics complained that he was losing his stuff even before the season started.[184] By mid-season, they started noting that his fastball wasn't as fast as it used to be.[185]

Regardless, he still had his days. On September 14, 1968, Veale shut out the Mets, 6–0. And his fastball could still strike batters out. On August 8, 1969, he struck out ten in a 7–1 win over San Diego.

Veale moved to the Pirates' bullpen in 1971. It wasn't his first shot as a reliever.

The Pirates had previously used him successfully out of the bullpen for a brief stint in 1967.[186] Still, he posted a 6–0 record for the year and notched one victory in the 1971 World Series as the Pirates won the world championship.

He also helped to make history. On September 1, 1971, manager Harry "The Hat" Walker put together the first all-black lineup in major league history. Veale didn't start the game, but he did enter it as a reliever, becoming one of ten African American players to participate in the historic game.[187]

His 7.04 ERA scared the Pirates, though, and they sold him to the Boston Red Sox late in the 1972 season.[188] In 1973, he recorded 11 saves for the Red Sox.

Veale retired from the major leagues with a 13-year career in which he posted a 120–95 lifetime record and a 3.07 career ERA. He appeared in 397 games, with 255 of those appearances as a starting pitcher. Always an iron man, Veale pitched 78 complete games, including 20 shutouts. He also tallied a total of 21 saves as a reliever. Above all, he was "the Pirates best pitcher for years."[189]

He did it all with a toughness and mental attitude that he got from his grandfather, which he described to historian Cal Fussman. "My granddaddy had a third-grade education," he said. "He didn't let nobody walk over him. He figured like this: Better to go through life as a lion for one day than to go through an entire life as a sheep."[190]

Veale looks back on his days with the Barons and with the Pirates fondly, but with a touch of nostalgia. "We're a dying breed," Veale said. "It seems like it was yesterday when I was at Rickwood chasing balls, when I was at Pittsburgh throwing balls, when I was out on the creek knocking turtles off the rocks with bricks."[191]

ARTIE WILSON

One of the most talented players who ever put on a Black Barons uniform was Arthur Lee "Artie" Wilson. Wilson played for the Barons for five years—1944 to 1948. During that time, he helped the Barons to two pennants (1944, 1948), played in four East-West All-Star Games,[192] and won two batting titles. Former Barons pitcher Bill Powell once described him as "one of the best shortstops ever to put on a glove."[193]

Wilson's skills on the baseball field were obvious, so much so that he made it to the major leagues. Unfortunately, timing was against him. He was already 26 years old when Jackie Robinson broke the major league color barrier. It would be another four years before he got his shot at the majors. By then he was 30 and past his prime. Still, accolades about his skills continue.

Wilson was born October 28, 1920, in Springville, Alabama, near Birmingham. He taught himself to hit by playing with a broomstick and rubber ball, later progressing to a larger ball made by wrapping thread around an old golf ball.[194] At the age of 16, while still in school, he started working part-time at ACIPCO — the Alabama Cast Iron Pipe Company — and playing on the company's industrial league baseball team. He lost a thumb in an accident at the plant, but it seemed to have little impact on his baseball skills.

The shortstop broke into the Negro Leagues in 1944 with the Birmingham Black Barons. He played a major role in the Barons claiming the Negro American League pennant in 1944. He stayed with the team for five seasons, through their 1948 pennant-winning campaign.

Wilson was the lead-off hitter for the Barons. He filled the role superbly, hitting for a high average and stealing bases once he reached first. He was consistently among the league leaders in both hitting and stolen bases during his four years in the Negro Leagues.

In his rookie year of 1944, Wilson hit .344 and finished second in the race for the batting title. In 1945, he upped his average to .374 and again finished second in the batting race. He had an off-year in 1946, dropping to .288, but he rebounded in 1947 by winning the batting title with a .370 mark.

He did even better in the Barons' championship season of 1948, hitting .402 and again claiming the batting title. Wilson's .402 mark in '48 makes him the last player in organized baseball to compile a .400-plus batting average.

In his later years, Wilson said he was able to reach the mark because fans were paying little attention to the Negro Leagues by then. The feat would be harder in the major leagues, he noted, "because every sportswriter, every newspaper, they want to write something about it. If he was like me, I wouldn't even worry about reading the sports pages. If you're under pressure to try and hit .400, going after pitches when normally you'd take them, then you start slowing down."[195]

Wilson's achievements made him a popular addition to Satchel Paige's All-Stars team. The team barnstormed the country while competing against Bob Feller's All-Stars. It was first-class traveling, but also made sure that the segregated norms of the day were maintained. Each team had its own plane.

Wilson was also a superb defensive player. As James Riley noted, Wilson was "a superior defensive shortstop who was a master at the double play ... [and] ... was generally regarded as the best shortstop in black baseball during the '40s."[196]

"I don't believe I ever saw him strike out," former teammate Sam Williams recalled. "I can't remember a single time when he walked back to the dugout with the bat. He could always make contact." Statistics from the Negro League are incomplete, but Wilson's major league record notes that he had only one strikeout during that tenure.

Following the '48 Negro League season, Wilson went to Puerto Rico to become player-manager for the Mayaguez team. New York Yankee scout Tom Greenwade spotted Wilson there. At that point, the Yankees did not have an African American on their team. Wilson could have potentially changed that,[197] and Greenwade offered him a Triple-A contract for $500 a month. That was less than the $750 per month Wilson was making with the Black Barons, but he initially accepted the deal because it offered a chance to reach the major leagues.

While the Yankees negotiated with the Black Barons, Wilson changed his mind, asking for a higher salary and a portion of the sale price from the Barons. Instead, the deal was cancelled, apparently with the support of both Tom Hayes, Jr., owner of the Black Barons, and the Yankees' Larry MacPhail.

The Barons subsequently sold Wilson's contract to Abe Saperstein, owner of the Harlem Globetrotters. Saperstein used his own money to essentially get the rights to Wilson's contract, apparently with the intention of re-selling it to a major league team.[198]

When he heard of the deal, Cleveland Indians owner Bill Veeck flew to Puerto Rico, where Wilson was playing winter ball, and tried to sign Wilson to the Cleveland Indians.[199] Moffi and Kronstadt reported that Veeck had trouble locating Wilson and requested that the island's radio stations announce that he was seeking him. Wilson and Veeck eventually got together and a contract was signed.[200]

The move would have sent Wilson to the San Diego Padres in the Pacific Coast League.[201] However, Yankee owner George Weiss complained about the deal. Baseball commissioner Happy Chandler stepped in. On May 13, 1949, Chandler ordered the Indians to trade Wilson to the Yankees for outfielder Luis Marquez.[202]

Wilson was assigned to the Oakland Oaks in the Pacific Coast League, where he roomed with future Yankee legend Billy Martin. Martin had volunteered to be his roommate after the team had initially said he must room alone since he was the only black on the team.

Wilson quickly demonstrated his skill in the Pacific Coast League. In 1949, he led the league in stolen bases with 47 and hit .348, becoming the first player to win the PCL batting crown without hitting a home run. After the season was over, he returned to Birmingham to play with the Black Barons in an October exhibition game against the Jackie Robinson All-Stars.[203] Wilson returned to the Oaks in 1950 and had another good year. He rapped out a .312 average in 1950 and led the league in runs (168) and hits (264).

His defense was superb. Lefty O'Doul, then the manager for the San Francisco Seals, recalled a double-header between Oakland and the Seals in which Wilson started three double plays and was the middle man in a fourth. "You don't see shortstop played better by anybody than you saw it today, O'Doul said. "I spent a few years in the majors, but I never saw anything like the exhibition Wilson staged."[204] But O'Doul did develop a way to counter Wilson's hitting skills, an approach that would be adopted by major league teams.

A trade between the Yankees and Giants organization resulted in Wilson ending up on the Giants' minor league team in Newark, New Jersey, at the end of the 1950 season. He was added to the major league roster of the New York Giants in 1951.

Major league defenses, though, were ready for his left-handed, opposite-field hitting style. The Giants' National League opponents used the same approach that O'Doul had used when the San Francisco Seals had faced Wilson. They merely shifted their defenses to the third base side of second base. The Dodgers had the prototype defense, shifting Jackie Robinson, Pee Wee Reese and Billy Cox between second and third. Right fielder Carl Furillo came in to play second base. Gil Hodges stayed at first base.

The Dodgers were essentially daring Wilson to pull the ball to right field. He couldn't do it. As former teammate and manager Tommy Sampson recalled, "He couldn't hit the ball to right field. You throw the ball and he's gonna hit it to left field anyway, or he's gonna hit it to the shortstop. He was always running from the plate; he hit running."[205]

Wilson got only 22 major league at-bats, hitting just .182, before the Giants called Willie Mays to the majors and sent Wilson back to the minor leagues.[206] He spent the rest of the '51 season with three different minor league teams before settling back in the

Pacific Coast League and playing with Portland, Oakland, and Sacramento.[207] He batted .316 in 1952 while leading the PCL in hits. He improved to .332 in 1953 and to .336 in 1954, leading the league in triples and batting during both seasons.

For 1955, he still hit above .300, reaching a .307 mark, but he dropped below that level in 1956 with .293. He dropped another 30 points — to .263 — in 1954. By then he was 36 years old and his prime playing days were behind him. He never received a second shot at the major leagues, but simply remained buried in the minor leagues.[208]

In 1962, at the age of 41, he tried to make a comeback with Portland but didn't make the team. He concluded the season and his baseball career with Kennewick in the Northwest League.

Afterword

SAVING THE SOUL OF A NATION

They played for the love of the game, often making meager wages during the baseball season and seeking some other way of making a living during the offseason. Some became baseball vagabonds, playing in the Negro Leagues during the summer and moving to winter leagues in Florida, the Caribbean, or South America during the rest of the year, making a living that was comparable to white blue-collar workers of the day.[1]

Five former members of the Birmingham Black Barons are currently honored with enshrinement in the National Baseball Hall of Fame in Cooperstown, New York. One — Willie Mays — earned the honor on the basis of his career in the major leagues. The other four — Leroy "Satchel" Paige, Mule Suttles, Bill Foster, and Willie Wells — received enshrinement based on their career in the Negro Leagues. Two of those — Paige and Suttles — had significant careers with the Birmingham Black Barons. The other two — Foster and Wells — had award-winning careers, but most of their reputation was garnered from other teams. Still, they were once part of the Black Baron tradition. Foster joined the Barons early in his career, and it served as the foundation for his Hall-of-Fame career. Wells joined the Black Barons after his playing career was over, serving as the team's manager in 1954. He brought a Hall of Fame career to a team and used that to inspire young players. These ties to the Black Barons are important ones that should be acknowledged.

They missed out on the big paydays that later black athletes would get. Most didn't even make the comfortable living that white players of the day could make. Instead, they had to play because (1) they really liked to play baseball, (2) it was more fun than digging ditches, and (3) if they watched their pennies, they could make a little money.

But as Eig noted, post-war America was changing, both demographically and sociologically.[2] The times were almost ready for the two races to work and play together.

Almost. But not quite. The nation needed something to prove it could work. Jackie Robinson and the Negro Leagues provided the proof. As Donnie Harris once said, "Jackie Robinson just wanted to play baseball, but I think that the civil rights movement really began when he stepped on that field in 1947."[3] Like Robinson, the members of the Birmingham Black Barons played for the love of the game, but displayed talent that was equal to or greater than their white counterparts. The heroes of this book spent their baseball career in those transition years in which talent did not always lead to major league contracts or monetary rewards. But they played anyway.

Their goal was not to break down barriers, but merely to pursue a personal dream. But, in doing so, they helped save the soul of a nation.

Chapter Notes

Preface

1. Christopher D. Fullerton, *Every Other Sunday* (Birmingham, AL: R. Boozer Press, 1999), 47–48.

PART I
Introduction

1. Lawrence D. Hogan, *Shades of Glory: The Negro Leagues and the Story of African-American Baseball* (Washington, DC: National Geographic, 2006).
2. David W. Zang, *Fleet Walker's Divided Heart: The Life of Baseball's First Black Major Leaguer* (Lincoln: University of Nebraska Press, 1998).
3. Jules Tygiel, *Baseball Great Experiment: Jackie Robinson and His Legacy* (New York: Random House, 1983); Jonathan Eig, *Opening Day: The Story of Jackie Robinson's First Season* (New York: Simon & Schuster, 2007),16.
4. William F. McNeil, *Black Baseball Out of Season: Pay for Play Outside of the Negro Leagues* (Jefferson, NC: McFarland, 2007).
5. Donn Rogosin, *Invisible Men: Life in Baseball's Negro Leagues* (New York: Atheneum, 1983).
6. S. Smith, "Baseball's Forgotten Pioneers," *Sports Illustrated* 76 (12), March 30, 1992.
7. Cal Fussman, *After Jackie: Pride, Prejudice, and Baseball's Forgotten Heroes.* (New York: ESPN Books, 2007).
8. Harry Edwards, "Invisible Men: Life in Baseball's Negro Leagues/Baseball's Great Experiment: Jackie Robinson and His Legacy," *Journal of Sport & Social Issues* 9 (1) (1985): 41–43; H. Hersch, "The Indifference Line," *Sports Illustrated* 72(25), June 18, 1990.
9. Randy Horick, "They Might Have Been Heroes," *Nashville Scene*, May 2, 1996: 23–30.
10. Hogan, *Shades of Glory*.
11. A. Rust, *Get That Nigger off the Field* (New York: Delacorte Press, 1976).
12. Robert Peterson, *Only the Ball Was White: A History of the Legendary Black Players and All-Black Professional Teams* (New York: Gramercy, 1970).
13. Christopher Hauser, *The Negro Leagues Chronology: Events in Organized Black Baseball, 1920–1948* (Jefferson, NC: McFarland, 2006).
14. Leslie A. Heaphy, *The Negro Leagues, 1869–1960* (Jefferson, NC: McFarland, 2003).
15. Brent P. Kelley, *Voices from the Negro Leagues: Conversations with 52 Baseball Standouts of the Period 1924–1960* (Jefferson, NC: McFarland, 1998); Brent P. Kelley, *The Negro Leagues Revisited: Conversations with 66 More Baseball Heroes* (Jefferson, NC: McFarland, 2000); Brent P. Kelley, *"I Will Never Forget": Interviews with 39 Former Negro League Players* (Jefferson, NC: McFarland, 2003); William F. McNeil, *Baseball's Other All-Stars* (Jefferson, NC: McFarland, 2000); Nick Wilson, *Voices from the Pastime: Oral Histories of Surviving Major Leaguers, Negro Leaguers, Cuban Leaguers and Writers, 1920–1934* (Jefferson, NC: McFarland, 2000).
16. Mark Lowery, "Negro League Players to Be Honored," *Black Enterprise* 25 (4) November 1994: 26; Bruce Chadwick, *When the Game Was Black and White* (New York: Abbeville Press, 1993); Phil Dixon and Patrick J. Hannigan, *The Negro Baseball Leagues: A Photographic History* (Mattituck, NY: Amereon House, 1992); John B. Holway, *Blackball Stars: Negro League Pioneers* (New York: Carroll & Graf, 1988); Bill Plott, "The Southern League of Colored Base Ballists," *Baseball Research Journal* (Cleveland, OH: Society for American Baseball Research, 1974); "Once They Were Kings," *Mudville Magazine: The Voice of Baseball* (May 2003): 2.
17. Ann Brown and Valerie Lynn Gray, Valerie Lynn "Black Museums Worth a Summer Visit," *Black Enterprise,* 28(11) June 1998: 336; Katherine House, "Jazz and Baseball in Kansas City," *New York Times*, February 15, 1998.
18. Rod Beaton, "Negro Leagues Museum Returns to Its Roots," *USA Today*, February 12, 2004, Sports: 10C.
19. Paul Gutierrez, "Up-To-Date in Kansas City," *Sports Illustrated* 88(1) January 12, 1998, 100.
20. Leslie A. Heaphy, ed., *Black Baseball and Chicago: Essays on the Players, Teams and Games of the Negro Leagues' Most Important City* (Jefferson, NC: McFarland, 2006); Paul DeBono, *The Chicago American Giants* (Jefferson, NC: McFarland, 2007).
21. Brad Snyder, *Beyond the Shadow of the Senators The Untold Story of the Homestead Grays and the Integration of Baseball* (New York: McGraw-Hill, 2003).
22. Darrell J. Howard, *Sunday Coming: Black Baseball in Virginia* (Jefferson, NC: McFarland, 2002).

23. Fullerton, *Every Other Sunday.*
24. Evan St. Lifer and Michael Rogers, "Birmingham Discovers Greatness," *Library Journal,* 120(8) (1995).

Chapter 1

1. Snyder, *Beyond the Shadow of the Senators.*
2. William Landson, "Ten Things You Never Knew About the Negro Leagues" *Sport,* December 1994, 17.
3. Fullerton, *Every Other Sunday,* 47–48, 23.
4. Charles Einstein, *Willie's Time: Baseball's Golden Age* (Peoria: Southern Illinois University Press, 1979): 304.
5. Fullerton, *Every Other Sunday,* 36.
6. *Ibid.,* 37.
7. William C. Rhoden. *$40 Million Slaves: The Rise, Fall, and Redemption of the Black Athlete* (New York: Crown, 2006).
8. Jacquelyn Hall, et al., *Like a Family: The Making of a Southern Cotton Mill World* (Chapel Hill: University of North Carolina Press, 1987); Margorie White, *The Birmingham District: An Industrial History and Guide* (Birmingham: Birmingham Historical Society, 1981); Robert J. Norrell, "Caste in Steel: Jim Crow Careers in Birmingham, Alabama," *Journal of American History* 73, (December 1986): 669–692.
9. Tim Cary, "Slidin' and Ridin': At Home with the 1948 Birmingham Black Barons," *Alabama History* (Fall 1986): 23.
10. Timothy Whitt, *Bases Loaded with History: The Story of Rickwood Field, America's Oldest Baseball Park* (Birmingham: R Boozer Press, 1995).
11. W.C. Kashatus, *Diamonds in the Coalfields: 21 Remarkable Baseball Players, Managers, and Umpires from Northeast Pennsylvania* (Jefferson, NC: McFarland, 2002).
12. Thomas K. Perry, *Textile League Baseball: South Carolina's Mill Teams, 1880–1955* (Jefferson, NC: McFarland, 2004); R.G. Utley and Scott Verner, *The Independent Carolina Baseball League, 1936–1938* (Jefferson, NC: McFarland, 2005).
13. James A. Riley, *The Biographical Encyclopedia of the Negro Baseball Leagues* (New York: Carroll & Graf, 1994).
14. *Ibid.*
15. *Ibid.*
16. Robert Charles Cottrell, *The Best Pitcher in Baseball: The Life of Rube Foster, Negro League Giant* (New York: New York University Press, 2001); Frank Holway, "Bill Foster," *Black Sports,* 3(9), (March 1974): 58–60; John B. Holway, "Rube Foster: Father of Black Game," *Sporting News,* 187(1) (January 6, 1979): 45; Charles E. Whitehead, *A Man and His Diamonds: A Story of the Great Andrew (Rube) Foster, the Outstanding Team He Owned and Managed, and the Superb League He Founded and Commissioned* (New York: Vantage Press, 1980).
17. Riley, *The Biographical Encyclopedia of the Negro Baseball Leagues.*
18. Donald Dewey and Nicholas Acocella, *The New Biographical History of Baseball* (Chicago: Triumph, 2002): 136.
19. Bill James, *The New Bill James Historical Baseball Abstract* (New York: Free Press, 2001): 191.
20. Don Jensen, *The Timeline History of Baseball* (New York: Palgrave McMillan, 2005): 7.
21. Peterson, *Only the Ball Was White.*
22. *Ibid.*
23. John B. Holway, *Voices from the Great Black Baseball Leagues* (New York: Da Capo Press, 1992); John Holway, "Hall Must Revive Negro League Committee," *USA Today Baseball Weekly,* May 6, 1992, 66; John B. Holway, "More Negro Leaguers for the Hall," *The National Pastime, Vol. 15* (Cleveland: Society for American Baseball Research, 1995): 91–95.
24. John B. Holway, "Negro League Great Bill Foster Finally Gets His Chance," *Sports Collectors Digest,* June 21, 1996; "Negro Leagues Pitcher William Foster Inducted in Baseball Hall of Fame," *Jet,* August 26, 1996.
25. Riley, *The Biographical Encyclopedia of the Negro Baseball Leagues.*
26. *Ibid.*
27. *Ibid.*
28. Peterson, *Only the Ball Was White.*
29. Dewey and Acocella, *The New Biographical History of Baseball,* 319.
30. Mac Davis, *Baseball's All-Time Greats: The Top 50 Players* (New York: Bantam, 1970).
31. Jeff Kisseloff, *Who Is Baseball's Greatest Pitcher?* (Chicago: Carus Books, 2003).
32. Mark Ribowsky, *Don't Look Back: Satchel Paige in the Shadows of Baseball* (New York: De Capo Press, 2000).
33. *Ibid.,* 53.
34. *Ibid.*
35. *Ibid.*
36. *Ibid.*
37. Leroy Paige and David Lipman, *Maybe I'll Pitch Forever* (Lincoln: University of Nebraska Press, 1993): 50.
38. *Ibid.,* 47.
39. *Ibid.*
40. Ribowsky, *Don't Look Back,* 53.
41. Paige, *Maybe I'll Pitch Forever,* 48.
42. *Ibid.,* 53.
43. *Ibid.*
44. Ribowsky, *Don't Look Back,* 52.
45. Paige, *Maybe I'll Pitch Forever,* 47.
46. Ribowsky, *Don't Look Back*; Joe Cuhaj and Tamara Carraway-Hinckle, *Baseball in Mobile* (Charleston, SC: Arcadia, 2003); Larry Powell, *At the Plate and on the Mound: Profiles from Baseball's Past* (San Jose, CA: Writer's Showcase, 2001).
47. Paige, *Maybe I'll Pitch Forever.*
48. *Ibid.*
49. *Ibid.*
50. *Ibid.*
51. *Ibid.*
52. *Ibid.*
53. *Ibid.*
54. Randy Horick, "They Might Have Been Heroes," *Nashville Scene,* May 2, 1996, 23–30.
55. Paige, *Maybe I'll Pitch Forever.*
56. Ryan Chamberlain, "SABR Nine Questions," *SABR Bulletin,* 37(1), (2007): 6–7.
57. Richard Goldstein, "Ted Radcliffe, Star of the Negro Leagues, Is Dead at 103," *New York Times,* August 12, 2005, A17.
58. Paige, *Maybe I'll Pitch Forever.*
59. *Ibid.*

60. Cal Fussman, *After Jackie: Pride, Prejudice, and Baseball's Forgotten Heroes* (New York: ESPN Books, 2007).
61. James (Red) Moore, "Baseball's Oldest Rookie," *Newsweek*, October 25, 1999, 50.
62. Paige, *Maybe I'll Pitch Forever*.
63. Chamberlain, "SABR Nine Questions."
64. *Ibid*.
65. Paige, *Maybe I'll Pitch Forever*.
66. Michael Bamberger, "Man of a Century," *Sports Illustrated*, July 15, 2002, 128–132.
67. Paige, *Maybe I'll Pitch Forever*.
68. Paige, *Maybe I'll Pitch Forever*.
69. *Ibid*.
70. *Ibid*.
71. Dewey and Acocella, *The New Biographical History of Baseball*, 320–321.
72. Bob Motley, *Ruling Over Monarchs, Giants, & Stars: Umpiring in the Negro Leagues & Beyond* (Champaign, IL: Sports Publishing, 2007): 84.
73. John Holway, *The Complete Book of Baseball's Negro Leagues: The Other Half of Baseball History* (Fern Park, FL: Hastings House, 2001).
74. Riley, *The Biographical Encyclopedia of the Negro Baseball Leagues*.
75. John B. Holway, "Harry Salmon, Black Diamond of the Coal Mines," *Black Sports*, November 1974.
76. Joe Posnanski, *The Soul of Baseball: A Road Trip Through Buck O'Neil's America* (New York: Morrow, 2007), 165.
77. Riley, *The Biographical Encyclopedia of the Negro Baseball Leagues*, 753–755.
78. Holway, *The Complete Book of Baseball's Negro Leagues*.
79. *Ibid*.
80. *Ibid*.
81. Larry Lester, *Black Baseball's National Showcase: The East-West All-Star Game, 1933–1953* (Lincoln: University of Nebraska Press, 2002).
82. *Ibid*.
83. John B. Holway, "Not All Stars Were White," *Sporting News*, August 2, 1983; John B. Holway, *Blackball Stars: Negro League Pioneers* (New York: Carroll & Graf, 1992).
84. Ed Harris, "At It Again," *Black Writers/Black Baseball: An Anthology of Articles from Black Sportswriters Who Covered the Negro Leagues* (Jefferson, NC: McFarland, 2007): 148–49.
85. Riley, *The Biographical Encyclopedia of the Negro Baseball Leagues*.
86. Holway, *The Complete Book of Baseball's Negro Leagues*.
87. *Ibid*.
88. William McNeil, *The California Winter League: America's First Integrated Professional Baseball League* (Jefferson, NC: McFarland, 2002).
89. Lawrence D. Hogan, *Shades of Glory: The Negro Leagues and the Story of African-American Baseball* (Washington, DC: National Geographic, 2006): 232.
90. John B. Holway, "More Negro Leaguers for the Hall," *The National Pastime*, Vol. 15 (Cleveland, OH: Society For American Baseball Research, 1995): 91–95.
91. "The Speedy Mule Suttles," *Our Sports*, 1(3), (July 1953): 72.
92. Riley, *The Biographical Encyclopedia of the Negro Baseball Leagues*.

Chapter 2

1. Fullerton, Christopher D. *Every Other Sunday* (Birmingham, AL: R. Boozer, 1999).
2. Moffi, Larry and Jonathan Kronstadt. *Crossing the Line: Black Major Leaguers, 1947–1959* (Lincoln: University of Nebraska, 1994): 11.
3. Kelley, Brent. *The Negro Leagues Revisited: Conversations with 66 More Baseball Interviews* (Jefferson, NC: McFarland, 2000): 126.
4. *Ibid*., 96.
5. Lester, Larry and Sammy J. Miller. *Black Baseball in Pittsburgh* (Charleston, SC: Arcadia, 2001).
6. Snyder, Brad. *Beyond the Shadow of the Senators: The Untold Story of the Homestead Grays and the Integration of Baseball* (New York: McGraw-Hill, 2003).
7. Smith, Curtis. *What Baseball Means to Me: A Celebration of Our National Pastime* (New York: Warner, 2002): 121.
8. Snyder, *Beyond the Shadow of the Senators*.
9. Riley, James A. *The Biographical Encyclopedia of the Negro Baseball Leagues* (New York: Carroll & Graf, 1994).
10. Kelley, *The Negro Leagues Revisited*, 184.
11. Snyder, *Beyond the Shadow of the Senators*.
12. *Ibid*.
13. Canada, Jim, with J.B. Holway. "Discoverer of Willie Mays." *Sports Quarterly*, June 1972.
14. Powell, Larry. Interview with Oliver Ferguson (Birmingham, AL, 2007).
15. Riley, *Biographical Encyclopedia of the Negro Baseball Leagues*.
16. *Ibid*.
17. *Ibid*.
18. *Ibid*.
19. *Ibid*.
20. *Ibid*.
21. *Ibid*.

Chapter 3

1. Fullerton, *Every Other Sunday*.
2. John B. Holway, *Voices from the Great Black Baseball Leagues* (New York: De Capo Press, 1992): 182.
3. Ed Krzemienski, "On the Initial Sack," *Nine: A Journal of Baseball History & Culture*, 14(2), (2006): 59–67.
4. Lester, *Black Baseball's National Showcase*.
5. Barry Swanton, *The Mandak League: Haven for Former Negro League Ballplayers, 1950–1957* (Jefferson, NC: McFarland, 2006).
6. Riley, *The Biographical Encyclopedia of the Negro Baseball Leagues*, 95–96.
7. Kelley, *The Negro Leagues Revisited*, 125.
8. Kyle McNary, "Negro Leaguer of the Month: Lyman Bostock, Sr.," *Pitch Black Baseball* (March 2005).
9. "Lyman W. Bostock," *Birmingham News*, June 30, 2005.
10. Tony McClean, "Remembering Lyman Bostock," *BASN Focus on History*, May 11, 2004.
11. Steven Travers, *Angels Essentials: Everything You Need to Know to Be a Real Fan* (Chicago: Triumph Books, 2007).
12. F. Russo and G. Racz, *Bury My Heart at Cooperstown: Salacious, Sad, and Surreal Deaths in the History of Baseball* (Chicago: Triumph Books, 2006).

13. Riley, *The Biographical Encyclopedia of the Negro Baseball Leagues*, 156.
14. *Ibid.*
15. Ted Radcliffe and John B. Holway, "Better Than the Majors," *Chicago Sun-Times Midwest Magazine*, July 11, 1971.
16. Kyle P. McNary, *Ted "Double Duty" Radcliffe: 36 Years of Pitching and Catching in Baseball's Negro Leagues* (McNary, 1995).
17. Michael Bamberger, "Man of a Century," *Sports Illustrated*, July 15, 2002: 128–132.
18. Riley, *The Biographical Encyclopedia of the Negro Baseball Leagues*, 684.
19. Lester, *The East-West All-Star Game*.
20. Holway, *Voices from the Great Black Baseball Leagues*.
21. Janet Bruce, *The Kansas City Monarchs: Champions of Black Baseball* (Lawrence: University of Kansas Press, 1985).
22. Motley, *Ruling over Monarchs, Giants, & Stars*, 89.
23. James Peter Rubin, "Now Pitching for Schaumburg: The Oldest Player in Pro Baseball," *Wall Street Journal*, April 5, 1999, B1.
24. "'Double-Duty' to Throw Out First Pitch," *Birmingham News*, July 22, 2005, 8D.
25. Richard Goldstein, "Ted Radcliffe, Star of the Negro Leagues, Is Dead at 103," *New York Times*, August 12, 2005, A17.
26. Holway, "Harry Salmon."
27. Riley, *The Biographical Encyclopedia of the Negro Baseball Leagues*.
28. "Former Negro League Player Spencer Dies," *Washington Post*, May 22, 2003.
29. Krzemienski, "On the Initial Sack."
30. Ben Green, *Spinning the Globe: The Rise, Fall and Return to Greatness of the Harlem Globetrotters* (New York: HarperCollins, 2005): 2.
31. George Vecsey, *The Harlem Globetrotters*, (New York: Scholastic, 1970).
32. Green, *Spinning the Glove*, 152–153.
33. Riley, *The Biographical Encyclopedia of the Negro Baseball Leagues*.
34. *Ibid.*
35. Vicki McClure, "Young Inspired Others," *Birmingham News*, August 18, 2002, 18A.
36. Kelley, "*I Will Never Forget*," 185.
37. McClure, "Young Inspired Others."
38. Kelley, "*I Will Never Forget*," 185.
39. McClure, "Young Inspired Others."

Part II

Introduction

1. Cary, "Slidin' and Ridin'," 23.
2. Hauser, *The Negro Leagues Chronology*.
3. Will Pascoe, *A Noble Game: A History of the Negro Leagues* (Charleston, SC: BookSurge, 2006).
4. R. Lavally, *Rights and Fights: An Analysis of the Social Movement That Led to Harry Truman's Order to Desegregate the U.S. Military*. Paper presented at the annual meeting of the National Communication Association. San Antonio, TX (2006).
5. Jarrett Bell, "Trailblazer with Stories," *USA Today*, November 22, 2006, 1C-2C.
6. Hogan, *Shades of Glory*.
7. "Jackie Robinson's All-Stars to Meet Black Barons Tonight," *Birmingham World*, October 18, 1949.
8. "Jackie Robinson's All-Stars Win Over Black Barons, 9–3," *Birmingham World*, October 21, 1949.
9. Ben Cook, *Good Wood* (Birmingham, AL: R. Boozer Press; 1995.)
10. Neil Lanctot, *Negro League Baseball: The Rise and Ruin of a Black Institution* (Philadelphia: University of Pennsylvania Press, 2004); John B. Holway, "Branch Rickey and the Destruction of Black Baseball," *The Village Voice*, October 18, 1984.
11. Fullerton, *Every Other Sunday*, 88.
12. Lowry, *Green Cathedrals*.
13. R. Swaine, *The Black Stars Who Made Baseball Whole: The Jackie Robinson Generation in the Major Leagues, 1947–1959* (Jefferson, NC: McFarland, 2006); David Q. Voight, *America Through Baseball* (Chicago: Nelson Hall, 1976).
14. Fullerton, *Every Other Sunday*, 90.
15. Mel Antonen, "Honored," *USA Today*, January 5, 2007, 6C.
16. Rob Trucks, *Cup of Coffee: The Very Short Careers of Eighteen Major League Pitchers* (New York: Smallmouth Press, 2002).
17. Fussman, *After Jackie*, 79.
18. Fullerton, *Every Other Sunday*, 91–92.
19. Larry Moffi and Jonathan Kronstadt, *Crossing the Line: Black Major Leaguers, 1947–1959* (Lincoln: University of Nebraska Press, 1994).
20. Watson Spoelstra, "Ike Brown Tigers' Jack-of-All-Trades," *Sporting News*, June 5, 1971, 12.
21. Peterson, *Only the Ball Was White*, 203.
22. *Ibid.*
23. Kelley, "*I Will Never Forget*."
24. Snyder, *Beyond the Shadow*.
25. Peter C. Bjarkman, *A History of Cuban Baseball, 1864–2006* (Jefferson, NC: McFarland, 2007).
26. Swanton, *The Mandak League*.
27. Fullerton, *Every Other Sunday*, vi–vii.
28. Heaphy, *The Negro Leagues, 1869–1960*.
29. William A. Nunneley, *Bull Connor* (Tuscaloosa: University of Alabama Press, 1991).
30. Fullerton, *Every Other Sunday*, 23.
31. Fussman, *After Jackie*.
32. David Falkner, *Great Time Coming: The Life of Jackie Robinson from Baseball to Birmingham* (New York: Touchstone, 1995).
33. Fullerton, *Every Other Sunday*, iv–v.
34. Fullerton, *Every Other Sunday*, ix.

Chapter 4

1. W.C. Madden and Patrick J. Stewart, *The Western League: A Baseball History, 1885 through 1999* (Jefferson, NC: McFarland, 2002).
2. Riley, *The Biographical Encyclopedia of the Negro Baseball Leagues*.
3. Fullerton, *Every Other Sunday*.
4. Kelley, *The Negro Leagues Revisited*, 56.
5. Riley, *The Biographical Encyclopedia of the Negro Baseball Leagues*.
6. Kelley, "*I Will Never Forget*," 185.
7. Kelley, *Voices from the Negro Leagues*, 281–282.
8. Riley, *The Biographical Encyclopedia of the Negro Baseball Leagues*.
9. *Ibid.*

10. W.C. Madden, *Baseball in Indianapolis* (Charleston, SC: Arcadia, 2003).
11. Larry Powell, interview with Cleophus Brown, Birmingham, AL. Other quotes from that interview appear elsewhere in his chapter.
12. Karen Lingo, "Alabama People and Places: Still in the Game," *Southern Living*, April 2006, 28–31.
13. Riley, *The Biographical Encyclopedia of the Negro Baseball Leagues*, 134.
14. Kelley, *Voices from the Negro Leagues*, 317.
15. Jimmy Bryan, "Glove Man Johnnie Cowan Remembered Fondly by Peers," *Birmingham News*, October 30, 1993, 1C, 9C.
16. *Ibid.*, 1C.
17. *Ibid.*, 9C.
18. *Ibid.*
19. *Ibid.*
20. Riley, *The Biographical Encyclopedia of the Negro Baseball Leagues*, 202.
21. Larry Powell, interview with Willie Curry, Birmingham, AL.
22. "Willie 'Boo Jack' Curry," *Birmingham News*, December 21, 2007.
23. Elizabeth Wallace, *Baseball in Colorado Springs* (Charleston, SC: Arcadia, 2003).
24. Kelley, "*I Will Never Forget,*" 43.
25. *Ibid.*, 43–44.
26. *Ibid.*, 43.
27. Larry Powell, interview with Henry Elmore, Birmingham, AL.
28. Sims, "Valvemen."
29. Sims, "Stockham Valvemen '65 Champions," *Stockham Bulletin*, 1965.
30. Powell, interview with Elijah Gilliam, Birmingham, AL.
31. "Elijah 'Slim' Gilliam, Sr.," *Birmingham News*, July 8, 2004.
32. Joel Hawkins, *The House of David Baseball Team* (Charleston, SC: Arcadia, 2002).
33. Fullerton, *Every Other Sunday*.
34. "Luis Charles Gillis, Sr.," *Birmingham News*, February 6, 2005.
35. Lester, *Black Baseball's National Showcase*.
36. Larry Powell, interview with Willie Harris, Birmingham, AL. Subsequent quotes from Willie Harris are from that interview.
37. Steve Penn and Tony Rizzo, "Special Players Relive Their Diamond Glory," *Kansas City Star*, November 2, 1997.
38. "Mr. Willie Harris," *Birmingham News*, January 13, 2006.
39. "Homegoing Celebration for Henry Fredo Howell," 45th Street Baptist Church Birmingham, AL, May 8, 1999.
40. Larry Powell, interview with James Ivory, Birmingham, AL, 2004.
41. Sims, "Stockham Valvemen '65 Champions."
42. Sims, "Valvemen."
43. Riley, *The Biographical Encyclopedia of the Negro Baseball Leagues*.
44. "Mr. Fayte Jones, Jr.," *Birmingham News*, March 4, 1999.
45. Riley, *The Biographical Encyclopedia of the Negro Baseball Leagues*, 463.
46. Randy Horick, "They Might Have Been Heroes," *Nashville Scene*, May 2, 1996, 23–30.
47. Kelley, *Voice from the Negro Leagues*, 317.
48. Riley, *The Biographical Encyclopedia of the Negro Baseball Leagues*.
49. Larry Powell, interview with Elmer Knox, Birmingham, AL, 2004.
50. Holly Crenshaw, "Elmer Knox, Negro Leagues Outfielder, Hobby Historian," *Atlanta Journal-Constitution*, November 18, 2007, E15.
51. *Ibid.*
52. *Ibid.*
53. Scott Kaufmann, "John "Blue Moon" Odom," *USA Today Baseball Weekly*, April 20, 1994, 38.
54. Larry Powell, interview with Leroy Miller, Birmingham, AL, 2005.
55. Lingo, "Still in the Game," 28–31.
56. "Willie Lee Patterson, Jr.," *Birmingham News*, August 27, 2004.
57. "Negro Leagues Player Pat Patterson Dies," *Mobile Register*, August 24, 2004.
58. C. Ray Hall, "Hits and Misses," *Louisville Courier-Journal Scene*, January 10, 1998, 12–14.
59. *Ibid.*, 12.
60. *Ibid.*
61. *Ibid.*
62. Riley, *The Biographical Encyclopedia of the Negro Baseball Leagues*.
63. *Ibid.*
64. Charley Pride, comments at the annual banquet of the Alabama Negro League Association, Birmingham, AL, 2005.
65. Kelley, *The Negro Leagues Revisited*, 115.
66. Fussman, *After Jackie*, 145.
67. *Ibid.*, 145–146.
68. Joe Posnanski, *The Soul of Baseball: A Road Trip through Buck O'Neil's America* (New York: William Morrow, 2007): 42.
69. Kelley, *The Negro Leagues Revisited*, 123.
70. *Ibid.*
71. *Ibid.*, 124.
72. *Ibid.*
73. *Ibid.*, 125.
74. *Ibid.*, 127.
75. Riley, *The Biographical Encyclopedia of the Negro Baseball Leagues*, 648–650.
76. Kelley, *The Negro Leagues Revisited*, 127.
77. *Ibid.*, 125.
78. Riley, *The Biographical Encyclopedia of the Negro Baseball Leagues*.
79. Kelley, *The Negro Leagues Revisited*, 356–359.
80. *Ibid.*, 356.
81. Larry Powell, interview with Eugene Scruggs, Birmingham, AL, 2005.
82. Kelley, "*I Will Never Forget,*" 154.
83. *Ibid.*, 155.
84. Kelley, *The Negro Leagues Revisited*, 357.
85. *Ibid.*
86. *Ibid.*, 357–358.
87. Kelley, "*I Will Never Forget,*" 155.
88. Kelley, *The Negro Leagues Revisited*, 358.
89. *Ibid.*
90. *Ibid.*, 359.
91. Kelley, "*I Will Never Forget,*" 157.
92. *Ibid.*
93. *Ibid.*, 154.
94. *Ibid.*, 286.
95. Riley, *The Biographical Encyclopedia of the Negro Baseball Leagues*.

96. *Ibid.*
97. Kelley, *Voices from the Negro Leagues,* 286.
98. Riley, *The Biographical Encyclopedia of the Negro Baseball Leagues.*
99. *Ibid.*
100. Larry Powell, interview with Robert Underwood, Birmingham, AL, 2004.
101. Riley, *The Biographical Encyclopedia of the Negro Baseball Leagues,* 648–650.
102. Dewey and Acocella, *The New Biographical History of Baseball,* 450.
103. John B. Holway, "Negro League Veterans Pick An All-Time Team," *Sporting News,* July 5, 1982, 37; Monte Irvin and Richard Watt, "Negro League All-Stars," *Sport* February 1984, 18.
104. Peterson, *Only the Ball Was White,* 234.
105. Riley, *The Biographical Encyclopedia of the Negro Baseball Leagues.*
106. Riley, *The Biographical Encyclopedia of the Negro Baseball Leagues*; Bob Rives, *Baseball in Wichita* (Charleston, SC: Arcadia, 2004).
107. Larry Lester, Sammy J. Miller and Dick Clark, *Black Baseball in Detroit* (Charleston, SC: Arcadia, 2000).
108. Larry Lester, Sammy J. Miller and Dick Clark, *Black Baseball in Chicago* (Charleston, SC: Arcadia, 2000).
109. Robert Cvornyek, *Baseball in Newark* (Charleston, SC: Arcadia, 2003).
110. "William (Bill) Byrd," *Sporting News,* January 28, 1991, 48.
111. John B. Holway, "Willie Wells: A Devil of a Shortstop," *Baseball Research Journal* (Cleveland, OH: Society for American Baseball Research, 1988): 50–53; Wendell Smith, "Introducing 'El Diablo' Wells of Mexico," *Pittsburgh Courier,* May 6, 1944; James A. Riley, *Dandy, Day, and the Devil* (Cocoa, FL: TK Publishers, 1987).
112. Willie Wells and John B. Holway, "'Devil' of an Infielder." *Black Sports Magazine,* 1983; John B. Holway, "Negro League 'Devil' Showed 40–40 Ability," *Chicago Tribune,* March 9, 1997; "Willie Wells, 82, Dies; Star in Negro Leagues," *New York Times,* January 25, 1989.
113. Posnanski, *The Soul of Baseball.*
114. Riley, *The Biographical Encyclopedia of the Negro Baseball Leagues.*
115. David Falkner, *Great Time Coming: The Life of Jackie Robinson from Baseball to Birmingham* (New York: Touchstone, 1995).
116. Madden, *Baseball in Indianapolis.*
117. Kelley, *The Negro Leagues Revisited,* 119.
118. James, *The New Bill James Historical Abstract,* 184.
119. Floyd Connors, *Baseball's Most Wanted: The Top 10 Book of the National Pastime's Outrageous Offenders, Lucky Bounces, and Other Oddities* (Dulles, VA: Brassey's, 2000): 45.
120. "Hall of Fame Inductees," *USA Today Baseball Weekly,* July 30, 1997, 7; "Negro League Player Willie Wells Selected for Induction into Baseball Hall of Fame—National Baseball Hall of Fame and Museum," *Jet,* March 24, 1997.
121. John B. Holway, "More Negro Leaguers for the Hall," *The National Pastime, Vol. 15* (Cleveland: Society For American Baseball Research, 1995): 91–95; John B. Holway, "For Wells, Hall Door Finally Opens," *Washington Post,* March 9, 1997.
122. Wells, 82.
123. Larry Powell, interview with Archie Young, Birmingham, AL, 2004.
124. Fullerton, *Every Other Sunday.*
125. *Ibid.*

Chapter 5

1. "Otha Bailey," *Sports Collectors Digest,* January 24, 1997.
2. Larry Powell, interview with Jessie Mitchell, Birmingham, AL, 2004.
3. Posnanski, *The Soul of Baseball,* 195.
4. *Ibid.*
5. Kelley, *Voices from the Negro Leagues,* 277–280.
6. *Ibid.,* 279.
7. *Ibid.,* 277.
8. *Ibid.,* 280.
9. Larry Powell, interview with Carl Holden, Birmingham, AL, 2005. Subsequent quotes by Holden are from that interview.
10. Kelley, *"I Will Never Forget,"* 85.
11. *Ibid.,* 86.
12. John Eisenberg, *From 33rd Street to Camden Yards: An Oral History of the Baltimore Orioles* (New York: Contemporary Books, 2001).
13. Kelley, *The Negro Leagues Revisited,* 86.
14. Larry Powell, interview with Tony Lloyd, Birmingham, AL, 2004. Other quotes by Tony Lloyd are from that interview.
15. C.V. Woodward, *The Strange Career of Jim Crow* (New York: Oxford University Press, 1974).
16. Fullerton, *Every Other Sunday,* 61.
17. Kelley, *"I Will Never Forget,"* 130.
18. Larry Powell, interview with John Mitchell. Birmingham, AL, 2006. Other quotes are from that inter-view.
19. Kelley, *"I Will Never Forget,"* 131.
20. *Ibid.*

Chapter 6

1. Larry Marthey, "Why Do Negro Stars Get Buried in the Minors?" *Our World,* October 1953.
2. Riley, *The Biographical Encyclopedia of the Negro Baseball Leagues.*
3. Swanton, *The Mandak League.*
4. Cathy Adams, "For Love of the Game," *Portico* (July/August 2002): 44–48.
5. Christopher D. Fullerton, *Every Other Sunday: Interviews with the Birmingham Black Barons* (University of Mississippi: Southern Voices CD).
6. Adams, "For Love of the Game," 45.
7. *Ibid.*
8. *Ibid.,* 45–46.
9. *Ibid.,* 46.
10. *Ibid.*
11. *Ibid.,* 47.
12. *Ibid.,* 48.
13. Larry Powell, interview with Earnest Harris, Birmingham, AL, 2004. Other quotes from Mr. Harris are from the same interview.
14. Heaphy, *The Negro Leagues, 1869–1960.*
15. Mark Langill, *The Los Angeles Dodgers* (Charleston, SC: Arcadia, 2004).

16. Kelley, *"I Will Never Forget,"* 114–116.
17. *Ibid.*
18. *Ibid.*, 115.
19. *Ibid.*, 114.
20. *Ibid.*
21. *Ibid.*
22. *Ibid.*, 115.
23. *Ibid.*, 116.
24. Kelley, *The Negro Leagues Revisited*, 303–308.
25. Larry Powell, interview with Carl Long, Birmingham, AL, 2008.
26. Kelly, *The Negro Leagues Revisited*.
27. *Ibid.*
28. Powell, Carl Long.
29. *Ibid.*
30. Kelley, *The Negro Leagues Revisited*.
31. Larry Powell, interview with Jessie Mitchell, Birmingham, AL, 2004. Other quotations from Jessie Mitchell are from this same interview.
32. Lingo, "Still in the Game," 28–31.
33. Sims, "Stockham Valvemen '65 Champions."
34. Sims, "Valvemen."
35. "They're Pro Ball Players," *The Rebel Review*, February 1956, 6.
36. Lingo, "Still in the Game."
37. Kelley, *"I Will Never Forget,"* 121.
38. *Ibid.*, 130.
39. Lingo, "Still in the Game."
40. Riley, *The Biographical Encyclopedia of the Negro Baseball Leagues*, 648–650.
41. Larry Lester and Sammy Miller, *Black Baseball in Pittsburgh* (Charleston, SC: Arcadia, 2001).
42. Kelley, *"I Will Never Forget,"* 176.
43. Riley, *The Biographical Encyclopedia of the Negro Baseball Leagues*.
44. Lanctot, *Negro League Baseball*.
45. Lester, *Black Baseball in Pittsburgh*, 2001.
46. Shirley Povich, *All Those Mornings at The Post* (New York: Perseus, 2005).
47. Einstein, *Willie's Time*, 299.
48. Kelley, Brent P. (1998). *Voices from the Negro Leagues: Conversations with 52 Baseball Standouts of the Period 1924–1960*. Jefferson, NC: McFarland.
49. Quoted by Kelley, *The Negro Leagues Revisited*, 307.
50. Quoted by Kelley, 1998, p. 260.
51. Kelley, *The Negro Leagues Revisited*. Bill Powell: 250 wins? In *The Negro Leagues Revisited: Conversations with 66 More Baseball Heroes* (pp. 215–221). Jefferson, NC: McFarland.
52. Kelley, *The Negro Leagues Revisited*; Riley, *The Biographical Encyclopedia of the Negro Baseball Leagues*, 648–650.
53. Kelley, *The Negro Leagues Revisited*, 215.
54. Riley, *The Biographical Encyclopedia of the Negro Baseball Leagues*.
55. Kelley, *The Negro Leagues Revisited*, 218.
56. Lester, *Black Baseball's National Showcase*.
57. Kelley, *The Negro Leagues Revisited*, 218.
58. *Ibid.*, 215.
59. *Ibid.*, 218.
60. *Ibid.*, 215.
61. Wallace, *Colorado Springs*.
62. Kelley, *The Negro Leagues Revisited*; Madden and Stewart, *The Western League*.
63. Kelley, *"I Will Never Forget,"* 216.
64. *Ibid.*
65. "William H. Powell," *Birmingham News*, August 25, 2004.
66. Larry Powell, interview with James A. "Jake" Sanders, Birmingham, AL, 2004. Other quotes from Mr. Sanders are from the same interview.
67. Lester, *Black Baseball's National Showcase*.
68. Kelley, *"I Will Never Forget,"* 175.
69. Larry Powell, interview with Sam Williams, Birmingham, AL, 2006. Unless otherwise attributed, subsequent quotes by Williams are from that interview.
70. John B. Holway, "Chet Brewer Just as Good as Satchel?" *Sporting News*, November 28, 1983; John B. Holway, "Papa Chet, Monarch of Los Angeles: An Interview with Chet Brewer," *Baseball History, 1* (Spring 1986).
71. "Jackie Robinson's All-Stars to Meet Black Barons Tonight," *Birmingham World*, October 18, 1949.
72. Kelley, *"I Will Never Forget,"* 177.
73. *Ibid.*, 176.
74. *Ibid.*
75. *Ibid.*
76. *Ibid.*, 177.
77. Kelley, *The Negro Leagues Revisited*, 197.
78. Sam Sciullo, *Tales from the Pitt Panthers* (Champaign, IL: Sports Publishing, 2004): 1.
79. Mary Schmitt Boyer, *Browns Essentials: Everything You Need to Know to be a Real Fan!* (Chicago: Triumph, 2006).
80. Andy Piascik, *The Best Show in Football: The 1946–1955 Cleveland Browns—Pro Football's Greatest Dynasty* (Lanham, MD: Taylor Trade Publishing, 2007): 1.
81. Kelley, *The Negro Leagues Revisited*, 197.
82. *Ibid.*, 198.
83. Phillip Merrill and Uluaipou-O-Maloaiono, *Baltimore* (Charleston, SC: Arcadia, 1999).
84. Herman Mason, Jr., *East Point* (Charleston, SC: Arcadia, 2001).
85. Tim Darnell, Roy E. Barnes and Bobby Dews, *The Crackers: The Early Days of Atlanta Baseball* (Athens, GA: Hill Street Press, 2003), 154.
86. Kelley, *The Negro Leagues Revisited*, 198.
87. Riley, *Biographical Encyclopedia of the Negro Baseball Leagues*, 893–894.
88. Kelley, *The Negro Leagues Revisited*, 199.
89. *Ibid.*
90. *Ibid.*, 203.
91. Lester, *Black Baseball's National Showcase*.
92. Kelley, *The Negro Leagues Revisited*, 201.
93. *Ibid.*, 200.
94. Madden and Stewart, *The Western League*.
95. Kelley, *The Negro Leagues Revisited*, 198.
96. *Ibid.*, 200.
97. *Ibid.*, 201.

Chapter 7

1. Riley, *The Biographical Encyclopedia of the Negro Baseball Leagues*, 50–51.
2. Mark Ribowsky, *A Complete History of the Negro Leagues* (Secaucus, NJ: Carol Publishing, 1995).
3. Floyd Connor, *Baseball's Most Wanted II* (Dulles, VA: Brassey, 2003).
4. Kelley, *The Negro Leagues Revisited*.
5. Riley, *The Biographical Encyclopedia of the Negro Baseball Leagues*.

6. Murray Polner, *Branch Rickey: A Biography* (New York: Signet, 1982).
7. Peterson, *Only the Ball Was White*.
8. Larry Moffi and Jonathan Kronstadt, *Crossing the Line: Black Major Leaguers, 1947–1959* (Jefferson, N.C.: McFarland, 1994): 11–13.
9. Tygiel, *Baseball's Great Experiment*.
10. Dan Gutman, *Jackie and Me* (New York: Avon, 1999).
11. Moffi and Kronstadt, *Crossing the Line*, 12.
12. Posnanski, *The Soul of Baseball*, 144.
13. *Ibid.*
14. *Ibid.*, 151.
15. "Baseball Preview: This Will Be One of Baseball's Hottest Years, Possibly, with Four Negroes in Big Leagues," *Our World*, April 1948, 46.
16. Tygiel, *Baseball's Great Experiment*, 262.
17. Sam Lacy, "Integration in Dixie Halts When Players Leave Field," *Baltimore Afro-American*, April 1, 1950.
18. Moffi and Kronstadt, *Crossing the Line*.
19. *Ibid.*
20. "Bankhead Plays First Base in Mexican League," *Jet*, August 13, 1953, 54.
21. Roberto Hernandez, "Bankhead Fired as Manager; Al Pinkston Fractures Arm," *Sporting News*, December 1, 1962, 41.
22. "Dan Bankhead," *New York Times*, May 7, 1976, 4–18.
23. Posnanski, *The Soul of Baseball*, 151.
24. John B. Holway, "Piper Davis," in *Baseball History, 4* (Westport, CT: Meckler Publishing, 1991), 62–74.
25. Shelley Smith, "Remembering the Game," *Sports Illustrated*, July 6, 1992, 80–92.
26. Trucks, *Cup of Coffee*, 38.
27. *Ibid.*
28. Dave Kindred, "From Miner to Majors: Negro Leagues' Star Piper Davis," *Sporting News*, June 30, 1997.
29. Theodore Rosengarten, "Reading the Hops: Recollections of Lorenzo Piper Davis and the Negro Baseball League," *Southern Exposure*, 1973, 62–79.
30. Vecsey, *The Harlem Globetrotters*.
31. Fullerton, *Every Other Sunday*, 81–82.
32. Kindred, "From Miner to Majors."
33. Phil Dixon and Patrick Hannigan, *The Negro Baseball Leagues: A Photographic History* (Mattituck, NY: Amereon House, 1992).
34. Fullerton, *Every Other Sunday*; Peterson, *Only the Ball Was White*.
35. Kelley, *Voices from the Negro Leagues*, 128–132; Willie Mays and L. Sahadi, *Say Hey: The Autobiography of Willie Mays* (New York: Simon & Schuster, 1988); Jim Riley, "Piper Davis: Willie Mays' Mentor," *Oldtyme Baseball News*, 1992, 13.
36. Tygiel, *Baseball's Great Experiment*, 39.
37. Holway, "Piper Davis," 1991; David Steele, "Time Wasn't Right for Robinson to Join Sox," *USA Today Baseball Weekly*, August 16, 1991, 31.
38. Peterson, *Only the Ball Was White*.
39. Riley, *The Biographical Encyclopedia of the Negro Baseball Leagues*, 217–218.
40. Tygiel, *Baseball's Great Experiment*, 262.
41. Kindred, "From Miner to Majors."
42. Fullerton, *Every Other Sunday*, 93.
43. "Negro Stars Threatened After Calif. Baseball Brawl," *Jet*, August 21, 1952, 52.
44. "Davis Plays Nine Positions in Ball Game," *Jet*, October 9, 1952, 50.
45. Kindred, "From Miner to Majors."
46. Jay Berman, "The 1956 Los Angeles Angels," *The National Pastime*, Vol. 17 (Cleveland: The Society for American Baseball Research, 1997): 81–84.
47. Riley, *The Biographical Encyclopedia of the Negro Baseball Leagues*.
48. Steve Wulf, "The Guiding Light," *Sports Illustrated*, September 19, 1994, 148–156.
49. Bruce Anderson, "Time Worth Remembering," *Sports Illustrated*, July 6, 1981, 46–47.
50. Kindred, "From Miner to Majors."
51. "Piper Davis, 79, Star Infielder and Manager in Negro Leagues," *New York Times*, May 23, 1997, A25.
52. Trucks, *Cup of Coffee*, 41; Riley, *The Biographical Encyclopedia of the Negro Baseball Leagues*.
53. Gary L. Bloomfield, *Duty, Honor, Victory: America's Athletes in World War II* (New York: Lyons, 2004).
54. Greg Garrison, "Black Marine Found Acceptance in Japan, But Not in the South," *Birmingham News*, May 30, 2004, 11A.
55. *Ibid.*
56. *Ibid.*
57. Lingo, "Still in the Game," 28–31.
58. Fullerton, *Every Other Sunday*.
59. Einstein, *Willie's Time*.
60. Fussman, *After Jackie*, 87.
61. Lester, *Black Baseball's National Showcase*.
62. Kelley, *Voices from the Negro Leagues*, 191.
63. *Ibid.*, 261.
64. Garrison, "Black Marine Found Acceptance in Japan."
65. Trucks, *Cup of Coffee*, 38.
66. Lingo, "Still in the Game."
67. Motley, *Ruling over Monarchs, Giants, & Stars*, 53.
68. Moffi and Kronstadt, *Crossing the Line*.
69. Tygiel, *Baseball's Great Experiment*.
70. Bruce Adelson, *Pushing Back Jim Crow: The Integration of Minor League Baseball in the South* (Charlottesville: University Press of Virginia, 1999).
71. Trucks, *Cup of Coffee*, 38.
72. "Negro Pitchers Make History in Texas Duel, *Jet*, August 21, 1952, 55; Tom Kayser and David King, *Baseball in the Lone Star State: The Texas League's Greatest Hits* (San Antonio: Trinity University Press, 2005).
73. Trucks, *Cup of Coffee*, 34.
74. Adelson, *Pushing Back Jim Crow*, 59.
75. Moffi and Kronstadt, *Crossing the Line*, 111.
76. Trucks, *Cup of Coffee*, 39.
77. "Yankees Bid for Pitcher Bill Greason," *Jet*, December 18, 1952, 53.
78. "Oklahoma City Refuses $100,000 Bids for Greason," *Jet*, December 25, 1952, 50.
79. Al Hirshberg, "Boston Needs a Negro Big-Leaguer," *Our Sports*, July 1953, 11–14.
80. Moffi and Kronstadt, *Crossing the Line*.
81. "St. Louis Cardinals Buy Pitcher Bill Greason," *Jet*, October 29, 1953, 55.
82. *Ibid.*
83. "The Minors' Ten Best Prospects," *Sport*, February 1954, 20–21.
84. Trucks, *Cup of Coffee*, 32–41.
85. Fussman, *After Jackie*.
86. Trucks, *Cup of Coffee*, 36.
87. Fussman, *After Jackie*, 88.

88. *Ibid.*, 89.
89. Trucks, *Cup of Coffee*, 36.
90. *Ibid.*, 37.
91. *Ibid.*, 36.
92. *Ibid.*
93. Peter Golenbock, *The Spirit of St. Louis: A History of the St. Louis Cardinals and Browns* (New York: Avon, 2000): 412.
94. Adelson, *Pushing Back Jim Crow*, 120.
95. Lingo, "Still in the Game."
96. *Ibid.*
97. *Ibid.*
98. *Ibid.*
99. Riley, *The Biographical Encyclopedia of the Negro Baseball Leagues*, 648–650.
100. Alan J. Pollock, *Barnstorming to Heaven: Syd Pollock and His Great Black Teams* (Tuscaloosa: University of Alabama Press, 2006): 111.
101. Fullerton, *Every Other Sunday.*
102. Pollock, 2006.
103. Moffi and Kronstadt, *Crossing the Line.*
104. Posnanski, *The Soul of Baseball,* 79.
105. Moffi and Kronstadt, *Crossing the Line.*
106. Herb Fagan, "Sam Hairston: Superstar Father and Coach," *Oldtyme Baseball News,*1998, 28–30.
107. George Vass, "They Follow in the Footsteps of Their Fathers," *Baseball Digest,* February 1982, 36–43.
108. "Former White Sox Sam Hairston," *Sports Collectors Digest,* November 28, 1997, 12; "Served Half a Century," *USA Today Baseball Weekly*, November 5, 1997, 43.
109. Fullerton, *Every Other Sunday.*
110. Riley, *The Biographical Encyclopedia of the Negro Baseball Leagues.*
111. Moffi and Kronstadt, *Crossing the Line.*
112. Riley, *The Biographical Encyclopedia of the Negro Baseball Leagues.*
113. Moffi and Kronstadt, *Crossing the Line.*
114. Louis Berney, *Tales from the Orioles Dugout* (Champaign, IL: Sports Publishing, 2004); James H. Bready, *Baseball in Baltimore: The First Hundred Years* (Baltimore: John Hopkins University Press, 1998); John Eisenberg, *From 33rd Street to the Camden Yards: An Oral History of the Baltimore Orioles* (New York: McGraw-Hill, 2002); Ted Patterson, *Day-By-Day in Baltimore Orioles History* (Champaign, IL: Sports Publishing, 1999).
115. Kweisi Mfune and Ronald I. Stodghill, *No Free Ride* (New York: Ballantine, 1996): 14.
116. "Mr. Jehosie Heard," *Birmingham News,* November 23, 1999.
117. Moffi and Kronstadt, *Crossing the Line.*
118. *Ibid.*
119. Mary Kay Linge, *Willie Mays: A Biography* (Westport, CT: Greenwood, 2005); John Grabowski, *Willie Mays* (New York: Chelsea House Publishers, 1990); Arnold Hano, *Willie Mays: The Say-Hey Kid* (New York: Bartholomew House, 1961); Willie Mays and Charles Einstein, *Willie Mays: My Life In and Out of Baseball* New York: E.P. Dutton, 1972); Willie Mays and Charles Einstein, *Born to Play Ball* (New York: G.P. Putnam's Sons, 1955); Mays and Sahadi, *Say Hey*; Milton J. Shapiro, *The Willie Mays Story* (New York: Julian Messner, 1960); Ken Smith, *The Willie Mays Story* (New York: Greenberg, 1954); George Sullivan, *Willie Mays* (New York: G.P. Putnam's Sons, 1973).
120. Jim Kisseloff, *Who Were Baseball's Greatest Hitters?* (New York: Henry Holt, 2001).
121. Kelley, *The Negro Leagues Revisited.*
122. Jim Canada and John B. Holway, "Discoverer of Willie Mays," *Sports Quarterly*, June 1972.
123. Kelly, *The Negro Leagues Revisited*, 127.
124. "Mays Homer Big Blow in Choo Choo Triumph," *Chattanooga Times*, May 15, 1948, 12.
125. Mays and Sahadi, *Say Hey*, 24.
126. *Ibid.*, 31.
127. Riley, *The Biographical Encyclopedia of the Negro Baseball Leagues*, 648–650.
128. Doug Segrest, "'Say Hey Kid' Comes Home," *Birmingham News*, February 14, 2007, 1C-2C.
129. Mays and Sahadi, *Say Hey*, 39.
130. *Ibid.*, 38.
131. *Ibid.*, 40
132. *Ibid.*, 41.
133. Kelley, *The Negro Leagues Revisited*, 218.
134. Motley, *Ruling Over Monarchs, Giants, & Stars*, 105.
135. Mays and Sahadi, *Say Hey*, 27.
136. *Ibid.*
137. *Ibid.*, 40.
138. Kelley, *The Negro Leagues Revisited*, 220.
138. *Ibid.*
139. Mays and Sahadi, *Say Hey*, 24.
140. *Ibid.*
141. *Ibid.*, 38.
142. Harvey Frommer, "Better Late Than Never," *108: Celebrating Baseball* (2007): 58–63.
143. Holway, *The Complete Book of Baseball's Negro Leagues.*
144. "Jackie Robinson's All-Stars to Meet Black Barons Tonight," *Birmingham World*, October 18, 1949.
145. Mays and Sahadi, *Say Hey*, 38.
146. Einstein, *Willie's Time*, 299.
147. Steve Bitker, *The Original San Francisco Giants: The Giants of '58* (Champaign, IL: Sports Publishing, 2001), 195.
148. Riley, *The Biographical Encyclopedia of the Negro Baseball Leagues.*
149. Robert Cole, *When Trenton Baseball Roared Like Thunder* (Trenton, NJ: Trenton City Museum, 1995).
150. Segrest, "'Say Hey Kid' Comes Home," 1C.
151. Davis, *Baseball's All-Time Greats*, 73.
152. *Ibid.*
153. Segrest, "'Say Hey Kid' Comes Home," 2C.
154. Frommer, "Better Late Than Never," 61.
155. Davis, "Better Late Than Never," 72.
156. Segrest, "'Say Hey Kid' Comes Home," 2C.
157. Posnanski, *The Soul of Baseball,* 33.
158. Dewey and Acocella, *The New Biographical History of Baseball*, 272.
159. Antonen, "Honored."
160. Mays and Sahadi, *Say Hey*, 24.
161. *Ibid.*, 23.
162. *Ibid.*, 25.
163. Posnanski, *The Soul of Baseball,* 31.
164. Fullerton, *Every Other Sunday.*
165. Brian Strickland, "Former Major Leaguer, Anniston Native, Smith Dies at Age 66," *Anniston Star*, January 18, 2006.
166. *Ibid.*
167. Rip Donovan, "A Long Trip to the Hall," *Anniston Star*, June 17, 2006.

168. Dave Finoli, *The Pittsburgh Pirates* (Charleston, SC: Arcadia, 2006).
169. Bob Veale, speech to the Triple Play Club, Birmingham, AL, 2006.
170. Fussman, *After Jackie*, 54.
171. "Bob Worked Out for Cards: Bucs' Scout Spotted Him," *Sporting News,* July 8, 1967, 3.
172. M. Frau, "Veale Maintains Big Wheel Role as Ponce Whiff Whiz," *Sporting News,* January 19, 1963, 33.
173. Les Biederman, "Eager Bucco Hurlers Jump Training Gun," *Sporting News,* March 2, 1963, 18.
174. James, *The New Bill James Historical Abstract.*
175. David Mananiss, *Clemente: The Passion and Grace of Baseball's Last Hero* (New York: Simon and Schuster, 2006), 208.
176. Les Biederman, "Veale Bread and Butter Beaut to Bucs: 'Bob No. 1 Lefty in N.L.,' Maintains Hill Coach King," *Sporting News,* July 8, 1967, 3.
177. Bill James and Rob Nevers, *The Never/James Guide to Pitchers* (New York: Fireside, 2004): 25.
178. Tim McCarver and Danny Peary, *Tim McCarver's Baseball for Brain Surgeons and Other Fans* (New York: Villard, 1998), 63.
179. Leonard Koppett, *Koppett's Concise History of Major League Baseball* (New York: Carroll & Graf, 2004): 322.
180. "Veale Victory Over Cards First Since July 22, 1964," *Sporting News,* May 13, 1967, 10.
181. Les Biederman, "Seven-run Bombing Makes Veale See Light," *Sporting News,* June 17, 1967, 10.
182. Les Biederman, "Veale Ignores an Aching Back: Buc Lefty Making Hitters Moan," *Sporting News,* May 27, 1967, 7.
183. Al Abrams, "Veale Discounts Wildness: If You Win, What Difference Do Walks Make," *Baseball Digest,* May 1965, 85–86.
184. Les Biederman, "Slaps at Veale Annoy Bucs' Brown," *Sporting News,* January 20, 1968, 28.
185. Les Biederman, "Smokeless Bob Veale a Puzzle to Redbirds," *Sporting News,* June 1, 1968, 13.
186. Les Biederman, "Veale, No Ham, Beefs Up Bucs with Bullpen Stint," *Sporting News,* May 6, 1967, 19.
187. Larry Powell, *Bottom of the Ninth: An Oral History on the Life of Harry "The Hat" Walker* (San Diego: iUniverse, 1999).
188. David S. Neft, Bob Carroll, Richard M. Cohen, Michael L. Neft, *Boston Red Sox Fan Book* (New York: St. Martin's Press, 2002).

189. Donald Hall, *Fathers Playing Catch with Sons: Essays on Sport* (New York: North Point Press, 1985).
190. Fussman, *After Jackie*, 189.
191. Veale, speech, 2006.
192. Lester, *Black Baseball's National Showcase.*
193. Kelley, *The Negro Leagues Revisited,* 218.
194. Riley, *The Biographical Encyclopedia of the Negro Baseball Leagues,* 866–867.
195. Eric Enders, "The Last .400 Hitter," EricEnders.com, 2002.
196. Riley, *The Biographical Encyclopedia of the Negro Baseball Leagues,* 866.
197. Milton Gross, "Will the Yankees Hire a Negro Player?" *Our Sports,* July 1953, 8–12.
198. Moffi and Kronstadt, *Crossing the Line.*
199. Bill Veeck and Gordon Cobbledick, "Baseball and Me: I Believe in Fireworks," *Sport,* April 1950, 28–32.
200. Moffi and Kronstadt, *Crossing the Line.*
201. Bill Swank, *Echoes from Lane Field: A History of the San Diego Padres 1936–1957* (Paducah, KY: Turner Publishing, 1997): 103–104.
202. Moffi and Kronstadt, *Crossing the Line.*
203. "Jackie Robinson's All-Stars to Meet Black Barons Tonight," *Birmingham World*, October 18, 1949.
204. Moffi and Kronstadt, *Crossing the Line,* 69.
205. Kelley, *The Negro Leagues Revisited*, 125.
206. Roger Kahn, "Of Galahad and Quests That Failed," *Sports Illustrated,* August 23, 1976, 28–35; Roger Kahn, *A Season in the Sun,* (New York: Harper & Row, 1977), 83–113; "Mays, Negro Star, Joins Giants Today," *New York Times,* May 25, 1951.
207. John Spalding, *Pacific Coast League Stars: One Hundred of the Best, 1903–1957* (San Jose, CA: John E. Spalding, 1994): 119–120.
208. Marthey, "Why Do Negro Stars Get Buried in the Minors?"

Afterword

1. William F. McNeil, *Black Baseball Out of Season: Pay for Play Outside the Negro Leagues* (Jefferson, NC: McFarland, 2007).
2. Jonathan Eig, *Opening Day: The Story of Jackie Robinson's First Season* (New York: Simon & Schuster, 2007).
3. Cathy Adams, "For Love of the Game," *Portico,* July/August 2002, 44–48.

Bibliography

Abrams, Al. "Veale discounts wildness: If you win, what difference do walks make." *Baseball Digest* 24(4), May 1965: 85–86.

Adams, Cathy. "For love of the game." *Portico* July/August, 2002: 44–48.

Adelson, Bruce. *Brushing Back Jim Crow: The Integration of Minor League Baseball in the American South.* Charlottesville: University Press of Virginia, 1999.

Anderson, Bruce. "Time worth remembering." *Sports Illustrated* 55(2), July 6, 1981: 46–47.

Antonen, Mel. "Honored." *USA Today* January 5, 2007: 6C.

"Bankhead Plays First Base in Mexican League." *Jet* 4(4), August 13, 1953: 54.

"Baseball Preview: This will be one of baseball's hottest years, possibly, with four Negroes in big leagues." *Our World* 3(4), April 1948: 46.

Berman, Jay. "The 1956 Los Angeles Angels." *The National Pastime* Vol. 17: 81–84. Cleveland: The Society for American Baseball Research, 1997.

Berney, Louis. *Tales from the Orioles Dugout.* Champaign, IL: Sports Publishing, 2004.

Biederman, Les. "Eager Bucco hurlers jump training gun." *The Sporting News* 155(6), March 2, 1963: 18.

_____. "Seven-run bombing makes Veale see light." *The Sporting News* 163(22), June 17, 1967: 10.

_____. "Slaps at Veale annoy Bucs' Brown." *The Sporting News* 165(1), January 20, 1968: 28.

_____. "Smokeless Bob Veale a puzzle to Redbirds." *The Sporting News* 165(20), June 1, 1968:13.

_____. "Veale bread and butter beaut to Bucs: 'Bob No. 1 lefty in N.L.,' maintains hill coach King." *The Sporting News* 163(25), July 8, 1967:

_____. "Veale ignores an aching back: Buc Lefty making hitters moan." *The Sporting News* 163(19), May 27, 1967: 7.

_____. "Veale, no ham, beefs up Bucs with bull-pen stint." *The Sporting News* 163(16), March 2, 1963: 19.

Bitker, Steve. *The Original San Francisco Giants: The Giants of '58.* Champaign, IL: Sports Publishing, 2001.

Bloomfield, Gary L. *Duty, honor, victory: America's athletes in World War II.* Guilford, CT: Lyons, 2004.

"Bob worked out for Cards: Bucs' scout spotted him." *The Sporting News* 163(25), July 8, 1967: 3.

Bready, James H. *Baseball in Baltimore: The First Hundred Years.* Baltimore: John Hopkins University Press, 1998.

Canada, Jim, w/ J.B. Holway. "Discoverer of Willie Mays." *Sports Quarterly* June, 1972.

Cole, Robert. *When Trenton Baseball Roared Like Thunder.* Trenton, NJ: Trenton City Museum, 1995.

Connor, Floyd. *Baseball's Most Wanted II.* Dulles, VA: Brassey, 2003.

"Dan Bankhead." *New York Times* May 7, 1976: 4–18.

Davis, Mac. *Baseball's All-Time Greats: The Top 50 Players.* New York: Bantam, 1970.

"Davis plays nine positions in ball game." *Jet* 2(24), October 9, 1952: 50.

Dewey, Donald and Nicholas Acocella. *The New Biographical History of Baseball.* Chicago: Triumph, 2002.

Dixon, Phil, and Patrick J. Hannigan. *The Negro Baseball Leagues: A Photographic History.* Mattituck, NY: Amereon House, 1992.

Donovan, Rip. "A long trip to the Hall." *Anniston Star.* June 17, 2006.

Eig, Jonathan. *Opening Day: The Story of Jackie Robinson's First Season.* New York: Simon & Schuster, 2007.

Einstein, Charles. *Willie's Time: Baseball's Golden Age.* Carbondale: Southern Illinois University Press, 1979.

Eisenberg, John. *From 33rd Street to the Camden Yards: An Oral History of the Baltimore Orioles.* New York: McGraw-Hill, 2002.

Fagan, Herb. "Sam Hairston: Superstar Father and

Coach." *Oldtyme Baseball News* 9(1), 1998: 28–30.

Finoli, Dave. *The Pittsburgh Pirates*. Charleston, SC: Arcadia, 2006.

"Former White Sox Sam Hairston." *Sports Collectors Digest* 24(48), November 28, 1997: 12.

Frau, M. "Veale maintains big wheel role as Ponce whiff whiz." *The Sporting News* 154(26), January 19, 1963: 33.

Frommer, Harvey. "Better late than never." *108: Celebrating baseball,* 1(2), 2007: 58–63.

Fullerton, Christopher D. *Every Other Sunday*. Birmingham, AL: R Boozer Press, 1999.

Fussman, Cal. *After Jackie: Pride, Prejudice, and Baseball's Forgotten Heroes*. New York: ESPN Books, 2007.

Garrison, Greg. "Black marine found acceptance in Japan, but not in the south."*Birmingham News* May 30, 2004: 11A.

Golenbock, Peter. *The Spirit of St. Louis: A History of the St. Louis Cardinals and Browns*. New York: Avon, 2000.

Grabowski, John. *Willie Mays*. New York: Chelsea House Publishers, 1990.

Gross, Milton. "Will the Yankees Hire a Negro Player?" *Our Sports*, 1(3), July 1953: 8–12.

Gutman, Dan. *Jackie and Me*. New York: Avon, 1999.

Hall, Donald. *Fathers Playing Catch with Sons: Essays on Sport*. New York: North Point Press, 1985.

Hano, Arnold. *Willie Mays: The Say-Hey Kid*. New York: Bartholomew House, 1961.

Hernandez, Roberto. "Bankhead fired as manager; Al Pinkston fractures arm." *The Sporting News,* 154(19), December 1, 1962:41.

Hirshberg, Al. "Boston needs a Negro big-leaguer." *Our Sports,* 1(3), July 1953: 11–14.

Holway, John. *The Complete Book of Baseball's Negro Leagues: The Other Half of Baseball History*. Fern Park, FL: Hastings House, 2001.

_____. "Piper Davis." In *Baseball History*, 4 (pp. 62–74). Westport, CT: Meckler Publishing, 1991.

"Jackie Robinson's All-Stars to meet Black Barons tonight." *Birmingham World,* October 18, 1949.

James, Bill. *The New Bill James Historical Abstract*. New York: Free Press, 2001.

James, Bill and Rob Nevers. *The Never/James Guide to Pitchers*. New York: Fireside, 2004.

Kahn, Roger. "Golden Triumphs, Tarnished Dreams." In *A Season in the Sun* (pp. 83–113). New York: Harper & Row, 1977.

_____. "Of Galahad and quests that failed." *Sports Illustrated,* 45(8), August 23, 1976: 28–35.

Kayser, Tom and David King. *Baseball in the Lone Star State: The Texas League's Greatest Hits*. San Antonio: Trinity University Press, 2005.

Kelley, Brent. *The Negro Leagues Revisited: Conversations with 66 More Baseball Heroes*. Jefferson, NC: McFarland, 2000.

_____. *Voices from the Negro Leagues: Conversations with 52 Baseball Standouts from the Period 1924–1960*. Jefferson, NC: McFarland, 1998.

Kindred, Dave. "From miner to majors: Negro Leagues' star Piper Davis." *Sporting News*. June 30, 1997.

Kisseloff, Jeff. *Who Were Baseball's Greatest Hitters?* New York: Henry Holt, 2001.

Koppett, Leonard. *Koppett's Concise History of Major League Baseball*. New York: Carroll & Graf, 2004.

Lacy, Sam. "Integration in Dixie Halts When Players Leave Field." *Baltimore Afro-American*. April 1, 1950. Reprinted in Jim Reisler. *Black Writers/Black Baseball: An Anthology of Articles from Black Sportswriters Who Covered the Negro Leagues*. Jefferson, NC: McFarland, 2007.

Lester, Larry. *Black Baseball's National Showcase: The East-West All-Star Game, 1933–1953*. Lincoln: University of Nebraska Press, 2002.

Linge, Mary Kay. *Willie Mays: A Biography*. Westport, CT: Greenwood Press, 2005.

Lingo, Karen. "Alabama people and places: Still in the game." *Southern Living,* 41(4), April 2006: 28–31.

Mananiss, David. *Clemente: The Passion and Grace of Baseball's Last Hero*. New York: Simon & Schuster, 2006.

Marthey, Larry. "Why do Negro stars get buried in the minors?" *Our World*, 1(5), October 1953.

Mays, Willie, with Charles Einstein. *Born to Play Ball*. New York: G.P. Putnam's Sons, 1955.

_____ and _____. *Willie Mays: My life In and Out of Baseball*. New York: E.P. Dutton, 1972.

_____. With Lou Sahadi. *Say Hey: The Autobiography of Willie Mays*. New York: Simon & Schuster, 1988.

"Mays, Negro Star, Joins Giants Today." *New York Times*. May 25, 1951.

"Mays homer big blow in Choo Choo triumph." *Chattanooga Times*. May 15, 1948: 12.

McCarver, Tim with Danny Peary. *Tim McCarver's Baseball for Brain Surgeons and Other Fans*. New York: Villard, 1998.

McNeil, William F. *Black Baseball Out of Season: Pay for Play Outside the Negro Leagues*. Jefferson, NC: McFarland, 2007.

Mfune, Kweisi, and Ronald I. Stodghill. *No Free Ride*. New York: Ballantine, 1996.

"The minor's ten best prospects." *Sport*. 16(2), February 1954: 20–21.

"Mr. Jehosie Heard." *Birmingham News*. November 23, 1999.

Moffi, Larry, and Jonathan Kronstadt. *Crossing the Line: Black Major Leaguers, 1947–1959*. Jefferson, NC: McFarland, 1994.

Motley, Bob. *Ruling Over Monarchs, Giants, & Stars: Umpiring in the Negro Leagues & Beyond*. Champaign, IL: Sports Publishing, 2007.

Neft, David S., Bob Carroll, Richard M. Cohen, and Michael L. Neft. *Boston Red Sox Fan Book*. New York: St. Martin's Press, 2002.

"Negro pitchers make history in Texas duel." *Jet,* 17(2), August 21, 1952: 55.

"Negro stars threatened after Calif. baseball brawl." *Jet,* 2(17), August 21, 1952: 52.

"Oklahoma City refuses $100,000 bids for Greason." *Jet,* 3(9), December 25, 1952: 50.

Patterson, Ted. *Day-by-Day in Baltimore Orioles History.* Champaign, IL: Sports Publishing, 1999.

Peterson, Robert. *Only the Ball was White: A History of the Legendary Black Players and All-Black Professional Teams.* New York: Gramercy, 1970.

"Piper Davis, 79, star infielder and manager in Negro leagues." *New York Times* May 23, 1997: A25.

Pollock, Alan J. *Barnstorming to Heaven: Syd Pollock and His Great Black Teams.* Tuscaloosa: University of Alabama Press, 2006.

Polner, Murray. *Branch Rickey: A Biography.* New York: Signet, 1982.

Posnanski, Joe. *The Soul of Baseball: A Road Trip Through Buck O'Neil's America.* New York: William Morrow, 2007.

Powell, Larry. *Bottom of the Ninth: An Oral History on the Life of Harry "The Hat" Walker.* San Diego: iUniverse, 1999.

Ribowsky, Mark. *A Complete History of the Negro Leagues.* Secaucus, NJ: Carol Publishing, 1995.

Riley, James A. *The Biographical Encyclopedia of the Negro Baseball Leagues.* New York: Carroll & Graf, 1994.

Riley, Jim. "Piper Davis: Willie Mays' Mentor." *Oldtyme Baseball News* 4(1), 1992: 13.

Rosengarten, Theodore. "Reading the hops: Recollections of Lorenzo Piper Davis and the Negro Baseball League." *Southern Exposure* 5(2–3), 1973: 62–79.

"St. Louis Cardinals buy pitcher Bill Greason." *Jet* 4(25), October 29, 1953: 55.

Segrest, Doug. "'Say Hey Kid' comes home." *Birmingham News* February 14, 2007: C-2C.

"Served half a century." *USA Today Baseball Weekly* 7(33), November 5, 1997: 43.

Shapiro, Milton J. *The Willie Mays Story.* New York: Julian Messner, 1960.

Smith, Ken. *The Willie Mays Story.* New York: Greenberg, 1954.

Smith, Shelley. "Remembering the game." *Sports Illustrated* 77(1), July 6, 1992: 80–92.

Spalding, John. "Artie Wilson." In *Pacific Coast League Stars: One Hundred of the Best, 1903–1957* (pp. 119–120). San Jose, CA: John E. Spalding, 1994.

Steele, David. "Time wasn't right for Robinson to join Sox." *USA Today Baseball Weekly* 1(20), August 16, 1991: 31.

Strickland, Brian. "Former major leaguer, Anniston native, Smith dies at age 66." *Anniston Star,* January 18, 2006.

Sullivan, George. *Willie Mays.* New York: G.P. Putnam's Sons, 1973.

Swank, Bill. "Artie Wilson." In *Echoes from Lane Field; A History of The San Diego Padres 1936–1957* (pp. 103–104). Paducah, KY: Turner Publishing, 1997.

Trucks, Rob. *Cup of Coffee: The Very Short Careers of Eighteen Major League Pitchers.* New York: Smallmouth Press, 2002.

Tygiel, Jules. *Baseball's Great Experiment: Jackie Robinson and His Legacy.* New York: Oxford University Press, 1983.

Vass, George. "They follow in the footsteps of their fathers." *Baseball Digest* 41(2), February 1982: 36–43.

Veale, Bob. Speech to the Triple Play Club. Birmingham, AL, 2006. Recorded by author.

"Veale victory over Cards first since July 22, 1964." *The Sporting News* 163(17), May 13, 1967: 10.

Veeck, Bill, with Gordon Cobbledick. "Baseball and me: I believe in fireworks." *Sport* 8(4), April 1950: 28–32.

Vecsey, George. *The Harlem Globetrotters.* New York: Scholastic, 1970.

Wulf, Steve. "The guiding light." *Sports Illustrated* 81(12), September 19, 1994:148–156.

"Yankees bid for pitcher Bill Greason." *Jet* 3(8), December 18, 1952: 53.

Index

Aaron, Hank 7, 86, 135, 137, 146, 189
Aaron, Tommie 135, 137
Abernathy, Robert 22
ACIPCO (Alabama Cast Iron Pipe Company) 1–2, 10–13, 95, 104, 106, 141, 147, 169, 195
Acocella, Nicholas 15, 19, 26, 107
Adams, Ben 156
Alabama A&M 114, 129
Alabama ByProducts 66
Alabama Negro League Players Association 3–4, 59, 128, 133
Alabama Sports Hall of Fame 49, 171
Alabama State University 162
Albany Giants 17
Alcorn State University 15
All-Star Game (Major Leagues) 194
Alvin, Gene 144
American Association 7, 152
Anderson, Harry 184
Anderson, Theodore "Bubbles" 12–13
Andrews, Herman "Jabo" 33
Anson, Cap 7
Apollo Theater 123
Arizona-Mexico League 64
Ashby, Earl 43
Asheville Blues 172
Ashford, Andy 162
Atlanta All-Stars 172
Atlanta Black Crackers 10, 34, 36, 70, 80, 82, 88, 149, 162, 172, 185
Atlantic City Bacharach Giants 28, 40
Atlantic Steel Company 88
Austin, Tank 33

Bailey, Otha 54–57, 114–115
Baker, Gene 173
Baltimore Black Sox 29, 39
Baltimore Elite Giants 27, 38–40, 50, 60, 70, 86, 98, 100, 108, 104, 162–163
Baltimore Orioles 26, 56, 58, 70, 78, 114, 145, 155–156, 165, 182–183
Bankhead, Dan 43, 55, 165–168, 170
Bankhead, Dan, Jr. 167–168
Bankhead, Fred 34
Bankhead, Joe 53, 62–63
Bankhead, Sam 33–34
Banks, Ernie 77, 95, 143, 189
Barnes, Bill 53
Barnes, Frank 121
Barnes, Harry 77
Barons Hall of Fame 168
Baseball Hall of Fame 15, 17, 19, 28–29, 31 108, 191, 199
Bass, Jesse 80
Bassett, Lloyd "Pepper" 44, 56, 63, 173
Baylis, Henry 56
Baylis, Henry J. "Hank" 63–64
Bell, "Cool Papa" 35, 40, 156
Bell, Herman 56, 64, 173
Bell, William "Lefty" Jr. 64
Bellville Grays 99
Benjamin, Jerry 35, 100
Berlin Wall 129
Beverly, William "Fireball" 64, 104–105, 174
Big State League 139
Biot, Charley 31, 86
Birmingham Black Eagles 140
Birmingham Public Library 8
Birmingham Stars 10, 99
Blaylock, Joe 88
Bodon, Jean iv, 4

Bolden, James "Fireball" 54, 64, 82
Bolin, Bob 141, 147
Bolin, James 67–68, 153–154
Bostock, Lyman, Jr. 45
Bostock, Lyman, Sr. 42–44, 53
Boston Blues 50
Boston Red Sox 19, 56, 112, 165, 168, 170, 177, 182, 195
Bouchee, Ed 184
Boudreau, Lou 125
Boyd, Bob 152
Boyer, Ken 118
Braidwood Coal Citys 14
Brewer, Chet 159, 188
Brewer, Sherwood 174
Bridgeforth, Sue 60, 163
Britton, Johnny 44, 65
Brooklyn Cuban Giants 64
Brooklyn (Los Angeles) Dodgers 3–4, 7, 43, 46, 48, 53, 55–56, 58, 70, 76, 81, 112, 133, 141, 152, 154–155, 165–166, 170, 175, 183–184, 191
Brooks, Edward "Eddie" 54, 65
Brown, Cleophus 4, 56, 66–69, 96
Brown, Ike 58
Brown, Larry "Iron Man" 13
Brown, Ralph 54
Bruton, Jack 35
Bryant, Paul "Bear" 128
Buffalo Bisons 194
Buford, "Black Bottom" 13
Bumpus, Earl 45
Bunch, Sidney 54, 142
Burgos, Jose 69–70
Butts, Tommy "Pee Wee" 70
Byrd, Bill 108

Calhoun, Don 128
California Angels 45
California League 46
California Winter League 31
Campanella, Roy 3, 112, 119, 140, 152; All-Stars 140
Canada, Jim 36, 54, 111, 120–121, 184
Carew, Rod 45
Carman Cardinals 44
Carolina League 139; Hall of Fame 140
Carter, Ernest "Spoon" 45
Central League 63
Cephus, Andrew 88
"Chalk Eye" 88
Chambers, Crip 120
Chandler, A.B. "Happy" 71, 197
Chattanooga Black Lookouts 19
Chattanooga Choo Choos 36, 64, 94, 111, 184–185
Chicago American Giants 8, 13–16, 18–19, 27–32, 39–41, 44–46, 47–49, 50–51, 64, 72, 75–76, 88, 94, 63–64, 100–101, 104–105, 108
Chicago Columbia Giants 33
Chicago Cubs 109, 128, 152, 192–194
Chicago White Sox 15, 24, 85, 89, 165, 168, 181, 183
Chism, Elijah "Eli" 70
Cincinnati Buckeyes 49, 71, 75
Cincinnati-Indianapolis Clowns 39, 50, 65, 85–86, 181
Cincinnati Reds 152, 192–194
Cincinnati Tigers 75
Clark, Fred 73
Clarkson, Buzz 179
Claybrook Tigers 39
Clemente, Roberto 179
Cleveland Bears 36, 39, 41
Cleveland Browns 161
Cleveland Buckeyes 41, 43, 46, 64, 70–71, 77, 104, 111, 126, 169–170
Cleveland Clippers 40
Cleveland Cubs 27, 40
Cleveland Giants 47
Cleveland Indians 48, 123, 126, 128, 145, 176, 182, 192, 197
Cleveland Red Sox 14, 18
Cleveland Stars 14
Clow Pipe 158
Cobb, Ty 7, 13
Coleman, Elliot "Junior" 54, 56, 70–71, 87, 104
Coleman, Melvin "Slick" 13
Cole's American Giants 32
Collins, Soc 88
Columbia American Giants 40

Columbus Buckeyes 40
Columbus Red Birds 177
Comiskey Park 60, 109, 132
Connie Mack Stadium 183
Connor, Eugene "Bull" 60–61
Connor Steel 106
Cooper, Anthony "Ant" 14
Cornelius, Willie "Sug" 14
Corrales, Pat 133
Country Music Hall of Fame 98
Cowan, Johnny 56, 71–72
Cox, Billy 197
Crawford, Sam 14
Cronin, Joe 170
Crowe, George 179
Crutchfield, John William "Jimmie" 72
Cuban League 152
Cuban Stars 32
Curry, Willie 4, 22, 55, 72–75, 180

Dallas Giants 18
Dallas Eagles 176
Daniels, Elbert May 93
Dapper, Cliff 160
Davenport, Lloyd "Ducky" 75
Davis, Lorenzo "Piper" 14, 36, 42, 44, 53, 55–56, 58, 71, 85, 87–88, 99, 100, 106, 119, 121, 129–130, 132, 147, 149, 162–163, 168–171, 173, 180, 185, 188–190
Dayton Marcos 31
Dean, Dizzy 19, 21, 126; All-Stars 126
Dennis, Wesley "Doc" 75
Detroit Senators 46, 101
Detroit Stars 17, 20, 32, 35, 40, 48, 60, 63, 71, 84–85, 102, 104–106, 120, 158
Detroit Tigers 56, 58, 71, 130, 135, 138, 171, 192
Detroit Wolves 28, 108
Devine, Bing 109
Dewey, Donald 107
DiMaggio, Joe 22, 126, 189
Dismukes, William "Dizzy" 15
Dixie Series 179
Doby, Larry 24, 53, 139, 144, 152
Dominican Republic League 168
Douglas, Jesse 75–76
Dropo, Walt 109, 170
Drummond, Charlie "Bulldog" 77–78
DuBose, Clifford 58, 76, 80
Dudley, James 63
Duncan, Melvin 151, 174

Dunsiath Giants 101
Durocher, Leo 190–191

Easley, James 88
East-West All-Star Game 14, 30, 34, 38–43, 47–48, 60, 70, 72, 75, 81, 94, 99, 105, 108–109, 120–121, 123, 126, 129, 132, 135, 143, 149, 151, 154, 163, 166, 170, 195
Eastern Illinois University 109
Ebbets Field 119, 131
Eig, Jonathan 199
Elliot, Joe 141
Elmore, Henry 4, 76–80, 85, 147
Elmwood Giants 64, 71, 75
Escogido Lions 168
Estrellas Elephants 168
Ethiopian Clowns 13, 65
Evans, Felix "Chin" 80–81
Evans, Frank 4, 55, 77, 102, 125–128, 154
Every Other Sunday 8

Fairfield Graystones 153
Feller, Bob 23, 166; All-Stars 23, 196
Ferguson, Oliver 36
Fernandez, Chico 183
Ferrara, Al 133
Fingers, Rollie 194
Finley, Red 87
Flood, Curt 139
Florida International League 70
Fort Worth Cats 171
Foster, Bill 15–18, 199
Fullerton, Christopher 3, 54, 57, 61, 169, 171
Furillo, Carl 197
Fussman, Cal 8, 195

Gardner, Jerry 19
Gatewood, Big Bill 17, 19–20
Gehrig, Lou 7, 16
Gehringer, Charlie 16
George Gibson League 88
Georgia State League 88
Get That Nigger Off the Field 8
Gibson, Alvin "Bubber" 45
Gibson, Josh 7, 27, 31, 38, 43, 86, 100, 105, 145, 158, 193
Gibson, Rufus 123, 135
Gilliam, Elijah 4, 81, 154, 156
Gilliam, Junior 70, 100, 152
Gillis, Louis "Sea Boy" 82
Gipson, Bubber 44
Golenbock, Peter 179
Gomez, Lefty 24
Gomez, Ruben 179
Grand Rapids Athletics 88
Grand Rapids Black Sox 135

Greason, William "Bill" 4, 22–24, 55–56, 58–59, 84, 165, 168, 170, 172–180, 189, 192
Great, Sollie 156
Green, Denny 145
Green, Pumpsie 168, 177
Greenwade, Tom 196
Griggs, Acie "Skeet" 82–83
Griggs, Wiley Lee "Diamond Jim" 82
Gulley, Napoleon "Nap" 46
Gurley, James "Jim" 17–18

Haggins, Raymond 58, 76
Hairston, Jerry 181
Hairston, John 181
Hairston, Sam 71, 163, 180–181
Hamilton, Art 120
Hankyu Braves 65, 87
Hardy, Paul 42
Harlem Globetrotters 41–42, 46, 48–50, 58, 63, 94, 98, 126, 169, 196
Harlem Satellites 129
Harrell, Billy 181–182
Harridge, Will 24
Harris, Donnie 51, 55, 128–135, 154, 199
Harris, Earnest 4, 55–56, 60
Harris, Luman 156
Harris, Victor "Vic" 38, 54, 56
Harris, Willie "Red" 4, 55, 57, 83–84, 143, 174
Harrisburg Giants 40, 88
Hayes, Tom 42–44, 60, 188, 190, 196
Heard, Jehosie "Jay" 55, 165, 173, 182–183
Hemus, Solly 184
Higgins, Jessie 80
Hodges, Gil 3, 197
Hoffman, Fred 114, 145
Holden, Carl 58, 60, 114–116
Hollingsworth, Curtis 84
Holway, John 29–31, 48, 62
Homestead Grays 8, 14, 18, 28–29, 32–33, 35, 38–41, 43, 45–48, 50, 53, 59, 63, 65, 71, 87, 99–100, 104–106, 149–151, 162, 169, 173
Hood, Cliff 88
Horick, Randy 8, 22
Horn, Luke 133
Hoskins, Dave 176
House of David 82, 98
Houston Black Buffaloes 14
Houston Eagles 30, 46, 50, 64–65, 82, 104, 108, 112, 119
Howard, Darrell 8
Howard, Frank 155
Howell, Henry F. "Hen" 84
Hubbard, J.D. 88

Huber, Butch 44
Huntsville Braves 114
Huntsville Giants 114
Huntsville Hawks 114
Huntsville Pirates 111
Huntsville Stars 111

Indianapolis ABCs 13, 15
Indianapolis Athletics 14
Indianapolis Clowns 8, 50, 60, 63, 77, 80, 107, 162, 174
Industrial League 2, 10–13, 76, 83, 104, 120, 129–130, 141, 147, 153, 158, 180
International League 152, 167, 179, 183, 194
Irvin, Monte 177, 190
Ivory, James "Sapp" 55, 85, 102, 147, 170
Iwo Jima 172

Jackson, Bozo 88
Jackson, R.T. 20
Jacksonville Red Caps 36, 39, 41, 47
James, Bill 108, 194
Japan, baseball in 65, 87
Javier, Gideon 77
Jenkins, James Edward "Pee Wee" 54, 85
Johnson, Abdul 102
Johnson, Judy 100
Johnson, Leroy 86
Johnson, Ralph 86
Jones, Casey 96, 160
Jones, Edgar "Special Delivery" 161
Jones, Fate 86
Jones, Reuben 10, 18
Jones, Sam 179
Jones, Stanley 144
Jordan, Michael 42

Kaline, Al 139; All-Stars 139
Kansas City Monarchs 8, 12, 15–16, 20, 22, 33, 39–40, 45–46, 48, 55, 57–58, 60, 63–64, 76, 86, 102–103, 105, 135, 138, 147, 151, 153, 156, 158, 160, 173–174, 183, 185, 189
Kansas City (Oakland) Athletics 19, 89, 129
Kansas City Royals 109, 128
Keane, Johnny 177
Kelley, Brent 76, 101, 103–194, 112, 114 135, 137, 139, 148, 151, 163
Kennedy, John Irvin 54–55, 57, 156, 165, 183–184
Kennimore, Ed 114
Kessinger, Don 193

Kimbro, Henry "Kimmie" 86
Kindred, Dave 169, 171
King, Clarence "Pijo" 54, 56, 87
Kisselford, Jeff 19
Knight, David iv, 4
Knox, Elmer 4, 11, 87–89
Knoxville Grays 88
Korean War 175

Lawrence, Brooks 179
Lee, Willie J. 55, 58, 102, 135–139
LeGrande, Larry 148
Leonard, Buck 53, 86, 107
Lester, Larry 24
Lewis, Carl 80
Lingo, Karen 148, 180
Little Richard 102
Little Rock Black Travelers 18
Lloyd, Anthony "Tony" 4, 55–56, 116–121, 170–171
Lloyd, John Henry 107
Lockett, Lester "Buck" 38, 44
Lollar, Sherm 181
Long, Carl 139–140, 149
Longhorn League 50, 164
Los Angeles Angels 171, 192–193
Lou Haney Stars 110
Louisville Black Caps 33, 45
Louisville Buckeyes 41, 104
Louisville Clippers 67, 74, 94–95, 106, 110
Louisville White Sox 14

Mack, Connie 9
MacPhail, Larry 196
Malacher, Dave 15, 30
Mandak League 39, 42, 44, 50, 59, 64, 70–71, 75–76, 87, 126
Marion, Marty 25, 108
Markham, Clarence M. 24
Marquez, Luis 197
Marthey, Larry 125
Martin, Billy 197
Martin, Bob "Pepper" 164
Martin, J.B. 170
May, Lee 171
Maybe I'll Pitch Forever 21
Mays, Willie 7, 28, 36, 47, 53, 55, 59, 87–88, 94, 98, 100–101, 120, 129, 143–144, 146–147, 149–150, 162, 165, 168, 170–173, 179, 184–192, 197–199; All-Stars 146–147
McAllister, George 18
McCarver, Tim 194
McCord, Butch 163
McCullum, Frank 73–74
McDowell, Ronald 59
McDuffie, Terris "Speed" 39

McLaurin, Felix 44, 47
McNair, Hurley 107
Memphis Red Sox 14–15, 17, 22, 27, 33–35, 41, 48, 58, 63, 65, 70–71, 76, 80, 83, 94, 102, 104–106, 119–121, 131, 135, 142, 158, 160, 165–166, 182
Meredith, Buford "Geetchie" 18
Mexican League 22, 26, 44, 47–49, 75–76, 85, 140, 149, 153, 161, 168
Miami Marlins 26
Mickelson, Ed 23, 25
Midwest League (Mississippi–Ohio Valley) League 49, 135, 161, 163
Miles College 87
Miller, Leroy 89–94
Milwaukee Bears 17, 31
Milwaukee Brewers 152
Minnesota Gophers 65
Minnesota Twins 58, 137
Minoso, Minnie 181
Mitchell, Jessie 4, 54–57, 61, 68, 85, 95, 97, 111, 119, 129, 131, 140–148, 156
Mitchell, John 55, 58, 68, 104–105, 119–124
Montague, Ed 149
Montgomery Grey Sox 18, 28, 39, 100
Montgomery Wings 128
Montreal Expos 128, 171
Morney, Leroy 44, 47
Morton, Charlie 7
Moss, Les 23
Motley, Bill 189
Motley, Bob 49, 175
Motley, Marion 53
Mumford, Pete 80
Murray, Mitch 19–20

Nagasaki 172
Napp, Larry 162
Nashville Black Vols 172
Nashville Elite Giants 13–14, 18, 27, 32–33, 35
Nashville Stars 75
National Baseball Congress 21, 89, 139
Navarro, Julie 193
Negro American League 36, 40–41, 46, 53, 59–60, 106
Negro League Legends Hall of Fame 69
Negro League Museum 8, 84
Negro National League 8, 10, 12, 59, 86, 105
Negro Southern League 10, 12, 18, 33, 71
Nelms, R.E. 102, 115

Nelson, Clyde 51
New England Patriots 128
New Haven Sailors 159
New Orleans Bears 81
New Orleans Black Pelicans 105
New Orleans Creoles 64
New Orleans Eagles 30, 46, 50, 64–65, 82, 104, 108, 112, 119
New Orleans Stars 36, 50, 60, 71
New York Bacharach Giants 29
New York Black Sox 14
New York Black Yankees 14, 27, 34, 36, 39–40, 47–48, 50, 86
New York Cuban Stars 27
New York Cubans 44, 50, 82, 94, 85, 100, 140
New York Giants 149, 165, 186–188, 190–191, 197
New York Lincoln Giants 13, 28, 100
New York Yankees 3, 15, 56, 70, 145, 166, 177, 197
Newark Dodgers 14, 39
Newark Eagles 30, 46, 50, 108, 112, 119
Newberry, Jimmy 44, 56, 87, 173, 185
Newcombe, Don 3, 54, 175
Northern League 183
Northwest League 46, 64, 76, 198

Oakland Oaks 41, 149, 171, 197
Odom, John "Blue Moon" 89
O'Doul, Lefty 197
Oklahoma City Indians 176
Omaha Tigers 169
O'Neil, Buck 29, 97, 107, 112, 167, 171, 173, 189, 191–192
Only the Ball Was White (Book) 8
Ott, Mel 171

Pacific Coast League 26, 41, 71, 105, 152, 171, 181–183, 197
Paige, Leroy "Satchel" 17, 18–27, 47, 59, 72, 78, 89–90, 113, 123, 126, 135, 145–146, 159, 166–167, 171, 189, 199; All-Stars 23, 46, 65, 76, 98, 104, 196
Paige, Robert 167
Parnell, Roy "Red" 26
Patkin, Max 160
Patterson, Willie "Pat" 41, 64, 94, 107, 154
Peach State League 88
Pepsi Cola Giants 89
Perdue, Frank 10
Perkins, Bill 27
Perkins, George 20

Perry, Alonzo 129, 148–151, 173, 185
Peterson, Robert 8, 19
Philadelphia Phillies 51, 55–56, 58, 132, 183–184, 191
Philadelphia Stars 13, 27, 33, 36, 39–40, 45, 47, 63, 75, 92, 94, 126
Phillips, Robert 94
Piedmont League 70
Pioneer League 139
Piper Coal Company 169
Pipkin, Robert "Black Diamond" 27
Pittsburgh Crawfords 14, 22, 27–28, 33–34, 38, 40, 45, 47–48, 50, 72
Pittsburgh Keystones 28
Pittsburgh Pirates 140, 165, 183, 193–195
Pittsburgh Stars 140
Poindexter, Robert 27
Pollard, Nathaniel "Nat" 95, 173
Pollock, Syd 181
Polo Grounds 52, 178, 188
Posnanski, Joe 112, 181
Powell, William "Bill" 53, 56, 58, 112, 151–153, 173, 189, 195
Pride, Charley 47, 54, 58, 67–58, 73, 95–98, 141, 144, 147
Providence Grays 7
Provincial League (Canada) 35, 64, 86, 94
Puerto Rican League 152
Purple Heart 86

Radcliffe, Ted "Double Duty" 24–25, 40, 42, 44, 46–49, 54, 58, 104, 180
Raleigh Tigers 60, 81, 126
Ramsey, Laymon 98
Rasberry, Ted 102–103, 135
Ray, Johnny 39
RCA 96–97
Redd, Ulysses 49, 108
Reed, Eddie Lee 76
Reese, Pee Wee 3, 15, 108, 197
Regan, Mark 145
Renfroe, Chico 31
Ribowsky, Mark 19–20
Rickey, Branch 39, 56, 140, 166–167, 170; League 88
Rickwood Classic 49
Rickwood Field 1–2, 9, 49, 53–55, 69, 77–78, 87, 96, 106, 119, 123, 129, 132, 143–144, 146–147, 149, 157, 193, 196
Riley, James 13, 62, 86–87, 105, 125, 196
Roberts, Curt 173
Robinson, Bobby 156

Index

Robinson, Earls 156
Robinson, Jackie 3, 7, 15, 24, 41–42, 48, 53–56, 58, 61, 64, 70–71, 78, 96, 119, 131, 140, 157–158, 165–166, 168, 170, 176, 178–180, 184, 195, 197, 199; All-Stars 42, 44, 53, 160, 162, 180, 190
Robinson, Norman 56, 98–99, 189
Rochester Red Wings 179
Rocket City Dodgers 114
Roe, Preacher 125
Rogosin, Donn 8
Rosairo, Luis 168
Rose, Pete 153
Runyon, Damon 48
Rush, Joe 10, 19
Rush Hotel 42
Rust, Art 8
Ruth, Babe 7, 16, 19, 184; All-Stars 21

Sacramento Saints 152
St. Louis Browns 23, 25–26, 175
St. Louis Cardinals 56, 58–59, 84, 109, 118, 121, 145, 165, 171, 177–179, 193
St. Louis Stars 17, 19, 28–29, 36, 50, 88, 107
Salmon, Harry 19, 28
Sampson, Tommy 34, 44, 99–100, 184–185, 197
San Antonio Black Aces 107
San Antonio Missions 145
San Diego Padres (minor league) 197
San Diego Padres (National League) 194
San Francisco Seals 197
Sanders, James "Jake" 4, 55–57, 93, 126, 153–158, 180
Sanford, Ron 179
Saperstein, Abe 42, 94, 126, 196
Saratoga Harlem Yankees 182
Saylor, Alfred "Greyhound" 44, 49
Scales, George "Tubby" 100
Schultz, Joe 145
Sciullo, Sam 161
Score, Herb 145, 177
Scott, Joe 100–101, 173
Scott, Johnny 44
Scruggs, Eugene 101–104, 125
Scruggs, Willie 104
Searcy, Kelly "Lefty" 54, 70, 104
Segrest, Doug 190
Sewell, Herb 173
Sewell, Joe 123

Shackleford, John 40
Shreveport Black Sports 101
Sienna College 182
Sierra, Pedro 120
Sisler, George 166
Smith, Clarence 33, 40
Smith, Hal 118, 144
Smith, Quincy 49
Smith, Taylor 104
Smith, Willie "Wonderful Willie" 55, 85, 119, 121, 192–193
Smithfield Library (Birmingham) 4
South Atlantic (Sally) League 152–153
Southern League 179, 181
Southwestern League 64
Spahn, Warren 191
Spencer, Joseph B. "J.B." 50
Sports Illustrated 8
Springfield, Billy 145
Stanky, Eddie 177–178
Steele, Ed "Stainless" 44, 53, 56, 72–73, 102, 104, 120, 162, 173
Stockham Valve 11, 76, 85, 106
Stoles, Walter 80
Stoll, Melvin 80
Stoneham, Horace 188
Streeter, Sam 19, 28
Strode, Woody 53
Sukeforth, Clyde 166
Sullivan, Bob 135, 137
Suttles, George "Mule" 28–31, 199
Sutton, Leroy 50

Tatum, Jim 176
Tatum, Reese "Goose" 42, 50, 78, 176
Taylor, Tony 156
Texas Black Spiders 101
Texas League 39, 71, 140, 163, 176–177
Thetford Miners 64
Thomas, "Showboat" 39
Thomas, Walter 105
Thompson, Frank 54, 59–60, 105
Thompson, James "Sandy" 31–32
Thompson, Jimmie 170
Thompson, Sam 154, 156
Thomson, Bobby 191
Threatt, "Slick" 130
Thurmond, Bob 179
"Tobacco John" 89
Toledo Blue Stockings 7
Toledo Crawfords 63
Toledo Tigers 17
Trucks, Rob 174, 176

Truman, Harry 53
Turner, Ted 106

Underwood, Robert 106
United Press All-American Team (basketball) 182
University of Alabama–Birmingham 4

Vance, Columbus "Luke" 32
Veale, Bob 61, 165, 193–195
Veeck, Bill 197
Vulcan Materials (Birmingham Slag) 74

Walker, A.M. 33, 40
Walker, Harry "The Hat" 195
Walker, Hoss 65
Walker, Jesse "Hoss" 106–107
Walker, Moses Fleetwood "Fleet" 7, 157
Walker, Welday 7, 157–158
Ward, Hollin 56 44
Washington, Kenny 53
Washington, Lafayette
Washington Elite Giants 40, 47, 86
Washington Nationals 133
Washington Pilots 30
Washington Potomacs 12–13
Washington Senators 25
Washington State College 89
Watkins, Willie 145
Watts, Andy 107
Watts, Richard "Dick" 56, 107
Weiss, George 197
Welch, Wingfield 42–44, 169
Wells, Willie 30, 47, 54, 107–108, 142, 199
West, James "Jim" 40, 77
West Baden Sprudels 15
West Texas–New Mexico League 160
Western Canada League 98
Western International League 182
Western League 70, 76, 152, 163, 181
Westfield, Ernest "Tennessee Ernie" 109
Whatley, David "Hammerman" 40
White, Bill 132
White, Stanky 156
White, William 7
Whitt 12
Wilder, Rich 88
Wilhite, Nick 133
Williams, Anita iv
Williams, Billy 119
Williams, Frank 119
Williams, John 60, 147

Williams, Poindexter 32
Williams, Sam 4, 56, 149, 158–161, 173, 192–193
Williams, Ted 126
Williams, Will "Curly" 54
Willis, Bob 53
Wilson, Artie 44, 55, 159, 165, 173, 180, 192, 195
Winnipeg Buffaloes 42, 44, 126
Woods, Parnell 41
Woodward, A.H. "Rick" 54, 68

World Series (Major League) 3, 89, 94, 179, 181, 195
World Series (Negro League) 13–14, 16, 24, 29, 38, 41, 43, 45, 47–48, 53, 59–60, 65, 71, 86, 104–106, 151, 162, 169, 173, 182
World War I 15
World War II 39, 41, 44, 50, 53, 82, 86–87, 89, 95, 101, 166, 172
Wright, Danny 54
Wright, Richard "Red" 54

Wrigley Field 22
Yancey, Bill 16
Yankee Stadium 42, 81, 119
Young, Archie "Dropo" 85, 109–111, 189
Young, Leandry 44
Young, Willie 51, 64, 143

Zapp, Jim 54–55, 80, 161–164, 172, 174
Zimmer, Don 179
Zulu Clowns 140
Zulu Grass Skirts 15

www.ingramcontent.com/pod-product-compliance
Lightning Source LLC
Chambersburg PA
CBHW081159230426
43666CB00016B/2862